Siegel's
PROFESSIONAL RESPONSIBILITY

Brian N. Siegel
J.D., Columbia Law School

Lazar Emanuel
J.D., Harvard Law School

and

Marsh C. Brilliant
J.D., Whittier Law School

The Siegel's Series
Essay and Multiple-Choice Questions and Answers

Aspen Law & Business
A Division of Aspen Publishers, Inc.
New York   Gaithersburg

Copyright ©2000 by Aspen Law & Business

All rights reserved. No part of this publication may be reproduced or transmitted in any form or by any means, electronic or mechanical, including photocopy, recording, or any information storage and retrieval system, without permission in writing from the publisher. Requests for permission to make copies of any part of this publication should be mailed to:

Permissions
Aspen Law & Business
1185 Avenue of the Americas
New York, NY 10036

Printed in the United States of America.

ISBN 0-7355-3468-3

This book is intended as a general review of a legal subject. It is not intended as a source of advice for the solution of legal matters or problems. For advice on legal matters, the reader should consult an attorney.

Siegel's, Emanuel, the judge logo, Law In A Flash and design, CrunchTime and design, Strategies & Tactics and design, and The Professor Series are registered trademarks of Aspen Law & Business.

About Aspen Law & Business Legal Education Division

Aspen Law & Business is proud to welcome Emanuel Publishing Corporation's highly successful study aids to its list of law school publications. As part of the Aspen family, Steve and Lazar Emanuel will continue their work on these popular titles, widely purchased by students for more than a quarter century. With the addition of the Emanuel title, Aspen now offers the most comprehensive selection of outstanding publications for the discerning law student.

Aspen Law & Business
A Division of Aspen Publishers, Inc.
A Wolters Kluwer Company
www.aspenpublishers.com

About The Authors

Professor Brian N. Siegel received his *Juris Doctorate* from Columbia Law School, where he was designated a Harlan Fiske Stone Scholar for academic excellence. He is the author of *How to Succeed in Law School* and numerous works pertaining to preparation for the California Bar examination. Professor Siegel has taught as a member of the adjunct faculty at Pepperdine School of Law and Whittier College School of Law, as well as for the UCLA Extension Program.

Lazar Emanuel is a graduate of Harvard Law School. In 1950, he became a founding partner of the New York firm now known as Cowan, Liebowitz & Latman. From 1960 through 1971, he was president of Communications Industries Corp., multiple licensee of radio and television stations in the Northeast. From 1987 to 2002, he served as Executive Vice President and General Counsel of Emanuel Publishing Corp. He has edited many of the publications in the Professor Series of study aids and in the Siegel's series of Essay and Multiple-Choice Question & Answer books.

Marsha C. Brilliant received her Bachelor of Arts (B.A.) from UCLA and her Juris Doctorate from Whittier Law School in 1994, where she graduated *cum laude*. She was Co-Executive Editor of the Whittier Law Review which published her student note, *Lee v. Weisman: The Establishment Clause: A Consideration of Its Protection Against Allowing Prayer in Public Schools*, 15 WHITTIER L. VER. 1193 (1994). Ms. Brilliant received American Jurisprudence Awards in Legal Process and Professional Responsibility. She is a member of the State Bar of California.

Preface

This book is a learning tool with two goals - to get you the best grade possible on your law school Professional Responsibility exam and to get you through the MPRE on your first try.

The book is broken up into two elements - ten essay questions and answers and 100 questions and answers of the multiple choice type. The essay questions will train you for your law school exam. The multiple choice questions are designed specifically to help you develop the skills you will need on the MPRE.

In the essay section, we offer complicated fact patterns and ask you to discuss all the issues arising under the facts. In the multiple-choice section, we offer MPRE-type questions. Our answers give you the right and wrong answers, but we tell you which one answer is right and why the other answers are wrong. Our objective in all this is to train you to pick out the important facts, find the issues they suggest, and then reason your way to the best answer.

This issue has been extensively revised to conform to recent changes in the Multistate Professional Responsibility Examination (MPRE). To the extent that they deal with the discipline of lawyers, the correct answers are now governed by the ABA Model Rules of Professional Conduct (the MR's). The Model Code of Professional Responsibility is no longer relevant to the MPRE.

Test items covering judicial ethics require knowledge and application of the ABA Model Code of Judicial Ethics (CJC).

In addition to questions testing the applicant's knowledge of the Model Rules, the test includes questions measuring knowledge of the rules, principles and common law regulating American lawyers as reflected in decided cases and in statutes and regulations. Wherever necessary to resolve procedural or evidentiary issues, the Federal Rules of Civil Procedure and the Federal Rules of Evidence are assumed to apply.

The MPRE gives varying weight to the different topics that comprise the subject of professional responsibility. In general, the weights are as follows:

1. Regulation of the Legal Profession — 8-12%

2. The Client-Lawyer Relatioship — 10-14%

3. Privilege & Confidentiality-Clients & Former Clients — 6-10%

4. Independent Professional Judgment-Conflicts of Interest- Client Consent — 12-16%

5. Competence, Legal Malpractice and Other Civil Liability — 8-12%

6. Litigation and Other Forms of Advocacy — 12-16%

7. Different Roles of the Lawyer — 4-8%

8. Safekeeping Property and Funds of Clients and Others — 4-8%

9. Communication about Legal Services — 6-10%

10. Lawyers and the Legal System — 2-6%

11. Judicial Ethics — 6-10%

Virtually all jurisdictions now require a passing grade on the MPRE for admission to the bar. The passing grade may vary from state to state. Many jurisdictions also require continuing education in ethics and professional responsibility for lawyers admitted to practic as part of their continuing legal education programs.

It's important that law students appreciate from the outset the importance of looking for ethical problems in all they do and think. I hope this book will be of some help to you in developing a sensitivity to these problems.

Lazar Emanuel

2000

Introduction

Although your grades are a significant factor in obtaining a summer internship or permanent position in a law firm, no formalized preparation for finals is offered at most law schools. Students, for the most part, are expected to fend for themselves in learning the exam-taking process. Ironically, law school exams ordinarily bear little correspondence to the teaching methods used by professors during the school year. They require you to spend most of your time briefing cases. Although many claim this is "great preparation" for issue-spotting on exams, it really isn't. Because you focus on one principle of law at a time, you don't get practice in relating one issue to another or in developing a picture of the entire course. When exams finally come, you're forced to make an abrupt 180-degree turn. Suddenly, you are asked to recognize, define and discuss a variety of issues buried within a single multi-issue fact pattern. In most schools, you are then asked to select among a number of possible answers, all of which look inviting but only one of which is right.

The comprehensive course outline you've created so diligently and with such pain, means little if you're unable to apply its contents on your final exams. There is a vast difference between reading opinions in which the legal principles are clearly stated and applying those same principles to hypothetical exams and multiple choice questions.

The purpose of this book is to help you bridge the gap between memorizing a rule of law and *understanding how to use it* in the context of an exam. After an initial overview describing the exam writing process, you will be presented with a large number of hypotheticals which test your ability to write analytical essays and to pick the right answers to multiple-choice questions. *Do them—all of them!* Then review the suggested answers which follow. You'll find that the key to superior grades lies in applying your knowledge through question and answers, not rote memory.

This book covers both the ABA Model Rules of Professional Conduct and the ABA Code of Judicial Conduct. It is an excellent tool for law school test preparation and for success on the MPRE.

GOOD LUCK!

Acknowledgement

The authors gratefully acknowledge the assistance of the California Committee of Bar Examiners which provided access to questions upon which many of the questions in this book are based.

Table of Contents

Preparing Effectively for Essay Examinations

The "ERC" Process	13.
Issue-Spotting	15.
How to Discuss an Issue	16.
Structuring Your Answer	19.
Discuss All Possible Issues	20.
Delineate the Transition From One Issue to the Next	21.
Understanding the "Call" of a Question	22.
The Importance of Analyzing the Question Carefully Before Writing	22.
When to Make An Assumption	23.
Case Names	24.
How to Handle Time Pressures	25.
Write Legibly	25.
The Importance of Reviewing Prior Exams	26.
As Always, A Caveat	27.

Essay Questions

Question 1 (Zealous Representation of Client; Duty of Confidentiality; Candor to Tribunal; Fairness to Adversary; Concealment of Physical Evidence; Testimony of Criminal Defendant; Perjury by Witness; Perjury by Party; Withdrawal by Counsel) .... 31.

Question 2 (Lawyer's Competence; Standards for Competency; Specialization; Declination of Representation; Association with Competent Attorney; Duty of Confidentiality; Factors for Reasonable Fees; Retainer Agreements; Duty to Communicate with Client) ...... 33.

Question 3 (Truthfulness on Bar Admission Application; Duty of Practitioner to Disclose Truth Regarding Bar Applicant; Attorney-Client Privilege; Duty of Confidentiality) .... 34.

Question 4 (Unauthorized Practice of Law; Supervision of Non-Lawyer Subordinates; Threatening Criminal Prosecution for Client Advantage; Attorney-Client Privilege; Duty of Confidentiality; Malpractice; Discipline of Non-Lawyers) .... 35.

Question 5 (Conflict of Interest; Instruments Creating Gifts to Lawyer; Former Client; Reasonableness of Fees; Contingent Fee Agreements; Prohibitions against Advancing Costs; Expenses of Litigation) .... 36.

Question 6 (Duty of Confidentiality; Future Crime Exception; Concealment of Physical Evidence; Obstruction of Justice; Duty to Supervise Subordinates; Control over Means of Communicating Client Confidence) .... 37.

Question 7 (Media Appearance; Client Solicitation; Direct Contact with Prospective Clients; Gifts to Media) .... 38.

Question 8 (Communications Concerning Services; False or Misleading Statements; Unjustified Expectations; Solicitation; Advertising by Mail) .... 39.

Question 9 (Duty to Discuss Fees; Contingent Fees; Writing Required for Contingent Fee Contracts; Liability for Costs; Reasonableness of Fee; Competent Representation; Client Controls Settlement Decision; Written Settlement Statement; Segregation of Funds; Notification of Receipt of Funds; Dispute over Fees) .... 40.

Question 10 (Conflicts of Interest; Duties of Loyalty and Confidentiality; Impairment of Judgment; Representing Both Sides of Transaction; Informed Consent; Source of Fee Payment; Mediation; Duty to Withdraw) .... 42.

Question 11 (Conflicts of Interest; Multiple Criminal Defendants; Difficulty of Maintaining Independence of Judgment; Duty to Withdraw; Payment of Fee by Third Person, not Client; Control by Client over Plea, Jury Trial and Decision to Testify) .... 43.

Question 12 (Conflicts of Interest; Former Government Lawyer; Negotiation for Private Employment; Representation of Private Client against Government Agency; Consent of Agency; Limitations on Use of Information Obtained during Government Service) .... 44.

Question 13 (Duty of Diligent and Zealous Representation; Duty to Consult with Client; Control of Case; Frivolous Claims; Harassment of Adversary; Abiding by Client's Decision; Identifying Client; Confidential Disclosures by Non-Client) .... 45.

Question 14 (Duty Not to Talk to Represented Client; Substitution of Lawyers; Impermissible Agreements over Media Rights; Duty to Communicate with Client; Control by Client over Plea; Lawyer's Crime of Moral Turpitude; Lawyer as Witness) .... 47.

Question 15 (Conflicts of Interest; Duties of Loyalty and Confidentiality; Current Client; Former Client; Consent after Consultation; Lawyer as Witness; Attorney-Client Privilege; Restraints against Lawyer's Partners; Reasonableness of Fees) .... 48.

TABLE OF CONTENTS

Question 16 (Diligent and Zealous Representation; Concealment of Documents; Withholding and Obstructing Evidence; Communication with Represented Party; Threat of Criminal Action for Advantage in Civil Matter; Asserting Opinion in Closing Arguments; Inflammatory Arguments) .... 49.

Question 17 (Acceptance of Gift by Judge; Obligation of Judge to Recuse Himself; Duty of Lawyer Not to Offer Gift to Judge; Membership by Judge in Discriminatory Organization; Improper Use of Influence by Judge; Political Activity by Judge) .... 50.

Question 18 (Campaign Contributions for Judge; Contributions by Lawyers; Solicitation of Funds by Judge; Campaign Committees; Use of Media for Campaign Publicity; Avoiding Appearance of Bias; Judge as Friend of Lawyer; Prohibition against Practice of Law by Judge) .... 51.

Question 19 (Improper Solicitation of Client; Misrepresenting Qualifications and Potential Outcome of Matter; Prejudicial Pre-Trial Publicity; Withholding Personal Opinions; Distorting Evidence) .... 52.

Question 20 (Misleading Advertising; Description of Services; Unlawful Practice of Law; Practice Limited to State of Admission; "How To" Books and Practice of Law; Reasonable Fees; Contingent Fee Agreements and Limitations; Writing Required for Contingent Fees; State in which Lawyer May Be Disciplined) .... 53.

Essay Answers

Answer to Question 1 .... 57.
Answer to Question 2 .... 61.
Answer to Question 3 .... 64.
Answer to Question 4 .... 67.
Answer to Question 5 .... 70.
Answer to Question 6 .... 72.
Answer to Question 7 .... 75.
Answer to Question 8 .... 77.
Answer to Question 9 .... 79.
Answer to Question 10 .... 81.
Answer to Question 11 .... 83.
Answer to Question 12 .... 85.
Answer to Question 13 .... 87.
Answer to Question 14 .... 89.

Answer to Question 15 .... 92.
Answer to Question 16 .... 94.
Answer to Question 17 .... 96.
Answer to Question 18 .... 99.
Answer to Question 19 .... 102.
Answer to Question 20 .... 104.

Multiple Choice Questions

Questions 1 through 100 .... 109.

Multiple Choice Answers

Answers to Questions 1 through 100 .... 155.

Tables & Index

Table of References to the Model Rules .... 212.
Table of References to the Model Code of Judicial Conduct .... 215.
Alphabetical index, listing issues by the number of the question
    raising the issue .... 217.

Preparing Effectively for Essay Examinations[1]

To achieve superior scores on essay exams, a student must (i) learn and understand "blackletter" principles and rules of law for each subject, and (ii) analyze how those principles of law arise within a test fact pattern. One of the most common misconceptions about law school is that you must memorize each word on every page of your casebooks or outlines to do well on exams. The reality is that you can commit an entire casebook to memory and still do poorly on an exam. Reviewing hundreds of student answers has shown us that most students can recite the rules. The ones who do **best** on exams understand how problems (issues) stem from the rules which they have memorized and how to communicate their analysis of these issues to the grader. The following pages cover what you need to know to achieve superior scores on your law school essay exams.

The "ERC" Process

To study effectively for law school exams you must be able to **"ERC"** (**E**lementize, **R**ecognize, and **C**onceptualize) each legal principle listed in the table of contents of your casebooks and course outlines. *Elementizing* means reducing the legal theories and rules you learn, down to a concise, straightforward statement of their essential elements. Without a knowledge of these precise elements, it is not possible to anticipate all of the potential issues which can arise under them.

For example, if you are asked, "what is self-defense?", it is *not* sufficient to say, "self-defense is permitted when, if someone is about to hit you, you can prevent him from doing it." This layperson description would leave a grader wondering if you had actually attended law school. An accurate elementization of the self-defense principle would be something like this: "Where one reasonably believes she is in imminent danger of an offensive touching, she may assert whatever force she reasonably believes necessary under the circumstances to prevent the offensive touching from occurring." This formulation correctly shows that there are four separate, distinct elements which must be satisfied for this defense to be successfully asserted: (i) the actor must have a *reasonable belief* that (ii) the touching which he seeks to prevent is *offensive*, (iii) the offensive touching is *imminent*, and (iv) the actor must use no greater force than she *reasonably believes is necessary under the circumstances* to prevent the offensive touching from occurring.

---

1. To illustrate the principles of effective exam preparation, we have used examples from Torts and Constitutional Law. However, these principles apply to all subjects. One of the most difficult tasks faced by law students is learning how to apply principles from one area of the law to another. We leave it to you, the reader, to think of comparable examples for the subject-matter of this book.

Recognizing means perceiving or anticipating which words within a legal principle are likely to be the source of issues, and how those issues are likely to arise within a hypothetical fact pattern. With respect to the self-defense concept, there are four ***potential*** issues. Did the actor reasonably believe that the person against whom the defense is being asserted was about to make an offensive contact upon her? Was the contact imminent? Would the contact have been offensive? Did the actor use only such force as she reasonably believed was necessary to prevent the imminent, offensive touching?

Conceptualizing means imagining situations in which each of the elements of a rule of law have given rise to factual issues. ***Unless a student can illustrate to herself an application of each element of a rule of law, she does not truly understand the legal principles behind the rule!*** In our opinion, the inability to conjure up hypothetical problems involving particular rules of law foretells a likelihood that issues involving those rules will be missed on an exam. It is therefore ***crucial*** to (i) ***recognize*** that issues result from the interaction of facts with the appropriate words defining a rule of law; and ii) develop the ability to ***conceptualize*** fact patterns involving each of the words contained in the rule

For example, an illustration of the "reasonable belief" portion of the self-defense principle in tort law might be the following:

> One evening, A and B had an argument at a bar. A screamed at B, "I'm going to get a knife and stab you!" A then ran out of the bar. B, who was armed with a concealed pistol, left the bar about 15 minutes later. As B was walking home, he suddenly heard running footsteps coming up from behind him. B drew his pistol, turned and shot the person advancing toward him (who was only about ten feet away when the shooting occurred). When B walked over to his victim, he recognized that the person he had killed was not A (but was instead another individual who had simply decided to take an evening jog). There would certainly be an issue whether B had a reasonable belief that the person who was running behind him was A. In the subsequent wrongful-death action, the victim's estate would certainly contend that the earlier threat by A was not enough to give B a reasonable belief that the person running behind him was A. B could certainly contend in rebuttal that given the prior altercation at the bar, A's threat, the darkness, and the fact that the incident occurred within a time frame soon after A's threat, his belief that A was about to attack him was "reasonable."

An illustration of how use of the word "imminent" might generate an issue is the following:

> X and Y had been feuding for some time. One afternoon, X suddenly attacked Y with a hunting knife. However, Y was able to wrest the knife away From X. At that point X retreated about four feet away from Y and screamed: "You were lucky this time, but next time I'll have a gun and you'll be finished." Y, having good reason to believe that X would subsequently carry out his threats (after all,

X had just attempted to kill Y), immediately thrust the knife into X's chest, killing him. While Y certainly had a reasonable belief that X would attempt to kill him the ***next time*** the two met, Y would probably ***not*** be able to assert successfully the self-defense privilege since the "imminency" element was absent.

A fact pattern illustrating the actor's right to use only that force which is reasonably necessary under the circumstances might be following:

D rolled up a newspaper and was about to strike E on the shoulder with it. As D pulled back his arm for the purpose of delivering the blow, E drew a knife and plunged it into D's chest. While E had every reason to believe that D was about to deliver an offensive impact on him, E probably could not successfully assert the self-defense privilege because the force he utilized in response was greater than reasonably necessary under the circumstances to prevent the impact. E could simply have deflected D's prospective blow or punched D away. The use of a knife constituted a degree of force by E which was ***not*** reasonable, given the minor injury which he would have suffered from the newspaper's impact.

"Mental gymnastics" such as these must be played with every element of every rule you learn.

Issue-Spotting

One of the keys to doing well on an essay examination is issue-spotting. In fact, issue spotting is ***the*** most important skill you will learn in law school. If you recognize all of the legal issues, you can always find an applicable rule of law (if there is any) by researching the issues. However, if you fail to perceive an issue, you may very well misadvise your client about the likelihood of success or failure. It is important to remember that (1) an issue is a question to be decided by the judge or jury; and (2) a question is "in issue" when it can be disputed or argued about at trial. The bottom line is that if ***you don't spot an issue, you can't discuss it***.

The key to issue-spotting is to approach a problem in the same way as an attorney would. Let's assume you're a lawyer and someone enters your office with a legal problem. He will recite the facts to you and give you any documents that may be pertinent. He will then want to know if he can sue (or be sued, if your client seeks to avoid liability). To answer your client's question intelligently, you will have to decide the following: (1) what are the pertinent facts; (2) what issues do they present; (3) what theories can possibly be asserted by your client; (4) what defense or defenses can possibly be raised to these theories; (5) what issues may arise if these theories and defenses are asserted; (6) what arguments can each side make to persuade the factfinder to resolve the issue in his favor; and (7) finally, what will the ***likely*** outcome of each issue be. ***All the issues which can possibly arise at trial should be discussed in your answer.***

How to Discuss an Issue

Keep in mind that *rules of law are the guides to issues* (i.e., an issue arises where there is a question whether the facts do, or do not, satisfy an element of a rule); a rule of law *cannot dispose of an issue* unless the rule can reasonably be *applied to the facts.*

A good way to learn how to discuss an issue is to start with the following mini-hypothetical and the two student responses which follow it.

Mini-Hypothetical

A and B were involved in making a movie which was being filmed at a bar. The script called for A to appear to throw a bottle (which was actually a rubber prop) at B. The fluorescent lighting at the bar had been altered, the subdued blue lights being replaced with rather bright white lights. The cameraperson had stationed herself just to the left of the swinging doors which served as the main entrance to the bar. As the scene was unfolding, C, a regular patron of the bar, unwittingly walked into it. The guard who was stationed immediately outside the bar had momentarily left his post to visit the restroom. As C pushed the barroom doors inward, the left door panel knocked the camera to the ground with a resounding crash. The first (and only) thing which C saw, was A (who was about 5 feet from C) getting ready to throw the bottle at B, who was at the other end of the bar (about 15 feet from A). Without hesitation, C pushed A to the ground and punched him in the face. Plastic surgery was required to restore A's profile to its Hollywood-handsome pre-altercation form.

Discuss A's right against C.

Pertinent Principles of Law:

1. Under the rule defining the prevention-of-crime privilege, if one sees that someone is about to commit what she reasonably believes to be a felony or misdemeanor involving a breach of the peace, she may exercise whatever degree of force is reasonably necessary under the circumstances to prevent that person from committing the crime.

2. Under the defense-of-others privilege, where the actor reasonably believes that someone is about to cause an offensive contact upon a third party, she may use whatever force is reasonably necessary under the circumstances to prevent the contact. Some jurisdictions, however, limit this privilege to situations in which the actor and the third party are related.

First Student Answer

Did C commit an assault and battery upon A?

"An assault occurs where the defendant intentionally causes the plaintiff to be reasonably in apprehension of an imminent, offensive touching. The facts state that C punched A to the ground. Thus, a battery would have occurred at this point. We are also told that C punched A in the face. It is reasonable to assume that A saw the punch being thrown at him, and therefore A felt in imminent danger of an offensive touching. Based upon the facts, C is liable for an assault and battery upon A.

Were C's actions justifiable under the defense-of-others privilege?

"C could successfully assert the defense-of-others and prevention-of-crime privileges. When C opened the bar doors, A appeared to be throwing the bottle at B. Although the "bottle" was actually a prop, C had no way of knowing this fact. Also, it was necessary for C to punch A in the face to assure that A could not get back up, retrieve the bottle, and again throw it at B. While the plastic surgery required by A is unfortunate, C could not be successfully charged with assault and battery."

Second Student Answer

Assault and Battery:

"C committed an assault (causing A to be reasonably in apprehension of an imminent, offensive contact) when A saw C's punch about to hit him, and battery (causing an offensive contact upon A) when he (i) C knocked A to the ground, and (ii) C punched A.

Defense-of-Others/Prevention-of-Crime Defenses:

"C would undoubtedly assert the privileges of defense-of-others (where defendant reasonably believed the plaintiff was about to make an offensive contact upon a third party, he was entitled to use whatever force was reasonably necessary to prevent the contact); and prevention-of-crime defense (where one reasonably believes another is about to commit a felony or misdemeanor involving a breach of the peace, he may exercise whatever force is reasonably necessary to prevent that person from committing a crime).

"A could contend that C was not reasonable in believing that A was about to cause harm to B because the enhanced lighting at the bar and camera crash should have indicated to C, a regular customer, that a movie was being filmed. However, C could probably successfully contend in rebuttal that his belief was reasonable in light of the facts that (i) he had not seen the camera when he attacked A, and (ii) instantaneous action was required (he did not have time to notice the enhanced lighting around the bar).

"A might also contend that the justification was forfeited because the degree of force used by C was not reasonable, since C did not have to punch A in the face after A had already been pushed to the ground (i.e., the danger to B was no longer present). However, C could argue in rebuttal that it was necessary to knockout A (an individual with apparently violent propensities) while the opportunity existed, rather than risk a drawn-out scuffle in which A might prevail. The facts do not indicate how big A and C were; but assuming C was not significantly larger than A, C's contention will probably be successful. If, however, C was significantly larger than A, the punch may have been excessive (since C could presumably have simply held A down)."

Critique

Let's examine the First Student Answer first. It mistakenly phrases as an "issue" the assault and battery committed by C upon A. While the actions creating these torts must be mentioned in the facts to provide a foundation for a discussion of the applicable privileges, there was no need to discuss them further because they were not the issue the examiners were testing for.

The structure of the initial paragraph of First Student Answer is also incorrect. After an assault is defined in the first sentence, the second sentence abruptly describes the facts necessary to constitute the commission of a battery. The third sentence then sets forth the elements of a battery. The fourth sentence completes the discussion of assault by describing the facts pertaining to that tort. The two-sentence break between the original mention of assault and the facts which constitute this tort is confusing; the facts which call for the application of a rule should be mentioned *immediately* after the rule is stated.

A more serious error, however, occurs in the second paragraph of the First Student Answer. While there is an allusion to the correct principle of law (prevention of crime), the *rule is not defined*. As a consequence, the grader can only guess why the student thinks the facts set forth in the subsequent sentences are significant. A grader reading this answer could not be certain that the student recognized that the issues revolved around the *reasonable belief* and *necessary force* elements of the prevention-of-crime privilege. Superior exam-writing requires that the pertinent facts be *tied* directly and clearly to the operative rule.

The Second Student Answer is very much better than the First Answer. It disposes of C's assault and battery upon A in a few words (yet tells the grader that the writer knows these torts are present). More importantly, the grader can easily see the issues which would arise if the prevention-of crime-privilege were asserted (i.e., "whether C's belief that A was about to commit a crime against B was reasonable" and "whether C used unnecessary force in punching A after A had been knocked to the ground"). Finally, it also utilizes all the facts by indicating how each attorney would assert those facts which are most advantageous to her client.

Structuring Your Answer

Graders will give high marks to a clearly-written, well-structured answer. Each issue you discuss should follow a specific and consistent structure which a grader can easily follow.

The Second Student Answer above basically utilizes the *I-R-A-A-O format* with respect to each issue. In this format, the *I* stands for the word *Issue*, the *R* for *Rule of law*, the initial *A* for the words *one side's Argument*, the second *A* for *the other party's rebuttal Argument*, and the *O* for your *Opinion as to how the issue would be resolved.* The *I-R-A-A-O* format emphasizes the importance of (1) discussing *both* sides of an issue, and (2) communicating to the grader that when an issue arises, an attorney can only advise her client as to the *probable* decision on that issue.

A somewhat different format for analyzing each issue is the *I-R-A-C format.* The *"I"* stands for *"Issue;"* the *"R"* for *"Rule of law;"* the *"A"* for *"Application of the facts to the rule of law;"* and the *"C"* for *"Conclusion."* I-R-A-C is a legitimate approach to the discussion of a particular issue, within the time constraints imposed by the question. The *I-R-A-C format* must be applied to each issue; it is not the solution to an entire exam answer. If there are six issues in a question, for example, you should offer six separate, independent *I-R-A-C* analyses.

We believe that the *I-R-A-C* approach is preferable to the *I-R-A-A-O* formula. However, either can be used to analyze and organize essay exam answers. Whatever format you choose, however, you should be consistent throughout the exam and remember the following rules:

First, *analyze all of the relevant facts.* Facts have significance in a particular case *only as they come under the applicable rules of law.* The facts presented must be analyzed and examined to see if they do or do not satisfy one element or another of the applicable rules, and the essential facts and rules must be stated and argued in your analysis.

Second, you must communicate to the grader the *precise rule of law* controlling the facts. In their eagerness to commence their arguments, students sometimes fail to state the applicable rule of law first. Remember, the *"R"* in either format stands for "Rule of Law." Defining the rule of law *before* an analysis of the facts is essential in order to allow the grader to follow your reasoning.

Third, it is important to treat *each side of an issue with equal detail.* If a hypothetical describes how an elderly man was killed when he ventured upon the land of a huge power company to obtain a better view of a nuclear reactor, your sympathies might understandably fall on the side of the old man. The grader will nevertheless expect you to see and make every possible argument for the other side. Don't permit your personal viewpoint to affect your answer! A good lawyer never does! When discussing an issue, always state the arguments for each side.

Finally, don't forget to *state your opinion or conclusion* on each issue. Keep in mind, however, that your opinion or conclusion is probably the *least* important part of an exam answer. Why? Because your professor knows that no attorney can tell her client exactly how a judge or jury will decide a particular issue. By definition, an issue is a legal dispute which can go either way. An attorney, therefore, can offer her client only her best opinion about the likelihood of victory or defeat on an issue. Since the decision on any issue lies with the judge or jury, no attorney can ever be absolutely certain of the resolution.

Discuss All Possible Issues

As we've noted, a student should draw *some* type of conclusion or opinion for each issue raised. Whatever your conclusion on a particular issue, it is essential to anticipate and discuss *all of the issues* which would arise if the question were actually tried in court.

Let's assume that a negligence hypothetical involves issues pertaining to duty, breach of duty, proximate causation and contributory negligence. If the defendant prevails on any one of these issues, he will avoid liability. Nevertheless, even if you feel strongly that the defendant owed no duty to the plaintiff, you *must* go on to discuss all of the other potential issues as well (breach of duty, proximate causation and contributory negligence). If you were to terminate your answer after a discussion of the duty problem only, you'd receive an inferior grade.

Why should you have to discuss every possible potential issue if you are relatively certain that the outcome of a particular issue would be dispositive of the entire case? Because at the commencement of litigation, neither party can be *absolutely positive* about which issues he will win at trial. We can state with confidence that every attorney with some degree of experience has won issues he thought he would lose, and has lost issues on which he thought victory was assured. Since one can never be absolutely certain how a factual issue will be resolved by the factfinder, a good attorney (and exam-writer) will consider *all* possible issues.

To understand the importance of discussing all of the potential issues, you should reflect on what you will do during the actual practice of law. If you represent the defendant, for example, it is your job to raise every possible defense. If there are five potential defenses, and your pleadings only rely on three of them (because you're sure you will win on all three), and the plaintiff is somehow successful on all three issues, your client may well sue you for malpractice. Your client's contention would be that you should be liable because if you had only raised the two additional issues, you might have prevailed on at least one of them, and therefore liability would have been avoided. It is an attorney's duty to raise *all* legitimate issues. A similar philosophy should be followed when taking essay exams.

What exactly do you say when you've resolved the initial issue in favor of the defendant, and discussion of any additional issues would seem to be moot? The answer is simple. You simply begin the discussion of the next potential issue with something like, "Assuming, however, the plaintiff prevailed on the foregoing issue, the next issue would be…" The grader will understand and appreciate what you have done.

The corollary to the importance of raising all potential issues is that you should avoid discussion of obvious non-issues. Raising non-issues is detrimental in three ways: first, you waste a lot of precious time; second, you usually receive absolutely no points for discussing a point which the grader deems extraneous; third, it suggests to the grader that you lack the ability to distinguish the significant from the irrelevant. The best guideline for avoiding the discussion of a non-issue is to ask yourself, "would I, as an attorney, feel comfortable about raising that particular issue or objection in front of a judge"?

Delineate the Transition From One Issue to the Next

It's a good idea to make it easy for the grader to see the issues which you've found. One way to accomplish this is to cover no more than one issue per paragraph. Another way is to underline each issue statement. Provided time permits, both techniques are recommended. The essay answers in this book contain numerous illustrations of these suggestions.

One frequent student error is to write a two-paragraph answer in which all of the arguments for one side are made in the initial paragraph, and all of the rebuttal arguments by the other side are made in the next paragraph. This is *a bad idea*. It obliges the grader to reconstruct the exam answer in his mind several times to determine whether all possible issues have been discussed by both sides. It will also cause you to state the same rule of law more than once. A better-organized answer presents a given argument by one side and follows that immediately in the same paragraph with the other side's rebuttal to that argument.

Understanding the "Call" of a Question

The statements *at the end of* an essay question or of the fact pattern in a multiple-choice question is sometimes referred to as the "call" of the question. It usually asks you to do something specific like "discuss," "discuss the rights of the parties," "what are X's rights?" "advise X," "the best grounds on which to find the statute unconstitutional are:," "D can be convicted of:," "how should the estate be distributed," etc. The call of the question should be read carefully because it tells you exactly what you're expected to do. If a question asks, "what are X's rights against Y?" or "X is liable to Y for:..." you don't have to spend a lot time on Y's rights against Z. You will usually receive absolutely no credit for discussing facts that are not required by the question. On the other hand, if the call of an essay question is simply "discuss" or "discuss the rights of the parties" then *all* foreseeable issues must be covered by your answer.

Students are often led astray by an essay question's call. For example, if you are asked for "X's rights against Y" or to "advise X", you may think you may limit yourself to X's viewpoint with respect to the issues. This is *not correct*! You cannot resolve one party's rights against another party without considering the issues which might arise (and the arguments which the other side would assert) if litigation occurred. In short, although the call of the question may appear to focus on one of the parties to the litigation, a superior answer will cover all the issues and arguments which that person might *encounter* (not just the arguments she would *make*) in attempting to pursue her rights against the other side.

The Importance of Analyzing the Question Carefully Before Writing

The overriding *time pressure* of an essay exam is probably a major reason why many students fail to analyze a question carefully before writing. Five minutes into the allocated time for a particular question, you may notice that the person next to you is writing furiously. This thought then flashes through your mind, "Oh, my goodness, he's putting down more words on the paper than I am, and therefore he's bound to get a better grade." It can be stated *unequivocally* that there is no necessary correlation between the number of words on your exam paper and the grade you'll receive. Students who begin their answer after only five minutes of analysis have probably seen only the most obvious issues, and missed many, if not most, of the subtle ones. They are also likely to be less well organized.

Opinions differ as to how much time you should spend analyzing and outlining a question before you actually write the answer. We believe that you should spend at least 12-18 minutes analyzing, organizing, and outlining a one-hour question before writing your answer. This will usually provide sufficient time to analyze and organize the question thoroughly *and* enough time to write a relatively complete answer. Remember that each word of the question must be scrutinized to determine if it (i) suggests an issue under the rules you've learned, or (ii) can be used in making an argument for the resolution of an issue. Since you can't receive points for an issue you don't spot, it is usually wise to read a question *twice* before starting your outline.

When to Make an Assumption

The instructions on an exam may tell you to *"assume"* facts which are necessary to the answer. Even where these instructions are *not* specifically given, you may be obliged to make certain assumptions with respect to missing facts in order to write a thorough answer. Assumptions should be made when you, as the attorney for one of the parties described in the question, would be obliged to solicit additional information from your client. On the other hand, assumptions should *never be used to change or alter the question.* Don't ever write something like "if the facts in the question were …, instead of …, then … would result." If you do this, you are wasting time on facts which are extraneous to the problem before you. Professors want you to deal with *their* fact patterns, not your own.

Students sometimes try to "write around" information they think is missing. They assume that their professor has failed to include every piece of data necessary for a thorough answer. This is generally *wrong.* The professor may have omitted some facts deliberately to see if the student *can figure out what to do* under the circumstances. In some instances, the professor may have omitted them inadvertently (even law professors are sometimes human).

The way to deal with the omission of essential information is to describe (i) what fact (or facts) are missing, and (ii) why that information is important. As an example, go back to the "movie shoot" hypothetical we discussed above. In that fact pattern, there was no mention of the relative strength of A and C. This fact could be extremely important. If C weighed 240 pounds and was built like a professional football linebacker, while A tipped the scales at a mere 160 pounds, punching A in the face after he had been pushed to the ground would probably constitute unnecessary force (thereby causing C to forfeit the prevention-of-crime privilege). If the physiques of the parties were reversed, however, C's punch to A's face would probably constitute reasonable behavior. Under the facts, C had to deal the *"knockout"* blow while the opportunity presented itself. The last sentences of the Second Student Answer above show that the student understood these subtleties and correctly stated the essential missing facts and assumptions.

Assumptions should be made in a manner which keeps the other issues open (i.e., prompts discussion of all other possible issues). Don't assume facts which would virtually dispose of the entire hypothetical in a few sentences. For example, suppose that A called B a "convicted felon" (a statement which is inherently defamatory, *i.e.,* a defamatory statement is one which tends to subject the plaintiff to hatred, contempt or ridicule). If A's statement is true, he has a complete defense to B's action for defamation. If the facts don't tell whether A's statement was true or not, it would ***not*** be wise to write something like, "We'll assume that A's statement about B is accurate, and therefore B cannot successfully sue A for defamation." So facile an approach would rarely be appreciated by the grader. The proper way to handle this situation would be to state, "if we assume that A's statement about B is not correct, A can not raise the defense of truth." You've communicated to the grader that you recognize the need to assume an essential fact and that you've assumed it in such a way as to enable you to proceed to discuss all other potential issues.

Case Names

A law student is ordinarily ***not*** expected to recall case names on an exam. The professor knows that you have read several hundred cases for each course, and that you would have to be a memory expert to have all of the names at your fingertips. If you confront a fact pattern which seems similar to a case which you have reviewed (but you cannot recall the name of it), just write something like, "One case held that ..." or "It has been held that ..." In this manner, you have informed the grader that you are relying on a case which contained a fact pattern similar to the question at issue.

The only exception to this rule is in the case of a landmark decision. Landmark opinions are usually those which change or alter established law.[2] These cases are usually easy to identify, because you will probably have spent an entire class period discussing each of them. *Palsgraf v. Long Island Rail Road* is a prime example of a landmark case in Torts. In these special cases, you may be expected to remember the case by name, as well the proposition of law which it stands for. However, this represents a very limited exception to the general rule which counsels against wasting precious time trying to memorize case names.

---

2. The only subject to which this does not apply is Constitutional Law, since here virtually every case you study satisfies this definition. Students studying Constitutional Law should try to associate case names with holdings and reproduce them in their exam answers.

How To Handle Time Pressures

What do you do when there are five minutes left in the exam and you have only written down two-thirds of your answer? One thing *not* to do is write something like, "No time left!" or "Not enough time!" This gets you nothing but the satisfaction of knowing you have communicated your personal frustrations to the grader. Another thing *not* to do is insert the outline you may have made on scrap paper into the exam booklet. Professors rarely will look at these items.

First of all, it is not necessarily a bad thing to be pressed for time. The person who finishes five minutes early has very possibly missed some important issues. The more proficient you become in knowing what is expected of you on an exam, the greater the difficulty you may experience in staying within the time limits. Second, remember that (at least to some extent) you're graded against your classmates' answers and they're under exactly the same time pressure as you. In short, don't panic if you can't write the "perfect" answer in the allotted time. Nobody does!

The best hedge against misuse of time is to **review as many old exams as possible**. These exercises will give you a familiarity with the process of organizing and writing an exam answer, which, in turn, should result in an enhanced ability to stay within the time boundaries. If you nevertheless find that you have about 15 minutes of writing to do and five minutes to do it in, write a paragraph which summarizes the remaining issues or arguments you would discuss if time permitted. As long as you've indicated that you're aware of the remaining legal issues, you'll probably receive some credit for them. Your analytical and argumentative skills will already be apparent to the grader by virtue of the issues that you have previously discussed.

Write Legibly

Make sure your answer is legible. Students should *not* assume that their professors will be willing to take their papers to the local pharmacist to have them deciphered. Remember, your professor may have 75-150 separate exam answers to grade. If your answer is difficult to read, you will rarely be given the benefit of the doubt. On the other hand, a legible, well-organized paper creates a very positive mental impact upon the grader.

Many schools allow students to type their exams. If you're an adequate typist, you may want to seriously consider typing. Typing has two major advantages. First, it should help assure that your words will be readable (unless, of course, there are numerous typos). Second, it should enable you to put a lot more words onto the paper than if your answer had been handwritten. Most professors prefer a typed answer to a written one.

There are, however, a few disadvantages to typing. For one thing, all the typists are usually in a single room. If the clatter of other typewriters will make it difficult for you to concentrate, typing is probably *not* wise. To offset this problem, some students wear earplugs during the exam. Secondly, typing sometimes makes it difficult to change or add to an earlier portion of your answer. You may have to withdraw your paper from the carriage and insert another. Try typing out a few practice exams before you decide to type your exam. If you do type, be sure to leave at least one blank line between typewritten lines, so that handwritten changes and insertions in your answers can be made easily.

If you decide against typing, your answer will probably be written in a "bluebook" (a booklet of plain, lined, white paper which has a light blue cover and back). It is usually a good idea to write only on the odd numbered pages (i.e., 1, 3, 5, etc.). You may also want to leave a blank line between each written line. Doing these things will usually make the answer easier to read. If you discover that you have left out a word or phrase, you can insert it into the proper place by means of a caret sign ("∧"). If you feel that you've omitted an entire issue, you can write it on the facing blank page. A symbol reference can be used to indicate where the additional portion of the answer should be inserted. While it's not ideal to have your answer take on the appearance of a road map, a symbol reference to an adjoining page is much better than trying to squeeze six lines into one, and will help the grader to discover where the same symbol appears in another part of your answer.

The Importance of Reviewing Prior Exams

As we've mentioned, it is *extremely important to review old exams.* The transition from reading blackletter law to writing an essay exam can be a difficult experience if the process has not been practiced. Although this book provides a large number of essay and multiple-choice questions, *don't stop here*! Most law schools have recent tests on file in the library, by the course. We strongly suggest that you make a copy of every old exam you can obtain (especially those given by your professors) at the beginning of each semester. The demand for these documents usually increases dramatically as "finals time" draws closer.

The exams for each course should be scrutinized *throughout the semester.* They should be reviewed as you complete each chapter in your casebook. Generally, the order of exam questions follows the sequence of the materials in your casebook. Thus, the first question on a law school test may involve the initial three chapters of the casebook; the second question may pertain to the fourth and fifth chapters, etc. In any event, *don't wait* until the semester is nearly over to begin reviewing old exams.

Keep in mind that no one is born with the ability to analyze questions and write superior answers to law school exams. Like any skill, it is developed and perfected only through application. If you don't take the time to analyze numerous examinations from prior years, this evolutionary process just won't occur. Don't just **think about** the answers to past exam questions; take the time to **write the answers down**. It's also wise to look back at an answer a day or two after you've written it. You will invariably see (i) ways in which the organization could have been improved, and (ii) arguments you missed.

As you practice spotting issues on past exams, you will see how rules of law become the sources of issues on finals. As we've already noted, if you don't **understand** how rules of law translate into issues, you won't be able to achieve superior grades on your exams. Reviewing exams from prior years should also reveal that certain issues tend to be lumped together in the same question. For instance, where a fact pattern involves a false statement made by one person about another, three potential theories of liability are often present — defamation, invasion of privacy (false, public light) and intentional infliction of severe emotional distress. You will need to see if any or all of these apply to the facts.

Finally, one of the best means of evaluating if you understand a course (or a particular area within a subject) is to attempt to create a hypothetical exam for that topic. Your exam should contain as many issues as possible. If you can write an issue-packed exam, you probably know that particular area of law. If you can't, then you probably haven't yet acquired an adequate understanding of how the principles of law in that subject can spawn issues.

As Always, a Caveat

The suggestions and advice offered in this book represent the product of many years of experience in the field of legal education. We are confident that the techniques and concepts described in these pages will help you prepare for, and succeed, at your exams. Nevertheless, particular professors sometimes have a preference for exam-writing techniques which are not stressed in this work. Some instructors expect at least a nominal reference to the ***prima facie*** elements of all pertinent legal theories (even though one or more of those principles is **not** placed into issue). Other professors want their students to emphasize public policy considerations in the arguments they make on a particular issue. Because this book is intended for nationwide consumption, these individualized preferences have **not** been stressed. The best way to find out whether your professor has a penchant for a particular writing approach is to ask her to provide you with a model answer to a previous exam. If an item is not available, speak to upperclass students who received a superior grade in that professor's class.

One final point. This book is based upon the authors' analysis of fact patterns raising common problems faced by lawyers in applying the ABA Rules of Professional Conduct and in analyzing the ABA Code of Judicial Conduct. Our analysis may be different from your professor's analysis of the same or similar problems. When a conflict exists between our formulation of a rule and the one which is taught by your professor, *follow the latter!* Since your grades are determined by your professors, their views should always supersede the views contained in this book.

Essay Exam Questions

Question 1

Mugsy Malone retained attorney Dee Fender to represent him on a federal bank robbery charge. The indictment charged that Malone had robbed Freedom Bank on Third Street. The prosecutor's case depended in part on photographic evidence obtained from hidden cameras in the bank. None of the photographs clearly depicted the robber's face.

At their first meeting, Malone told Fender that, at the time of the robbery, he was watching television at the home of his friend Dolly Moll.

While reviewing the evidence, Fender noticed that one of the bank photographs showed the robber wearing a ring on the fourth finger of his right hand. Later, at one of their trial preparation sessions, Fender saw that Malone had a ring on the same finger. Fender mentioned this to Malone, and the following conversation occurred:

> Malone: "So what? Lots of people wear rings on that finger and lots of rings look like this one."
>
> Fender: "Yours has a 'B' on it."
>
> Malone: "You can't see the one in the bank photo clearly enough to see if there's a 'B' on that one."
>
> Fender: "You might be able to if they blow it up."

After the meeting ended, Malone removed the ring and Fender never saw it again. In a subsequent meeting, Fender noticed a tan ring line on Malone's finger and said, "The DA may ask you about the ring line on your finger." Malone did not respond.

During the trial, but before he testified, Malone asked Fender what he should do if the prosecutor asks him if he owned a ring with a 'B' on it.

"If you insist on testifying, you have to tell the truth," Fender said.

The night before closing arguments were scheduled to begin, Malone gave Fender the balance of her legal fee in $100 bills. Fender noticed that the serial numbers on fourteen of the $100 bills corresponded to the the serial numbers identified during the testimony of a bank officer as the numbers on some of the stolen bills.

Fender returned the fourteen $100 bills to Malone and told him to bring an equivalent sum in other denominations. The following morning, Malone came to court with bills in various denominations, which Fender accepted.

In her closing argument, Fender argued that the prosecutor was going after the wrong man and urged the jury to believe Dolly Moll's testimony confirming Mugsy's alibi.

What standards of professional responsibility, if any, has Fender violated by her conduct in representing Malone? Discuss.

Question 2

Marcia, an attorney, has been in general practice for two years. Alice, a potential client, meets with Marcia and asks for legal advice on a complex property matter. Marcia listens closely to Alice as she relates her problem and then asks Alice for a $500 retainer to accept the case, which Alice pays. Over the course of the next six months, Marcia neither writes nor initiates a call to Alice regarding the status of her case. During this time, Alice calls Marcia eight times. Marcia never takes Alice's phone calls but does return four of them, telling Alice each time that she has been "busy researching the problem." After the last phone call from Alice, Marcia actually does begin researching the question of property law controlling Alice's case. Marcia becomes very discouraged when she realizes that she does not understand the issues. She spends about fifteen hours attempting to learn the subject but is not confident that she has mastered it. Marcia then telephones Jan, an attorney who specializes in property law, and asks her to associate herself with Marcia in Alice's matter. Jan agrees to act as co-counsel, with the understanding that Alice will pay her $250 per hour. Marcia consents to Jan's fee without consulting Alice.

A few days later, Marcia writes Alice the following letter:

> "Dear Alice:
>
> You will be pleased to know that I am making progress on resolving your case. I have spent fifteen hours researching the subject and am enclosing a bill for $2,250, which covers my fee of $150 per hour. In addition, I have associated with a well known expert on property law to co-represent you. Her name is Jan. She will be billing you separately at $250 per hour for her services. Please call if you have any questions.
>
> Sincerely, Marcia"

Has Marcia violated any standards of professional responsibility? Discuss.

Question 3

Joe Isuzu is a third year law student in the state of Shock and is in the process of filling out his bar application. One question asks if the applicant has ever been convicted of a crime, including traffic-related violations. Joe has a misdemeanor drunk driving conviction on his record. Joe convinces himself that the authorities are really concerned only with felony convictions, and he answers "no" to the question. Six months later, Joe takes and passes Shock's bar examination and joins a large downtown law firm as an associate.

Joe becomes friendly with John, another associate at the firm. One night, Joe and John go out to dinner. Over drinks, Joe confesses that he was once arrested and convicted for drunk driving. John asks him, "How did you handle that on your application for the bar?" Laughing, Joe says, "Those knuckleheads never found out about the conviction. I didn't put it on my application and they never asked." The next day, now sober, Joe notices that John is keeping his distance and acting remote and unresponsive. Fearful that John will report him to the grievance committee, Joe goes to see Perry Mason, an old family friend and well-known criminal defense attorney. Joe asks Perry for advice on what to do now that John knows about the drunk driving conviction. Mason advises Joe to notify the state bar about the conviction. Mason says, "Confession before John reports you is the best step. You've had a good record since you were admitted and the Committee may take no action. But you have to tell them." Joe leaves Mason's office and does not notify the bar. Neither John nor Mason ever reports Joe to the bar.

A year later, Joe decides to move to the state of Euphoria. The bar application in Euphoria asks only if there have been any prior *felony* convictions. Joe honestly replies no. Joe asks Mason to write a letter of recommendation for his admission to the Euphoria state bar. Mason consents and sends the letter to the bar. Mason says nothing about his interview with Joe or about his conviction. Joe is admitted to practice law in the state of Euphoria.

Are Joe, John, and/or Mason subject to discipline? Discuss.

Question 4

Henry, out of work and down on his luck, has been living in an old residential hotel near skid row. He lives with his big bad dog, Woof. While walking downtown one day, he sees a sign advertising, "Downtown Legal Center: Free Legal Services for Those in Need." Henry walks in and is assigned to Dan, an experienced legal aid attorney. Dan tells Henry, "I'm a little busy right now but my partner, Larry, can help you with whatever you need." When Henry asks Larry if he is also an attorney, Larry, still within Dan's earshot, replies, "I do most of the work around here." Larry is actually a student at the local law school who is doing an internship at the center.

Henry tells Larry his landlord is threatening to evict him for keeping an animal in his room, despite the fact that other tenants have pets. Larry takes the information down and tells Henry he'll get started on the landlord issue immediately, and to come back and see him in two weeks to discuss the progress of his case.

Larry tells Dan about Henry's problem with his landlord, and Dan says he knows just the solution. Dan writes a letter to the landlord stating that if the landlord doesn't stop harassing Henry about his dog, Dan will have his friends in the district attorney's office file criminal charges against the landlord for building code violations. Influenced by the letter, the landlord agrees to let Henry continue to live in the building with Woof.

A few days later, Henry takes Woof for a walk and sees an armored truck parked next to the local bank. Henry watches as the driver opens the back door of the truck, removes satchels of money and walks into the bank. Henry notices that the driver has neglected to lock the back door, and the door swings open. Henry reaches into the truck, grabs a bag of money and runs. Later, Henry discovers that he has taken $50,000 in large bills.

When Henry returns to the legal center for his appointment, both Larry and Dan meet with him. They notice that Henry is clean shaven and is wearing a new shirt, slacks, and shoes. Henry tells them in confidence that he stole money from an armored truck so that he could provide a better life-style for Woof. "I'm scared I'll get caught. I didn't know what I was doing and I think I may have left some fingerprints on the door. What should I do?" Dan and Larry discuss Henry's options, including the option of going to the police and offering a confession. Henry says he will think about the confession and leaves. After he leaves, Dan hears Larry call the police and report Henry's theft. Henry is arrested, tried and convicted, largely as a result of Larry's testimony against him.

What claims, if any, does Henry have against *Dan*, and what standards of professional conduct, if any, has *Dan* violated? Also, is there any avenue of recourse against Larry?

Question 5

Marvin Mogul retains Suzanne Ellis to represent him in the acquisition of an investment property. The negotiations are extremely tense, but Ellis manages to close the deal at the lowest price Mogul could have hoped for. Elated with the results, he tells Ellis he wants to give her a bonus: a $50,000 bequest in his will. He asks Ellis to draft the codicil herself. "I don't think that would be a good idea. You should really have an independent attorney do that." Mogul insists that Ellis do it herself, and she finally agrees.

Two years later, Alice Johnson comes to see Ellis. Johnson has been Mogul's assistant for the last 18 months and wants to sue him for sexual harassment. The facts of her case are compelling and Ellis agrees to take the case. Johnson has been so distraught over her working conditions that she is no longer capable of working at all. She has no money to offer Ellis, and is not sure she can withstand the pressures of going forward with a trial.

Ellis tells Johnson that she can take the case on a contingent fee basis. She presents her with a written agreement specifying the amount she will recover in the case of settlement (20 percent) or trial (30 percent), and explaining that all relevant expenses will be deducted from the recovery before calculation of the contingent fee award. She then offers to advance Johnson the costs of a qualified therapist to help give Johnson the emotional resolve necessary to pursue her claim. "You can pay me back if you win. If you don't, consider it a gift."

Has Ellis violated any rules of professional conduct? Discuss.

Question 6

Dreisdale is a criminal defense attorney. He uses an office intercom to communicate with Ethel Hathaway, his paralegal, whose desk is outside his office. When Dreisdale is not meeting with a client, he usually leaves the intercom on so he can call to Hathaway without leaving his desk. Hathaway has worked for Dreisdale for two months when one afternoon, Clampett, a client, rushes past Hathaway and into Dreisdale's office. Clampett shouts, "I have to tell someone. I killed a man last night." Dreisdale tells Clampett to sit down and tell him the details. Clampett explains, "I got into a fight with a guy who was flirting with my girlfriend. I followed him to an alley behind his house and shot him. It was dark and I don't think anyone saw me." Clampett then asks Dreisdale, "I have the gun I used — what should I do with it?" Dreisdale replies, "I have to advise you to turn the gun over to the police. If you give the gun to me, I will give it to the police." Clampett throws the gun on Dreisdale's desk and says, "OK, you know what to do with it."

Obviously agitated, Clampett gets up to leave and Dreisdale asks, "Where are you going?" Clampett replies, "To finish the job I started. The guy had a friend who was also bothering my girlfriend. I'm going to make sure he can never do that again." Clampett rushes out and Dreisdale carefully picks the gun up with a pencil. He places it in a paper bag, and drops it in a trash can next to a fast food restaurant. Dreisdale then calls the police anonymously and tells them where they can find the weapon.

Returning to his office, Dreisdale realizes that the intercom was on during his meeting with Clampett and that Hathaway heard everything. Hathaway confesses that she called a friend at the local newspaper and gave him the scoop on the latest murder in town. The next day, Dreisdale learns that the police have arrested Clampett for murder after reading the article.

Has Dreisdale committed any ethical violations by his conduct? Discuss.

Question 7

Mansfield is a successful criminal defense attorney. For the past six months, she has been doing televised trial commentary on a notorious murder trial involving a former football star. Her comments are considered sharp and perceptive and she has gained national recognition. She has recently received numerous other offers to appear on television. One afternoon, Mansfield appears on a live talk show with three other attorneys to discuss the general state of the law. The panel takes questions from phone callers. The callers are asked to use their first names only in order to protect their privacy.

A young woman named Julie calls and directs her question to all of the lawyers on the panel: "I have just received a subpoena to be a witness at my brother's criminal trial and I don't want to testify. Is there anything I can do to avoid appearing?" Just as one of the other attorneys is about to answer the question, Mansfield interrupts, "I believe that I'm the most qualified person to help Julie with her problem because I have such extensive criminal trial experience and am looked upon across the country as an expert in this area. Julie, before I can help you, I need to know more about why you don't want to testify." Julie responds, "I'm afraid that I might be arrested if they find out I helped my brother." Mansfield responds, "Julie, why don't you call my office at 555-4387 to set up an appointment. You are definitely in need of professional help, but your situation requires more detailed advice than I can give you here or over the phone. Don't worry, I have gotten many a client out of similar jams."

When the television program ends, Mansfield stops by the station's news room and delivers two front-row tickets to the most popular play in town to the news director. Mansfield says to the director, "This is just my way of saying thank you for the interview that you did with me last week. My phone has been ringing off the hook ever since. Lots of new clients."

Has Mansfield violated any standards of professional responsibility? Discuss.

Question 8

Joey Bologna has just graduated from law school and is newly admitted to the state bar of Montansas. Joey was an average student in law school and never had time to participate in extra curricular activities as he worked almost full time at a delicatessen. Joey opens his own practice and waits for the phone to ring. When it doesn't, he decides to mail the following letter to solicit new business:

> Offices of Dr. Joe Bologna
>
> 1234 Main Street
>
> Rapid Falls, Montansas 90001
>
> Dear Neighbor:
>
> My name is Dr. Joey Bologna and I'm an attorney. I was born and raised in Montansas and have been practicing law for quite a while in Rapid Falls. I graduated from Montansas Law School where I was a member of the moot court honors team and also participated in other trial competitions.
>
> When you hire me, you don't just get a lawyer, you get a doctor — my degree is: "Juris Doctor." This qualifies me to handle medical malpractice cases. I also consider myself to be a specialist in personal injury law and I'm pretty knowledgeable about other areas of the law as well.
>
> When you compare my prices and service to those of other lawyers in this area, I can't be beat. I charge a low hourly fee and/or a percentage of the recovery, depending on the type of case. The first meeting with me is always free. So pick up your phone and give me a call.
>
> I look forward to meeting with you soon.
>
> Sincerely,
>
> Joey Bologna

Joey mails 1,000 copies of his completed letter to potential clients, some of whom he surmises have a need for legal services. Joey mails the letters out in plain white envelopes marked only with the client's address and his return address.

Has Joey violated any standards of professional responsibility? Discuss.

Question 9

Adam is injured in an auto accident and quickly sustains $5,000 in medical bills. In addition, his car is badly damaged and requires extensive repairs. Adam retains Swanson, an attorney, to sue MaGoo, the other driver.

In their first meeting, Adam describes the accident to Swanson and Swanson concludes that Adam was at least partially responsible for the accident. He advises Adam that recovery will be difficult and that a quick settlement without litigation would be advisable. He reviews with Adam a contingent fee agreement under which Swanson will advance all costs of litigation and Adam will pay nothing until the settlement or judgment is received. Under the terms of the agreement, if no money is received, Adam will not have to repay Swanson any costs advanced by him. If there is a recovery, whether from a settlement or judgment, then Swanson is authorized to deduct the costs he may have advanced from the amount recovered. The remaining sum is to be divided 1/3 to Swanson and 2/3 to Adam. Adam agrees in writing to be bound by the contingent fee agreement, which contains a provision authorizing Swanson to settle for any amount over $25,000.

Swanson addresses a letter to Magoo and soon receives a call from one of the adjusters for Magoo's insurer. Swanson argues the merits of Adam's case, stressing his large medical bills. The adjuster calls back within a few days and offers $30,000, which Swanson accepts on Adam's behalf. The insurance company forwards a settlement letter and release agreement to Swanson. Swanson explains the release agreement to Adam and obtains his signature to the agreement. Shortly thereafter, Swanson receives the check for $30,000. In all, Swanson has spent approximately five hours on Adam's case and has not needed to advance any costs.

Swanson places the entire $30,000 in his client trust account. He then writes Adam a letter as follows:

> Dear Adam:
>
> You will be pleased to learn that I have just received the $30,000 check in settlement of your case. Of that, you owe me no money for costs advanced. Therefore, per our agreement, my fee is $10,000 and the remaining $20,000 is your settlement. Enclosed is your copy of the settlement agreement signed by all parties, and a check to your order in the amount of $20,000 drawn upon my client trust account. I trust this is a satisfactory resolution of your claims. Please call me if you have any questions.
>
> Sincerely,
>
> Swanson

Adam calls Swanson a few days later, acknowledges that he has received the check and asks how much time Swanson spent on the case. Swanson replies, "A few hours, which is not out of the ordinary for this type of case." Adam expresses his anger that he has to pay $10,000 to Swanson for so few hours of work. After a short exchange, Swanson advises Adam to consult with other counsel if he believes the fee arrangement was unfair.

After they hang up, Swanson writes Adam another letter explaining again how contingent fee arrangements work, and reminding Adam that he had advised him that a settlement before trial would be advisable and that he was authorized to settle for anything over $25,000. Swanson advises Adam once again to hire another attorney and suggests that he may wish to consult the state bar about the reasonabless of the fee. Four weeks pass without any further contact by Adam, and Swanson writes himself a check for $10,000 out of his client trust account and deposits it into his business account.

Has Swanson violated any standards of professional responsibility? Discuss.

Question 10

Ross Piranha has been offered a position as CEO of Megatron, a large multinational electronics corporation. Piranha and the president of the Megatron board, Tom Shark, meet to discuss the terms of the agreement. They sketch out a compensation plan which includes a hefty salary and stock options worth several million dollars. In the spirit of cooperation, Shark suggests that they use the same attorney to draw the agreement, and agrees to have Megatron pick up the tab. They set up a meeting with Leslie Connors, a well-respected local business attorney.

In the initial meeting, Shark tells Connors, "We have already outlined all the key factors to Ross's contract and just need you to help us formalize the terms. Now I want you to consider yourself as acting for Ross and for Megatron, but Megatron will be solely responsible for your fees. So what do you say, can you help us move this thing forward?"

Connors responds that she would be happy to help them out. She explains that she charges $185 an hour for her services, and provides Shark with a written fee agreement. The parties then discuss the specifics of their deal.

Shortly thereafter, she phones Piranha to clarify some of the terms. In particular, she wants to know how long the vesting period is supposed to be for the stock options. "Well, to tell you the truth, we never really discussed that. Make it two years. The fact is, I have already committed to move to Tokyo in two and a half years when my daughter graduates from law school here. I plan to work for another company over there. Please don't mention that to Tom. It could kill our deal."

Connors then calls Shark and asks him what he thinks the vesting period is supposed to be. "I guess we forgot to spell that out in our prior discussions but Megatron's standard vesting policy is 20 percent after three years, another 30 percent after five years and then the balance after seven years. Just put that in."

After talking to Shark, Connors decides, in fairness to both parties, to "split the difference." She writes up the agreement and presents it to both parties to sign.

Has Connors acted properly under the rules of professional conduct? Discuss.

Question 11

Linda Bigbucks is the wealthy mother of two spoiled teenagers, Ruth, age 18, and Ralph, age 19. One night, as a misguided prank, Ruth induces Ralph to join her in breaking into the home of their neighbors, Mr. and Mrs. Jones. They blindfold the Jones' 13 year-old daughter and take her for a cruise in their new BMW. Ralph is driving. Without realizing it, he crosses the line into the adjoining state. Ruth finds that she has accidentally dropped her scarf— embroidered with her initials— in the Jones' house. The next morning, Ruth and Ralph return home with the girl, who is unharmed. By this time, however, the police have been called and they arrest Ruth and Ralph for burglary, kidnapping and endangering the safety of a minor.

Linda immediately calls and visits Edward Alvarez, a prominent criminal defense attorney. Linda asks Edward if he will defend both Ruth and Ralph in their upcoming trial. Linda tells Edward that she will pay all of Ruth and Ralph's legal fees, and insists that Edward consult with her about all aspects of the case. Before leaving Edward's office, Linda says, "I don't want Ralph to testify at the trial under any circumstances. He's quick to lose his temper and Ruth is much more articulate and convincing. In any case, I think the jury will be more sympathetic to a pretty girl."

Can Edward properly take the case under these circumstances? Discuss.

Question 12

The Department of Justice has recently brought criminal charges against Logaway, a logging company in the Pacific Northwest, charging that Logaway has violated federal environmental laws by polluting the local river near the company plant. Logaway is also involved in a lawsuit against a major logging competitor, Woodchuck. The dispute is over the title to some land which both companies need for a new operating plant.

Logaway's general counsel is Jerry Blake. Two years ago, while working as an environmental attorney for the Department of Justice, Jerry was one of twenty lawyers who investigated citizen complaints against logging companies in the northwest involving the pollution of rivers and streams. Logaway and Woodchuck were among the companies involved. A vice president of Woodchuck turned government informant and gave Jerry and his colleagues important information about company policies and operations. These "tips" led to the filing of charges against Woodchuck for violation of several environmental laws. The investigation of Logaway, on the other hand, showed no violations by the company. At the end of the investigation, Jerry accepted an offer of employment from Logaway to become its general counsel.

Has Jerry violated any rules of professional responsibility and may he represent Logaway in its defense against the criminal charges and in the civil action with Woodchuck? Discuss.

Question 13

Margie is corporate legal counsel for Sweetums Corporation, a manufacturer of both regular and diabetic chocolate candy, both called Sweetums. To protect against misuse by diabetics, the regular candies are packed in a red box with a prominent black "warning" sign and the diabetic candies are packed in a green box with the prominent legend "For Diabetics." Henry, a confirmed diabetic, rushes into a BVF drug store, takes a box off the shelf, eats five pieces while waiting at the register to pay for them, and is rushed to the hospital in diabetic shock. In the excitement, a BVF employee throws the box out, along with the remaining pieces of candy. That night, the box and candy are carted away with the daily store trash. Alleging that Sweetums put regular chocolate in the green box marked "For Diabetics," Henry sues Sweetums for his injuries and his medical expenses.

Concerned that the company will be bombarded with law suits, Frank, Vice President of Sweetums, tells Margie to deny all of Henry's charges and to assert a contributory negligence defense. He says, "We have the BVF clerk as witness. She'll testify that Frank rushed into the store, grabbed a red box and then gulped down several pieces of candy without pausing for a second. It's all his fault." Frank tells Margie to bombard Henry with numerous and massive discovery requests to induce him to settle his lawsuit. Frank also tells Margie to send an investigator out to interview as many people as possible who may have seen Henry at the store to back up Sweetums' contributory negligence defense.

Margie is uncomfortable with Frank's directives. Her files show that Henry experienced severe physical pain and harm as a result of eating the candy and that he has been unable to return to work since the incident, and she feels sorry for him and his family. She's also concerned that the jury may conclude that Henry is telling the truth and that the candy was packed in the wrong box. After giving the matter some thought, Margie decides against following Frank's instruction. She doesn't assert any affirmative defenses; she does not hire any investigators to interview other witnesses; and she limits her discovery requests to a single deposition at which Henry insists on his version of the facts.

One day, while Margie is working on Henry's case, Ellen, an assembly line worker, rushes into her office and insists on telling Margie that Sweetums' management is unfair to the workers on the line. Margie patiently explains to Ellen that, as corporate counsel, Margie represents the Corporation, not the workers, and that Ellen's statements to Margie are not privileged. Margie advises Ellen to seek advice from independent counsel, but Ellen persists, "I don't care what you say. I'm telling you, if conditions on the line don't change by tomorrow, expensive equipment may begin to disappear." Ellen then storms out of Margie's office.

Margie immediately phones the Sweetums plant manager and tells him about Ellen's complaint and threat. The next morning, Sweetums places armed guards throughout the assembly line plant to protect its equipment.

Has Margie violated any rules of professional responsibility? Discuss.

Question 14

Hilly Solightly, madam to the stars, is arrested for pandering and other vice counts. Hilly has made some bad investments and is now broke. The court appoints Sally Goode to represent her. Hilly is very unhappy with Sally, who personifies all that is good and virtuous.

One day, while out on bail, Hilly runs into Tony Dee, a top criminal defense attorney and one of her most ardent former clients. Hilly asks Tony to defend her against the charges. Hilly explains that she can't afford Tony's fees. Sensing that Hilly's story will make a dilly of a movie, Tony suggests that Hilly sign over to him all her literary and movie rights to her life story. Hilly agrees and Tony drafts an agreement under which Hilly assigns all her rights to him in payment of her legal fees and in consideration of Tony's promise to pay her 25% of the profits realized by Tony from the assignment.

One week later, the prosecutor informs Tony that she is willing to negotiate a plea bargain with Hilly. Tony communicates this information to Hilly in passing but advises her that it is in her best interest to go to trial and win a "big" acquittal. He tells Hilly, "You've had some hard times and some great times. You've known the lowest and the greatest. What a story. Let it all play out and you'll never have to walk the streets again."

Shortly before the trial is scheduled to begin, the prosecutor moves to disqualify Tony on the grounds that he is a potential witness in the case because of his former relationship with Hilly.

Has Tony violated any rules of professional responsibility? Should he be disqualified as Hilly's attorney? Discuss.

Question 15

Reggie, an attorney, prepared Milt's will fifteen years ago. Milt is now dead. His will left $250,000 to his wife and split $250,000 between two of his sons, Earl and Ed, who had worked for their father. The will also left $5,000 to Milt's third son, Fred, who had dropped out of high school against his father's wishes and, in Milt's opinion, was a "loafer." Shortly after Milt's death, Fred came to see Reggie and told him that he wished to attack his father's will. As he was leaving Reggie's private office, Fred ran into Larry, Reggie's law partner. "You must be Milt's boy. You're a dead ringer for your father—no pun intended. Reggie tells me you got the short end of the stick in his will. Sorry about that, son. Life's not always fair. Why don't you join me for lunch one day. We can talk things over." One week later, Fred received a bill in the mail from Reggie for $100 for an initial consultation fee.

1. Is it proper for Reggie to represent Fred in challenging the will?

2. What should Reggie have said to Fred during their meeting?

3. Would it be proper for Larry to take Fred's case?

4. Was it proper for Reggie to bill Fred for the consultation?

Question 16

Tonya, a civil trial attorney, represents George, the plaintiff in a medical malpractice case against Dr. Hackem. Dr. Hackem undertook to perform minor plastic surgery on George's cheek to cover a small discoloration, but George ended up with a large, permanent scar running from his forehead to his chin. In the exchange of discovery, defense counsel requested that plaintiff produce certain medical and employment records. Tonya reviewed the appropriate records. After rejecting some as seriously damaging, she copied the others on her photocopy machine at a light setting which made them virtually impossible to read. Tonya then sent only the photocopied documents to counsel, withholding the others.

Tonya then wrote to Dr. Hackem. suggesting that he "settle this lawsuit soon, first because of the time and expense involved in going to trial, and second, because it would avoid the necessity of my contacting the district attorney regarding your unorthodox billing practices." At trial, during closing arguments, Tonya referred to Dr. Hackem as a "butcher" who had "destroyed" George's life. Tonya also stated, "If it were up to me, this poor excuse for a doctor would never be allowed to practice medicine again." The jury finds for George and awards him a punitively large sum of money in damages.

Is Tonya subject to discipline? Discuss.

Question 17

Judge Stern is a state court judge. State court judges in this state have general civil and criminal jurisdiction, including over capital crimes. He is assigned to preside over a bitter contract dispute between two large computer companies, Bitty Bytes and RAM DOS. In his spare time, he relaxes by listening to opera and playing golf. Lisa Larson is the lead attorney for RAM DOS. She was a classmate of Judge Stern's 15 years ago at Yallard Law. While in school, they both took the same torts class, along with 150 other students. Except for an occasional greeting at bar committee meetings, their paths have never crossed again. A few weeks before the trial, which is heavily publicized, Larson calls Judge Stern at his home. "I was just flipping through our old law school year book and thinking about all the fun we had back then. I was wondering if you would care to get together to reminisce about the good ol' days at Yallard? I know how much you like opera and I happen to have two box seats for Placido Domingo in Wagner's *Tristan und Isolde* this weekend. I feel so lucky because the performance is completely sold out. Would you like to join me?" Judge Stern jumps at the chance. They are both careful not to discuss the upcoming case during their evening together.

The following Saturday morning, Judge Stern rushes out to make his 9:00 a.m. tee time at his private club, Club Anglo, to which he and about 250 other men belong. On the way, he is stopped by a traffic cop for speeding. The Judge says, "Have you ever appeared before me? You look so familiar. My name is Judge Harry Stern. I'm a state court judge." The officer shakes his head "no" and writes the judge a ticket.

Two months later, during Judge Stern's re-election campaign, he is interviewed by a local reporter. The reporter asks him about his position on the death penalty and he answers truthfully, "I think the penalty is inhumane. I could never bring myself to impose it." The reporter then asks him what he thinks about the other local races. "Well, as a judge I don't like to get too involved in politics — but I do like Sally Smith for city council."

Has Judge Stern acted properly? How about Lisa Larson?

Question 18

Joanne and Mary, both successful attorneys in West Dakota, are good friends. They have never practiced together or become associated in any matter. For the past five years, Joanne, Mary, and their husbands and children have rented a condo in Colorado and have gone skiing together during Christmas break. When celebrating the Christmas holiday, Joanne and Mary's families exchange generous presents with one another.

Mary is running for election as superior court judge in her jurisdiction. Joanne believes that Mary will make an excellent judge and donates $5,000 to Mary's campaign committee. During her well organized campaign for judicial office, Mary pays for several television and radio advertisements supporting her candidacy and appears at three Democratic Party gatherings. Mary is elected to the superior court and is sworn in.

During her campaign and before being sworn in as judge, Mary worked on an appeal to the United States Supreme Court for an indigent client. She would like to see this one case through to its conclusion. She does not intend to accept any compensation for the matter.

Shortly after being sworn in, Mary is assigned to preside over a personal injury case in which Joanne is the plaintiff's attorney.

1. Has Joanne behaved properly?

2. Did Mary behaved properly during the course of her campaign?

3. Should Mary disqualify herself from Joanne's upcoming trial?

4. Is it proper for Mary to conclude her case before the United States Supreme Court after being sworn in as a judge?

Question 19

Thaddeus Mueller, Attorney at Law, is walking back to his office after a brief lunch break when he happens upon the scene of a car accident. He watches while Arnie Simpson is placed onto a stretcher by paramedics. Mueller elbows his way through the crowd to talk to Simpson. "Are you OK? I am so sorry about your accident, but I think I may be able to help you. I am a personal injury lawyer. I have obtained pretty amazing results for my clients. Why just last week I got a $3 million verdict for a kid injured in a bicycle accident. Listen, I know you're in no position to talk, but here's my card. Give me a call when you are feeling up to it." Mueller hands Simpson his business card and returns to his office.

A week later, Simpson calls Mueller and retains him to represent him. It turns out that the driver of the other car was a famous pop music star, Padrona. Mueller calls a reporter friend of his and tells her about the case. "Padrona doesn't have a chance. We have photographic evidence from a store surveillance camera that proves the accident was his fault. Not only that, but he refused to submit to drug and alcohol testing after the accident. We're pretty sure he was high as a kite at the time." The reporter runs the story in the local daily newspaper and it is picked up by the national wire services.

Several months later, the jury trial begins. During opening arguments, Mueller refers to Padrona as a "drugged out rock and roll star who thinks rules just don't apply to him." Actually, despite extensive discovery on the issue, Mueller never uncovered anything which would lead him to believe Padrona has ever used drugs or abused alcohol, and Mueller has no plans to introduce any evidence on that issue.

Has Mueller violated any rules of professional conduct? Discuss.

Question 20

Donald Quack is an attorney licensed to practice law in State A. He is also a physician, licensed to practice medicine in State B. Quack opens up a store-front clinic in State B, called "Quack's Quick Clinic for Victims of Personal Injury." As soon as patients enter the clinic, the receptionist hands them a free book authored by Quack entitled, "How to File Your Own Personal Injury Lawsuit."

Quack follows the same procedure with each patient who enters the clinic for treatment. He first conducts a physical examination of the patient to determine the extent of injury and then interviews him or her to get a medical history and to review the circumstances which caused the injuries to decide whether the patient has a legal claim. If Quack believes there is a legal claim, he explains to the patient how the patient can litigate that claim *pro se*. He then provides the patient with the necessary forms to initiate a case in state court, and offers to help the patient fill out the forms. If the patient decided to proceed, the doctor's secretary helps him or her to fill out the forms.

Quack charges each patient $500 for this initial visit or, if the patient prefers, 50% of the amount of money the patient receives in settlement of his or her medical claim. Quack offers no actual treatment or follow-up medical care to the patients. If the patient specifically requests it, he gives the patient a copy of his medical record.

Has Quack violated any rules of professional conduct? If so, where will he be subject to discipline?

Essay Exam Answers

Answer to Question 1

An attorney has a duty to represent her client with diligence and zeal, and to preserve her client's confidences. MR 1.3 and MR. 1.6. These duties are not absolute, however. They are limited by an attorney's countervailing duties of candor to the tribunal and fairness to the opposing party. MR 3.3 and MR 3.4.

Fender's Actions and Advice Regarding Malone's Ring

During a pre-trial meeting, Fender notices that Malone wears a ring similar to the one worn by the robber in the photograph. She cannot tell from the photo, however, whether the rings are the same. Furthermore, her client has asserted his innocence and has presented an alibi, and at this early stage she has no reason to doubt his story. In addition, she doesn't know whether the prosecution intends to blow up the photograph to make a more definitive comparison. Although the ring may have potential evidentiary value to the prosecution, it's not Fender's job to prove the prosecutor's case. It is her job, however, to anticipate the prosecution's case and to prepare against it to the best of her ability.

A lawyer has a duty not to conceal, alter or destroy objects having potential evidentiary value, and not to assist another in so doing. MR 3.4(a). This does not, however, include an affirmative duty to come forward with items of potential relevance if they may prove harmful to her client's case.

Fender has not suggested to Malone that he destroy the ring or that he have it re-engraved with a different emblem. This would clearly be improper. Rather, she has suggested only that the ring may ultimately become an issue at the trial. She's made the same suggestion about the ring line on Malone's skin. Her actions can be likened to those of an attorney in a case involving a crime committed by a person described as wearing jeans and a t-shirt who counsels her client to wear a suit to court. Fender is under no obligation to reveal her own observations to the prosecution. It is up to the prosecution to investigate the possibility that Malone has a similar ring, and to uncover it through legal means such as a search warrant. (It can be argued, however, that Fender had an affirmative duty to advise Malone not to alter, conceal or destroy the ring.)

Fender's Advice to Malone Regarding Testifying at Trial

As Malone's attorney, Fender has a duty of candor toward the tribunal and must counsel her client to tell the truth. MR 3.3(a)(4). In a criminal defense, the lawyer should confer with the defendant about the wisdom of allowing the defendant to testify. After discussing the potential consequences of a vigorous cross-examination by the prosecutor, the lawyer must advise the defendant that the decision whether or not to testify is his alone to make. MR 1.2(a). During the trial, but before Malone testified, he asked Fender what might happen if the prosecutor asked him if he had a ring with a "B" on it. Fender advised him, "If you insist on testifying, you have to tell the truth." Fender has advised Malone that his testimony must be truthful. She has satisfied her duty of candor to the court with this admonition. She is entitled to assume that Malone will tell the truth if the prosecutor pursues an inquiry into the ring.

Malone's Payment of Legal Fees

Under Fender's duties of candor to the court and fairness to opposing counsel, she must not unlawfully obstruct another party's access to evidence, unlawfully alter, destroy or conceal a document or other item having potential evidentiary value, or counsel or assist another to do any of these things. MR 3.4(a). On the night before closing arguments, Malone gave Fender the balance of her legal fee in $100 bills. Fender immediately realized that these bills had evidentiary value and were, in all likelihood, the "fruits" of the crime in question. Nevertheless, she asked Malone to take them back and give her different ones instead.

Most courts have recognized that criminal defense attorneys have a special duty to make available to the prosecution physical evidence that comes into their possession. This duty generally applies to evidence that is either the product of the crime (i.e., stolen property) or the instrumentality of the crime (i.e., a weapon). Upon receipt of the $100 bills from Malone, Fender had a duty to turn this evidence over to the prosecution, especially since the numbers on the bills had already been disclosed in the bank officer's testimony. MR 3.4, Comment [2]. By returning the fourteen $100 bills to Malone, Fender breached her duty to the court and opposing counsel by both obstructing the prosecution's access to evidence and by concealing the bills which she knew had evidentiary value. Further, by telling Malone to bring an equivalent amount of money in other denominations, Fender, in effect, counseled Malone to obstruct, conceal and possibly destroy valuable evidence. All of the above would subject Fender to discipline.

Fender's Discovery of Possible Perjury By Both Moll and Malone

A lawyer has a duty not to present false evidence. MR 3.3(a)(4). This duty includes an obligation to take remedial measures if the false nature of the evidence becomes apparent only after the evidence has been presented. At trial, both Moll and Malone assumedly testified that Malone was watching TV with Moll during the time of the bank robbery. Fenders was entitled to present this evidence at the time because she did not yet know for a fact that it was false. However, upon receipt of the $100 bills from Malone, Fenders could reasonably have concluded that Malone in fact committed the crime. If Fenders was convinced that Malone and Moll had lied with respect to the alibi testimony, she had a duty to correct this false testimony. Her duties with respect to Malone's and Moll's testimony differ somewhat, however.

[Ordinarily, Fender would not be required to disclose the source of the bills under her duty of confidentiality to the client. MR 1.6. However, the duty of confidentially can conflict with the duty of candor to the tribunal under MR 3.3. In criminal cases, this conflict is generally resolved in favor of maintaining confidentiality even in the face of client perjury. But not all courts agree with this resolution. *See* MR 3.3, Comments [7]-[10]. Because the facts here suggest that Malone has probably already taken the stand to testify and has testified falsely, Fender has a duty to correct the impact of the perjury. Because closing argument will occur the next day, Fender must take steps immediately to prevent the jury from reaching a verdict without all the evidence. After telling Malone that she has a duty not to assist him in committing perjury, Fender should advise the court of the circumstances under which she came into possession of the bills. MR 1.2(d) tells a lawyer not to assist a client in conduct the lawyer knows to be criminal.]

Fender's Duty to Correct Malone's Perjury

When a lawyer learns that her criminal-defendant client has given false testimony, she must (a) attempt to persuade the client to reveal the perjury, (b) attempt to withdraw, if that will remedy the situation, or — if neither of these can remedy the problem, (c) reveal the perjury to the court. MR 3.3. Under the present facts, withdrawal is no longer a practical option because all testimony is in. Malone claimed he was innocent and assumedly testified falsely that he was with Dolly at the time of the crime. If the $100 bills convinced Fender that Malone's testimony was false, she had a duty to attempt to get Malone to recant his testimony. If he refused to do so, she had a duty to report Malone's perjury to the court. Her failure to do so would subject her to discipline.

Fender's Duty to Correct Moll's Perjury

Fender does not owe a duty of confidentiality or loyalty to Moll because Moll is not her client. Her responsibility to correct Moll's perjury is therefore more straightforward: she must inform the court that Moll has lied. Fender would be subject to discipline for failing to do so. MR 3.3(a)(4), Comment [4].

Fender's Closing Argument

Once again, Fender has a duty of candor to the tribunal which requires that she not offer false evidence. When Malone gave Fender what appeared to be the money stolen in the bank robbery, the inescapable conclusion was that Malone had played a part in the robbery. Therefore, she violated her duty of candor by arguing that the prosecutor had gone after the wrong man and by urging the jury to believe Malone's and Molly's testimony. She will be subject to discipline for arguing facts she knew or suspected to be false. MR 3.3(a),(b): a lawyer must not knowingly make a false statement of material fact to a tribunal or fail to disclose a material fact when disclosure is necessary to avoid assisting in a criminal act by the client.

Answer to Question 2

Alice has retained attorney Marcia to handle a complex property matter for her. Upon entering into an attorney-client relationship, Marcia becomes subject, among other duties, to the duties of competence, confidentiality, and diligence, as well as the duty to charge a reasonable fee. I will discuss each of these duties and how Marcia may have violated them.

Marcia's Duty of Competence

The very first of the Model Rules (MR 1.1) provides that a lawyer shall provide competent representation to the client. This means that the lawyer must possess the legal knowledge, skill, thoroughness, and preparation reasonably necessary to carry out the representation. In general, the standard is that of the *general* legal practitioner. When the case is particularly complex or technical and requires specialized knowledge, or when the lawyer holds herself out as a specialist or expert, the lawyer will be held to a higher standard.

When a lawyer lacks the necessary knowledge or skill to represent a client competently, the lawyer may do one of three things: 1) decline to accept the client's representation all together (or, if she accepts the matter and later finds that it's beyond her skills, she may withdraw from the representation after making sure that the client's interests are protected by helping the client to retain other, competent counsel); 2) accept the representation with the understanding that she will obtain the necessary competence through study and investigation — as long as the lawyer can accomplish this without unreasonable delay or expense to the client, or 3) associate with other counsel of established competence.

These facts show clearly that Marcia was not competent to handle Alice's matter when she accepted the representation. Some problems in property law are very complex and require specialized knowledge. Alice should have recognized her relative lack of knowledge and skill and declined the matter. Instead, she accepted the case and decided to "study up" to increase her competence. "A lawyer can provide adequate representation in a wholly novel field through necessary study." MR 1.1, Comment [2]. However, good intentions are not sufficient. —The necessary competence must be achieved within the requisite time **and** at minimal cost to the client. Marcia was not able to achieve this. Her efforts to learn property law were fruitless; and she added cost to injury by billing her client for the time in trying to learn. Marcia has violated MR 1.1 by failing to provide competent representation in the first place and by failing to acquire the necessary skills through study, especially after assuring the client that she was "busy researching the problem."

Marcia's Act of Associating Jan in as Co-Counsel

Marcia attempted to salvage the representation by associating with other, more competent counsel. She did this without consulting the client. This brings to the fore the issue of client confidentiality. A lawyer "shall not reveal information relating to representation" unless the client consents after consultation. MR 1.6. But this obligation is not absolute. A lawyer is permitted to reveal the client's confidences "when they are impliedly authorized in order to carry out the representation." The issue here is which controls: the Rule or the exception. Is disclosure to a more competent attorney with whom the lawyer associates "impliedly authorized?"

The better view is probably that Marcia violated her duty of confidentiality to Alice by sharing the details of Alice's case with Jan without first getting Alice's consent to do so. There was nothing to prevent Marcia from consulting with Alice first except Marcia's embarrassment in disclosing her ignorance and her lack of diligence in pursuing the representation. The failure to consult with Alice led also to Marcia's commitment to Jan to secure Alice's payments of $250 per hour. Marcia had no authority from Alice to do this. Of course, the facts do not tell us if Jan proceded to do any work after talking with Marcia. There may in fact be no liability by anyone to Jan.

Marcia's Retainer and Hourly Fees

The fee which a lawyer charges the client must be reasonable. MR 1.5. When the lawyer has not regularly represented the client—the case here—she must communicate the basis or rate of the fee to the client within a reasonable time after commencing the representation, "preferably in writing." MR 1.5. Factors which a lawyer may consider in fixing a fee: 1) The time and labor required, novelty and difficulty of the questions involved, and skill required to perform the services; 2) the likelihood, if apparent to the client, that acceptance of the particular employment will preclude other employment by the lawyer; 3) the customary fee charged for similar work in that locality; 4) the amount of the client's claim or interest and the results obtained; 5) the time limitations imposed either by the client or circumstances; 6) the length and nature of the professional relationship with the client; 7) the experience, reputation and ability of the lawyer or lawyers who perform the services; and 8) whether the fee is contingent or fixed. MR 1.5.

Here, Marcia has charged a retainer of $500. Because Alice has a complex property question that is likely to take substantial time and labor, the retainer seems reasonable. In every other respect, Marcia has violated the letter of MR 1.5. First of all, she never communicated either the basis or the rate of her fee to Alice. The first notice to Alice of the basis upon which the fee would be calculated was contained in Marcia's letter to Alice which was not sent for at least six months after the representation began. Secondly, she failed to reduce the fee to writing at the beginning of the representation. Lastly, she used the fee of $2,250 solely to educate herself in property law, and then without benefit to the client. To the extent the lawyer must spend excessive amounts of time preparing for tasks that are routine for an experienced lawyer, she should not expect the client to pay for her education. *In re Estate of Larson,* 694 P.2d 1197 (Wash. 1995). Furthermore, although we do not see a copy of the bill, the accompanying letter intimates that Marcia expects Alice to pay the full $2,250 — without crediting or accounting for the $500 retainer. The retainer must be applied to Alice's balance. It is not a "signing bonus" to be retained by the attorney.

Attorney's Duties of Diligence and Communication

No single failure is more irritating to a client or is more likely to lead to a complaint to the disciplinary authorities than the neglect of the client's matter or the failure to keep the client informed on a regular basis. MR 1.3, Comment [2]; MR 1.4. A lawyer must act with reasonable diligence and promptness in representing a client. MR 1.3. To act with diligence means that the attorney must work zealously to further the client's interests, within the bounds of the law, and represent the client until the work is completed. Promptness means that the lawyer must represent the client efficiently and without unreasonable delay. A lawyer's duty of communication means she must keep a client reasonably informed about the status of a matter and promptly comply with reasonable requests for information. MR 1.4.

Marcia did not even begin to work on the research needed for Alice's case for at least six months. She never wrote to Alice about the status of her case, nor did she take any of Alice's eight calls. The first time Marcia initiated any communication with Alice was to send her a bill. Marcia did manage to return half of Alice's calls, but used the calls only to misstate the status and scope of her work: she claimed she was continuing her research, but the reality was that she hadn't even begun it. It is axiomatic that a lawyer's duty of communication requires that she be truthful in her reports. Marcia has violated the Model Rules by failing to represent Alice promptly or zealously, and by failing to keep Alice informed about the status of her matter. By so doing, she has prevented Alice from making informed decisions about the representation. MR 1.4(b).

It's hard to believe that Marcia's delays and neglect over more than six months have not adversely affected Alice's substantive interests in the property involved. If so, Marcia may be liable to Alice on a claim for malpractice.

Answer to Question 3

Membership in the legal profession carries with it many benefits and rewards. To earn these benefits, every lawyer is expected to maintain his own integrity and also help to maintain the integrity of the entire bar. Several rules have been developed to help lawyers understand and carry out the resulting duties. Joe, John, and Mason each had specific duties which they failed to fulfill. I will discuss their respective violations below.

Joe's Bar Application

An applicant for admission to the bar must not knowingly make a false statement of material fact, MR 8.1(a), or knowingly fail to respond to a lawful demand for information from an admissions authority MR 8.1(b). In filling out his application for Shock's state bar, Joe recognized the dilemma caused by the question on prior convictions. At the least, he had a duty to call or write to the admissions committee and ask whether a conviction for a misdemeanor traffic violation had to be reported. If the answer turned out to be yes, Joe was under an obligation to report it, whatever the consequences. Instead, Joe turned a blind eye to the dilemma and simply answered "no." This was both a false statement of what was probably a material fact and a failure to respond to the bar's demand for information. Joe is subject to discipline.

John's Duty to Report Joe

A lawyer who knows that another lawyer has committed a violation of the rules of professional conduct that raises a substantial question as to that lawyer's honesty, trustworthiness, or fitness as a lawyer in other respects, shall inform the appropriate professional authority. MR 8.3.

When Joe confessed to John that he had failed to disclose his conviction for drunk driving on his application to the bar, John had a duty to consider what action he should take. Because Joe had been drinking, John probably needed to confirm the facts after Joe sobered up. This could be accomplished by asking Joe directly about the conviction. Once Joe confirmed the facts, John had a duty to advise the appropriate grievance committee because the confession would raise substantial questions about Joe's honesty, trustworthiness, and fitness as a lawyer. MR 8.3, which confirms the duty to disclose, contains no statute of limitations, so the fact that two years had elapsed since Joe's application did not diminish John's obligation to report the infraction.

If Joe claimed that he always distorted the truth when he was drunk, repudiated his confession and denied his conviction, John would probably not have an obligation to investigate further or to make any disclosure to the grievance authorities.

Joe's conversation with Mason

Joe consulted Mason regarding his failure to report his drunk driving conviction on his bar application. Their conversation is protected by the attorney-client privilege and the duty of confidentiality. MR 1.6. Although all attorneys are under a general duty to report another lawyer's violations of the rules of professional conduct, there is an exception for information gained in the course of an attorney-client relationship. MR 8.3(c): "This Rule does not require disclosure of information otherwise protected by Rule 1.6..." Also, "The duty to report professional misconduct does not apply to a lawyer retained to represent a lawyer whose professional conduct is in question..." MR 8.3, Comment [4]. Unless Joe consented to disclosure, Mason had an ethical obligation *not* to disclose what Joe had told him about his drunk driving conviction and his failure to disclose the conviction on the Shock bar application. Mason did the right thing under the circumstances by not reporting Joe's violation to the state and by advising Joe that he should report the violation himself. Mason has complied with the Code.

Mason's Letter of Recommendation to State of Euphoria Bar

A lawyer who has knowledge of conduct by another lawyer which raises a substantial question about that lawyer's honesty, trustworthiness or fitness as a lawyer, shall inform the appropriate professional authority. MR 8.1. Mason was excused from complying with this Rule both because he was bound by the lawyer-client privilege and the duty of confidentiality, and because he had been retained in connection with a possible question about Joe's professional conduct. However, he did not have to write the letter of recommendation. He wrote the letter with knowledge that Joe had lied on his application for admission to the bar in the state of Shock, thereby violating the rules of professional conduct. Although Mason could not reveal to the state bar authorities in either Shock or Euphoria the existence of Joe's prior conviction or the fact that he had lied on his Shock bar application, neither could he endorse Joe for membership in Euphoria's state bar knowing of conduct which reflected on Joe's honesty and fitness. He should have refused to write the letter. By recommending Joe despite his knowledge of Joe's ethical violations, Mason has committed his own ethical violation of the Code and will be subject to discipline in the state of Shock, where he is admitted and conducts his practice.

Joe's Euphoria Bar Application

Although Joe answered the "prior convictions" question truthfully on his application for admission to the bar of Euphoria, his obligation did not end there. An applicant for admission to the bar must not knowingly make a false statement of material fact or fail to disclose a fact necessary to correct a misapprehension known to him. MR 8.1. Joe had a duty to disclose to the

Euphoria admissions committee that he had lied on his prior bar application. His failure to do so will subject him to discipline. After his admission to practice in the state of Euphoria, he will be subject to discipline by the disciplinary authorities of both Shock and Euphoria.

Answer to Question 4

These facts raise several issues about the conduct of Dan and Larry. Among them: the unauthorized practice of law, improperly implying a law partnership where none exists, insufficient supervision by a lawyer of his nonlawyer subordinates, improper use by a lawyer of the threat of criminal prosecution to advance the interests of a client, breach of the attorney-client privilege and breach of the duty of client confidentiality. In addition, the facts suggest the possibility of a suit for malpractice.

Unauthorized Practice of Law

The unauthorized practice of law is a crime in most jurisdictions. A lawyer must not aid a nonlawyer in the unauthorized practice of law. MR 5.5(b). Most law schools conduct student clinics which enable law students to participate as interns in the work of the clinics. They are allowed to interview clients and even to make court appearances, but they are always under the supervision and direction of a faculty member who is a member of the local bar. In no event are the students allowed to claim membership in the bar. Here, when Dan assigned Henry to Larry at the Downtown Legal Center, he referred to Larry as his "partner," and assured Henry that Larry could "help you with whatever you need." Also, Dan remained silent when he heard Larry state, "I do most of the work around here," when Henry asked Larry if he was also a lawyer. Dan led Henry to believe that Larry was a lawyer capable of handling all aspects of the representation. In doing so, he aided Larry in the unauthorized practice of law in violation of the rules of professional conduct. Dan is therefore subject to discipline.

Dan Improperly Held Himself Out As Larry's Partner

Dan misled Henry into thinking not only that Larry was a licensed attorney, but that he was Dan's partner as well. In so doing, he violated at least two ethical rules. MR 7.5(d) prevents a lawyer from claiming a partnership with another lawyer unless a partnership exists in fact. The same Rule would also certainly prevent a lawyer from claiming a partnership to practice law with a non-lawyer. Further, a partnership agreement between Dan and Larry would be absolutely void: *a lawyer shall not form a partnership with a nonlawyer if any of the activities of the partnership consist of the practice of law.* MR 5.4(b). (Note that fee splitting with a nonlawyer is also a violation of the Code. However, the facts here indicate that services of the Clinic were free so this prohibition does not come into play.) Dan is subject to discipline for holding himself out as the partner of a non-lawyer in an organization whose function is to deliver legal services.

Threatening Criminal Prosecution

Unlike the Code of Professional Responsibility, the Model Rules of Professional Conduct do not specifically prohibit a lawyer from threatening a party with criminal charges solely to obtain an advantage in a civil matter. However, the provisions of MR 8.4 dealing with lawyer misconduct are sufficient to deal with this issue. Thus, MR 8.4(b) forbids a lawyer to commit a criminal act that reflects adversely on a lawyer's honesty or fitness as a lawyer. MR 8.4(c) forbids a lawyer to engage in conduct involving deceit or misrepresentation. MR 8.4(d) forbids a lawyer from conduct that is prejudicial to the administration of justice. And MR 8.4(e) forbids him to state or imply an ability to influence a government official improperly. Here, Dan wrote a letter to Henry's landlord in which he threatened to have his friends in the district attorney's office bring criminal charges against the landlord if he did not stop harassing Henry about Woof. The landlord was persuaded by Dan's letter to allow Henry to keep Woof. Dan will be subject to discipline for writing the letter to Henry's landlord. If he did not have the ability to persuade his friends in the DA's office to bring charges against the landlord, he was guilty of misrepresentation. If he had the ability, he was nevertheless guilty of violating the provisions of MR 8.4 above.

Dan's Failure to Properly Supervise Larry With Respect to Client Confidences

A lawyer who has direct supervisory authority over a nonlawyer must make reasonable efforts to ensure that the non-lawyer's conduct conforms with the professional obligations of the lawyer. MR 5.3(b). Also, a lawyer is *responsible* for the conduct of a nonlawyer if the same conduct by a lawyer would represent a violation of the Code and if the lawyer either authorizes or ratifies the non-lawyer's conduct. MR 5.3(c).

Under MR 1.6, a client has the right to assume that the matters he confides to his lawyer will be confined to employees of the lawyer who have an absolute need to know and that they will not be divulged by anyone working for the lawyer who comes into possession of them. Here, Henry told both Dan and Larry about his theft of money from the armored truck under the assumption that the information would be privileged. Unbeknownst to Henry, Larry was not actually an attorney and could not be disciplined under the Code. For this reason, and because Dan knew that Henry believed Larry to be a lawyer, Dan had a clear obligation to take reasonable measures to ensure that Larry did not reveal Henry's secret. He should have remonstrated with Larry not to reveal the secret to anyone. And when Dan heard Larry speak with the police, he had a clear duty to take steps to remedy the matter and minimize the impact of the disclosures. Yet he said and did nothing. His failure to control Larry, his lack of adequate instruction to Larry, and his failure to remedy Larry's actions will all subject him to discipline. Furthermore, they could subject him to liability for malpractice because, as a supervising attorney who knew about Larry's breach and failed to do anything about it, he would be deemed responsible for Larry's actions in an action by Henry to recover for his damages.

Disciplinary Action Against Larry

The state bar has no disciplinary jurisdiction over Larry because he is not actually an attorney. However, upon discovering that Larry is practicing law without a license, the state bar will probably report him to the police and district attorney's office and recommend that they file criminal charges against him under the appropriate state statute prohibiting the practice of law by a non-lawyer.

Answer to Question 5

Ellis Should Not Have Drafted the Codicil Because Doing So Created an Impermissible Conflict of Interest

The relationship between lawyer and client contains within it the potential for conflicts of interest. The lawyer must be zealous to recognize and avoid these conflicts. MR 1.8, Comment [1]. For example, a lawyer shall not prepare an instrument that gives the lawyer a substantial gift from the client, including a testamentary gift, unless the client is related to the lawyer. MR 1.8(c), Comment [2]. The rationale is that the lawyer will be inescapably influenced to protect his own interests in the document, and that these interests may conflict with the client's interests. When faced with this dilemma, a lawyer should insist that the document be prepared by independent counsel.

In the facts presented, Mogul wants to make a testamentary gift to Ellis and asks her to draft the document herself. Ellis correctly recommends that Mogul have an independent attorney draft the document instead. However, when Mogul insists that she do it herself, she gives in. Ellis should have explained to Mogul that her professional obligations prohibited her from undertaking the assignment. She should have refused to draft the codicil. Her failure to do so will subject her to discipline.

Ellis Probably Should Not Have Accepted Johnson's Case Against Mogul

Another source of conflict between lawyer and client arises when the lawyer undertakes to represent a client whose interests are adverse to another present or former client. The rules applicable to current clients differ from those applicable to former clients. The rule with respect to former clients is as follows: A lawyer who has formerly represented a client in a matter cannot later represent another person in the same or a substantially related matter if that person's interests are materially adverse to those of the former client, unless the former client consents after consultation. MR 1.9(a).

The facts state that Mogul was a client of Ellis for the acquisition of the piece of investment property and for the subsequent drafting of the will codicil. It does not appear that the attorney-client relationship continued beyond those matters. Mogul would be considered a "former client" for purposes of applying the conflict of interest rules. The gravamen of Johnson's complaint is that Mogul sexually harassed her. This new case is not in any respect similar to either of the matters on which Ellis formerly represented Mogul, nor is it substantially related to either one. Therefore, Ellis would ordinarily be free to take on Johnson's case without violating any conflict of interest rules.

However, our analysis doesn't end there. We musn't forget that Ellis is the testimentary beneficiary of a $50,000 gift from Mogul and that Mogul is apparently still alive. Also, Ellis drafted the codicil to Mogul's will (improperly, of course) under which she acquired an interest in Mogul's estate and nothing in these facts indicates that the codicil has been revoked or modified. Under these facts, Ellis has a continuing duty to Mogul not to reveal any of his confidences and not to represent a person with interests adverse to Mogul's. As it relates to these facts, Ellis' duty to Mogul is not specifically defined in MR 1.8 or MR 1.9, but falls instead under the definition of conduct by a lawyer which is both deceitful and prejudicial to the administration of justice. MR 8.4.

Ellis' Contingent Fee Agreement With Johnson is Appropriate

A lawyer's fees must be reasonable. MR 1.5. Except in certain matrimonial matters and in all criminal matters, a lawyer is permitted to enter into a contingent fee arrangement with a client, provided the agreement is in writing and states the method by which the fee is to be determined. MR 1.5(c),(d). Ellis entered into a contingent fee agreement with Johnson in order to carry on Johnson's case. The agreement was in writing, the amount was reasonable, and the formula for calculating the fee was clearly stated. Ellis acted properly with respect to the contingent fee arrangement.

Ellis' Offer To Advance Johnson's Therapy Costs is Impermissible

A lawyer must not provide financial assistance to a client in connection with pending or contemplated litigation, with the exception of advances for court costs and the expenses of litigation. The rationale behind this rule is to prevent the attorney from having a vested interest in the outcome of the case which could affect the attorney's judgment or her loyalty to her client. In other words, the greater the lawyer's outlays and advances, the greater her instinct to protect her own funds rather than the client's interests. MR 1.8(e).

In addition to their fairly standard contingent fee arrangement, Ellis and Johnson entered into an unusual agreement with respect to the costs of Johnson's psychotherapy. Ellis offered to advance the costs of Johnson's therapy in order to provide her with the emotional support she needed to continue with her case. Ellis offered to let Johnson pay her back if she won, but to keep the advances if she lost. The costs of psychotherapy are not court costs, nor are they the expenses of litigation. Ellis is prohibited from advancing these costs to Johnson.

Answer to Question 6

Dreisdale's Possible Ethical Violations:

Duty of Confidentiality With Respect To The Killing

A lawyer shall not reveal a confidence or secret of his client unless the client consents after full disclosure, except for disclosures that are impliedly authorized to carry out the representation (and except to prevent the client from committing a criminal act that the lawyer believes is likely to result in imminent death or substantial bodily harm). MR 1.6.

Clampett came to see his attorney, Dreisdale, for professional advice and to confess that he had killed someone. All of Clampett's statements to Dreisdale are protected by the attorney-client privilege and the duty of confidentiality. Dreisdale cannot reveal them to the police or anyone else. There is no indication that he ever disclosed the statements to anyone. However, as we will discuss below, he may be subject to discipline for the consequences of Hathaway's disclosures to her journalist friend.

Dreisdale's Duty With Respect To Clampett's Statement About The Dead Man's Friend

Although the general rule is that a lawyer must not reveal his client's confidences, there is an exception for certain prospective crimes. MR 1.6(b)(1). A lawyer **is permitted** to reveal the intention of his client to commit certain crimes in order to help prevent the commission of those crimes. Under the Model Rules, this exception is narrowly limited to criminal acts which are likely to result in imminent death or substantial bodily harm. Note that this "prospective crimes" exception does not *require* the lawyer to disclose the confidence. Instead, it gives him the option to disclose or not to disclose. MR 1.6, Comment [9]. The framers of the Model Rules felt that it was better to encourage full and open communication between lawyer and client (thereby enabling the lawyer to counsel against wrongful conduct), than to require the lawyer to disclose a client's criminal purpose.

Before leaving Dreisdale's office, Clampett said that he intended to "finish the job" by preventing the dead man's friend from bothering Clampett's girlfriend again. Under the circumstances, Dreisdale could reasonably believe that Clampett intended another murder and was therefore justified in reporting the conversation to the police. However, he had no obligation to report the conversation and will not be subject to discipline for not doing so. Indeed, disclosure of the prospective crime would almost certainly have led to disclosure of Clampett's confession of the earlier crime. This would have involved Dreisdale in a violation of the attorney-client privilege and the duty of confidentiality.

Under these facts, Dreisdale probably took the wiser course in not disclosing Clampett's intentions.

Dreisdale's Duty With Respect to the Gun

A lawyer must not unlawfully obstruct another party's access to evidence or unlawfully alter, destroy or conceal a document or other material having potential evidentiary value. A lawyer must not counsel or assist another person to do any such act. MR 3.4(a). The attorney's duty of confidentiality does not extend to physical evidence of a crime. When Clampett waved his gun in front of Dreisdale, Dreisdale correctly advised Clampett to turn the gun over to the police. When Clampett gave the gun to Dreisdale instead, Dreisdale's choices narrowed. Most courts have recognized that criminal defense attorneys have a duty to turn over to the police or prosecution physical evidence that comes into their possession relating to the commission of a crime. This applies both to any product of the crime (i.e., stolen property) or to the instrumentalities of the crime (i.e., a weapon). Upon receipt of the gun from Clampett, Dreisdale had a duty to turn this evidence over to the police.

Instead, Dreisdale dropped the weapon into a trash can and anonymously called the police to tell them where they could find it. Looking at his conduct most sympathetically, we might argue that he was attempting to protect his client's confidences by withholding any information about the source of the weapon. However, Dreisdale's actions certainly made the authorities' job more difficult. It was foreseeable, for example, that the trash can would be picked up and emptied before the police got to it. It's true that he did not alter the evidence and took care to preserve any fingerprints, but his real duty was simply to turn over the gun directly. In failing to do this, he may well have crossed the fine line to the crime of obstruction of justice.

Hathaway's Disclosure of Clampett's Confidential Information

A lawyer having direct supervisory authority over a nonlawyer shall make reasonable efforts to ensure that the nonlawyer's conduct is compatible with his own obligations. MR 5.3(b). Among other things, he must exercise reasonable care to prevent his employees and associates from disclosing or using confidences or secrets of a client. Dreisdale had hired Hathaway only two months before, so short a period as to require special vigilance by Dreisdale. He had an obligation to instruct Hathaway in the preservation of client's confidences. Also, he had a duty not to permit conferences with clients to be broadcast over an office intercom. His neglect of sound office procedure and his failure to train and supervise Hathaway will probably subject him to discipline.

Even if Hathaway were a long-standing, well-trained and trusted employee, Dreisdale's method of communicating with her was fraught with problems. By leaving the intercom on at all times except during client meetings, Dreisdale created the risk that he might forget to turn it off when necessary, or that Hathaway or someone else would overhear him during a telephone call about a client. A lawyer must organize and run his office in a manner which assures protection of client confidences and secrets.

Answer to Question 7

Mansfield's Appearance on Television Program

Lawyers are not discouraged from speaking or writing on the law. On the contrary, because our legal system is such an integral part of our society, comment by lawyers is encouraged. Many lawyers participate in TV discussions of general legal issues and even the facts of particular cases. And many lawyers write articles of comment for magazines and newspapers. The attorney's ability to speak, however, is not unbridled. The Model Rules place limits essentially on two areas of speech: 1) Extrajudicial statements by a lawyer who is participating in the investigation or litigation of a matter (MR 3.6); and 2) statements and other communications which may be broadly construed as advertising and solicitation (MR 7.1 through MR 7.5).

Thus, an attorney shall not make a false or misleading statement about her services. A statement is false or misleading if it is likely to create an unjustified expectation about the results the lawyer can achieve, or if it compares the lawyer's services with other lawyers' services, unless the comparison can be substantiated factually. MR 7.1(b),(c). Here, Mansfield has boasted before a TV audience that she is a nationally recognized criminal law expert and that she has "gotten many a client" out of a jam similar to Julie's. Also, she has claimed herself to be "the most qualified person" to help Julie, thereby claiming a level of superiority over other lawyers which she cannot possibly substantiate. In her enthusiasm before a large audience, Mansfield has exceded the bounds prescribed by the Rules and is subject to discipline.

Mansfield's Request That Julie Schedule An Appointment

As part of his duty to avoid improper solicitation of clients, a lawyer shall not, by in-person or live telephone contact, "solicit professional employment from a prospective client with whom the lawyer has no family or prior professional relationship when a significant motive for the lawyer's doing so is the lawyer's pecuniary gain". MR 7.3(a). The Rule does not by its terms prohibit impromptu TV solicitation, but certainly the facts here would require that the Rule be applied. Mansfield was talking directly to Julie when she urged her to telephone her to set up an appointment. In describing Julie as "definitely in need of professional help," she was stressing the importance of the appointment. This is definitely the kind of direct one-on-one solicitation MR 7.3 was intended to prevent.

Further, the solicitation of clients from the general public by means of TV advertising is specifically covered by MR 7.3(c). This section anticipates that TV advertising will have a written script and will be broadcast through recordings. It requires that all such advertising be clearly labelled "Advertising Material" at the beginning and ending of each recorded communication. MR 7.2(b) requires that all written and recorded advertising scripts be maintained by the lawyer for a period of two years to facilitate inspection in the event of a complaint. Mansfield's tactics here show why this Rule was needed.

Although Mansfield might argue that Julie solicited the legal advice when she called in, the fact is that Julie did not expect to have her request for free guidance converted into a lawyer's solicitation of a new client. Mansfield should simply have said, "It sounds to me as though you need competent advice by a specialist in criminal matters. I would consult a lawyer as soon as possible. If you don't know one, contact your local bar association."

Giving Theater Tickets to News Director

With very limited exceptions, a lawyer shall not give anything of value to another person for recommending the lawyer's services. MR 7.2(c). Mansfield gave two tickets to a popular play to the news director to thank him for airing an interview with her on the network news. Mansfield's remarks confirm that she considered the interview a source of new clients and that she was specifically rewarding the news director for helping her to get these clients. Although it may be argued that theatre tickets are of nominal value, they represent the very kind of thing the Rule was intended to prevent. Mansfield is subject to discipline.

Answer to Question 8

Joey's Letter Contains Numerous Statements that are False and Misleading

All advertising by a lawyer through public media is controlled by MR 7.2. This Rule permits a lawyer to advertise through written or recorded communication, subject to the requirements of MR 7.1 and MR 7.3. These Rules specify, among other things, that a lawyer shall not make a false or misleading communication about herself or her services. A communication is false or misleading if it: (a) contains a material misrepresentation of fact or law, or omits a fact necessary to make the statement considered as a whole not materially misleading; (b) is likely to create an unjustified expectation about the results the lawyer can achieve, or states or implies that the lawyer can achieve results by means that violate the rules of professional conduct or other law; or (c) compares the lawyer's services with other lawyers' services, unless the comparison can be factually substantiated. MR 7.1.

In his letter, Joey has made the following statements, all of which are misleading:

1) He refers to himself as Dr. Joey Bologna, a designation that suggests training in the medical sciences, and then says, "When you hire me, you don't just get a lawyer, you get a doctor", etc. Although he qualifies this by admitting that he's writing as a lawyer, the implication persists that he may have some special medical skills. This is misleading, at best. While all lawyers now earn the degree of Juris Doctor, they are not generally referred to as "Doctor", at least, not in the U.S. or the U.K.

2) He claims that he has been practicing law for "quite a while." This statement as false. We are told that he has just graduated from law school and is newly admitted to the bar.

3) He claims that he was a member of his law school's moot court honors team and participated in other trial competitions. From the facts, we know this statement is false as well. In fact, Joey was an average student, and he never had time for extra-curricular activities. He could not have participated either in moot court or in other trial competition.

4) He suggests that the degree of Juris Doctor somehow qualifies him to handle medical malpractice cases. Obviously, there is no basis for this claim and it constitutes a statement which is completely false and misleading.

5) He claims that he is a "specialist" in personal injury law. Claims of special training or skills by a lawyer are very carefully circumscribed and scrutinized. Lawyers shall not state or imply that they have been recognized or certified as specialists in a particular field of law, except that: 1) lawyers who have been admitted to practice patent law before the US Patent and Trademark Office may

use the designation "Patent Attorney"; lawyers engaged in Admiralty practice may use the designation "Admiralty"; and 3) lawyers who have been certified as specialists in a field of law by a regulatory authority empowered to grant certification of specialization in that field may communicate the fact of certification. MR 7.4. No jurisdiction recognizes a specialty in personal injury law and no lawyer may claim it. A lawyer may say, "My practice is limited to personal injury law" or even "Personal injury law is my only business," but he may not claim that he is recognized or certified in that field. Joey's statement is especially misleading not only because he is not a specialist but because he has no experience in the field. His claim that he is "pretty knowledgable" is improper for the same reason.

6) He claims that if his prices and services are compared with those of other lawyers in the area "I can't be beat." This claim is improper for two reasons. First of all, it violates the Rule against comparing one's services with the services of other lawyers "unless the comparison can be factually substantiated" MR 7.1(c). Secondly, as a new attorney, Joey cannot possibly have accummulated the knowledge of local practice necessary to substantiate this statement. The statement is patently false and misleading.

For all of the above, Joey has violated the standards of professional responsibility and is subject to discipline.

Joey's Solicitation by Mail to People Known to be in Need of Legal Services

Lawyers are permitted to advertise their services. The rationale is that this fulfills the public's need to know about available legal services and also satisfies the general requirements of free speech. But the Model Rules impose controls which are intended to prevent abuses in solicitation. Thus, every written or recorded communication from a lawyer soliciting professional employment from a prospective client known to be in need of legal services in a particular matter, and with whom the lawyer has no family or prior professional relationship, must include the words "Advertising Material" on the outside envelope or at the beginning and ending of any recorded communication. MR 7.3(c). Joey mailed 1,000 of his solicitation letters to prospective clients. Giving Joey the benefit of the doubt, it's at least possible that some of these prospects needed legal services. But Joey failed to include the words "Advertising Material" on any of his envelopes and it does not appear that he had a family or prior professional relationship with any of these people. Therefore, Joey violated the terms of MR 7.3 and is subject to discipline.

Answer to Question 9

Swanson's Fee Agreement with Adam

When a lawyer has not regularly represented a client, the basis or rate of the fee shall be communicated to the client, preferably in writing, within a reasonable period of time. MR 1.5(b). This provision would control here because this is the first meeting between Swanson and Adam. The fee can be paid in a number of ways, e.g., under a fixed hourly rate or as a percentage of the recovery. As a matter of sound practice, the attorney should offer the client a number of payment options. Although there is no evidence that Swanson offered Adam the option of paying him on an hourly basis, we do know that Swanson told Adam that recovery was problematic, that Adam had already sustained a large medical bill, and that Swanson was going to advance the costs. It is reasonable to conclude from these facts that payment in cash was probably not a viable option for Adam.

The Model Rules require that a contingent fee agreement be in writing. MR 1.5(c). Swanson reviewed the agreement with Adam before he signed it and has met the requirements of the Rule.

A contingent fee agreement is valid as long as it is in writing and states the method by which the fee is to be determined, including the percentage that will accrue to the lawyer if successful, the expenses to be deducted, and whether they should be deducted before or after calculating the contingent fee. MR 1.5(c). A contingent fee is not permitted in any criminal case or in most domestic relations matters. MR 1.5(d). [Many jurisdictions prescribe by statute or rule the percentage which may be paid to the lawyer under a contingency fee agreement in a personal injury matter.] Here, Swanson's agreement clearly stated that costs would be deducted off the top, and that the remainder of any recovery would be split 1/3 to Swanson and 2/3 to Adam. The agreement also makes it clear that if there were no recovery, Adam would not be responsible to repay Swanson for any costs advanced. This arrangement is fine under the Model Rules (MR 1.8(e)). [In some jurisdictions which still observe the terms of the original ABA Model Code, advances for costs must be reimbursed by the client and may not be contingent.]

The Amount of the Contingent Fee

A lawyer's fee must be reasonable. MR 1.5. A contingent agreement which provides the attorney one-third of the recovery after costs is not unusual in personal injury cases. Contingent fees usually result in greater compensation to the lawyer than fixed fees because the attorney must bear the risk of loss and may have to advance costs which may or may not ever be repaid. Therefore, under the circumstances, Swanson's fee is reasonable.

Settlement of the Claim

A lawyer must provide competent representation to the client. Competent representation requires the legal knowledge, skill, thoroughness and preparation reasonably necessary for the representation. MR 1.1. A lawyer also must act with reasonable diligence and promptness in representing a client. MR 1.3. A lawyer must abide by a client's decision whether to accept an offer of settlement on a matter; he has no inherent authority to settle, but authority may be express or implied. Here, Swanson had the express authority conferred in the contingency agreement itself. He was able to settle Adam's claim with the insurance company in just a few hours and for $30,000, $5,000 more than Adam had expressly authorized. By settling the case in this manner, Swanson was able to avoid litigation costs which he would have deducted from the total settlement. Considering all of the above, Swanson's settlement of the case was proper.

Placement of the $30,000 in Swanson's Client Trust Account

Upon conclusion of a contingent fee matter, the lawyer shall provide the client with a written statement stating the outcome of the matter and, if there is a recovery, showing the remittance to the client and the method of determination. MR 1.5(c). A lawyer must keep separate from the lawyer's personal and business property all client property in the lawyer's possession. Funds must be kept in a separate account maintained in the state where the lawyer's office is situated, or elsewhere with the consent of the client. MR 1.15(a). Upon receiving funds or other property in which a client has an interest, a lawyer must promptly notify the client. Here, Swanson followed the rules exactly: upon receipt of the settlement check, he deposited the full amount into his trust account. He then wrote a letter to Adam informing him that he had received the money, detailing his calculations under the contingent fee agreement, and remitting Adam's portion of the funds.

Swanson's Fee

A few days after Swanson delivered to Adam his 2/3 amount of the settlement, Adam expressed his dismay over the size of Swanson's fee. If a dispute arises concerning the respective interests of the lawyer and client in funds held by the lawyer, the portion in dispute must be kept separate in the lawyer's trust account until the dispute is resolved. MR 1.15(c). Swanson therefore was correct in leaving his 1/3 of the fee in the client trust account while he waited to see if Adam would actually take some action to contest it. In addition, he recommended to Adam that he seek other counsel if he wished to dispute the fee. Swanson waited four weeks to see if Adam intended to dispute his fee. This was probably not an unreasonable time to wait before disbursing the funds to himself. Swanson is not subject to discipline for his conduct under these facts.

Answer to Question 10

This question presents several problems in the area of conflicts of interest.

Connors' Representation of Both Piranha and Megatron

A key duty for a lawyer is to recognize and avoid actual or potential conflicts of interest. She owes each client the duties of loyalty (MR 1.7) and confidentiality (MR 1.6). These duties are hard to satisfy in a transaction involving two clients with different interests. This means that a lawyer should not undertake or continue the representation of a client if the representation will be directly adverse to another client unless both clients consent after consultation. MR 1.7. The lawyer also owes each client the duty of confidentiality. This means that a lawyer should avoid the representation when she might be required to divulge another client's confidences and secrets.

Comment [12] to Model Rule 1.7 warns, "For example, a lawyer may not represent multiple parties to a negotiation whose interests are fundamentally antagonistic to each other, but common representation is permissible where the parties are generally aligned in interest..." Generally speaking, no negotiation is more fraught with real and potential antagonism in interests than an employment contract, especially one dealing with stock options worth several million dollars, as here.

MR 1.7 does permit a lawyer to undertake joint representation if she reasonably believes the representation of one will not adversely affect her relationship with the other *and if both clients consent after consultation.*

Piranha and Megatron, the two parties to the proposed employment, requested that Connors represent them both. This did not relieve her of the responsibility to inquire extensively into their respective interests and to warn them each of the many issues that might arise in her negotiation and drafting of specific terms of an involved agreement.

It doesn't appear that Connors considered any of this or that she mentioned her duties under the Rules to either Piranha or Shark before agreeing to accept the representation. She would be subject to discipline for her failure to obtain both parties' informed consent before entering into the dual-representation relationship. The facts themselves show the kind of problem that can arise when a lawyer attempts dual representation in situations like this: the parties had never discussed the vesting period, let alone resolve it. This was obviously an issue on which they had antagonistic interests and on which zealous advocacy on behalf of one would be adverse to the other.

Payment of Connors' Fee

A key ingredient in the relationship between lawyer and client is the negotiation and payment of the lawyer's fee. In our society, compensation is usually the price of loyalty. For this reason, a lawyer shall not accept compensation for representing a client from someone other than that client, unless (1) the client consents after consultation; (2) there is no interference with the lawyer's independence of professional judgment or with the client-lawyer relationship; *and* (3) information relating to the representation of the client is kept confidential from the person paying the fee. MR 1.8. Here, Connors' entire fee will be paid by Megatron, even though Connors is representaing Piranha's interests as well. Reasonable reflection should have convinced Connors that Pirhana's consent could not dispel the problems created by the payment of her fees by Megatron. First of all, her resulting loyalty to Megatron would inevitably interfere with her independence of judgment. And secondly, she would inevitably — as indeed, she did — receive information relating to her representation of Piranha which she was under a duty to protect but which she might be required to disclose to Megatron under her duty of loyalty to Megatron.

Connors didn't appear to give these issues any thought at all. She certainly didn't discuss the potential risks with Piranha, nor did she even attempt to obtain his consent. Connors has violated her duty of professional responsibility by failing to take the necessary precautions against an impermissible conflict of interest created by the payment from Megatron. She will be subject to discipline.

Connors' Handling of the Stock Option Vesting Question

Shortly after Connors took on the joint representation, she was informed by Piranha that he intended to leave Megatron after two and half years. Obviously, his plans would have caused Shark to reconsider his offer of employment to Piranha; no company would offer a hefty salary and stock options worth several million dollars to a transient president. Piranha's intentions also explain why he wanted his stock options to vest after two years. Pirhana's confession to Connors of his intended disloyalty to Megatron should have caused her a sleepless night. And when Connors called Shark and learned the company's policy on stock vesting, she was confronted with the kind of dilemma that is virtually certain to occur when a lawyer attempts to represent two clients with potentially adverse interests. There was now only one course of action for Connors that would adequately protect the confidences and the interests of each client. She was obliged to withdraw from representing either and both. "If such a conflict arises after representation has been undertaken, the lawyer shall withdraw from representation." Continued representation of either client under these circumstances would represent a violation of the rules of professional conduct, mandating withdrawal. MR 1.16.

Answer to Question 11

Edward has several potential problems to consider in his possible representation of both Ruth and Ralph.

Conflict of Interest Problems in Representing Multiple Criminal Defendants

A lawyer shall not represent a client if the representation of that client may be materially limited by the lawyer's responsibilities to another client or to a third person...unless the lawyer reasonably believes the representation will not be adversely affected *and* the client consents after consultation. MR 1.7(b). When an attorney undertakes to represent multiple clients in a single matter, he must explain the implications of joint representation and the advantages and risks involved to each client. In a criminal matter especially, the potential for conflict in representing more than one defendant is so great that ordinarily a lawyer should decline to represent more than one codefendant. MR 1.7 Comment [7]. Consider the facts in this question: Either Ralph or Ruth may want to cooperate with the police and implicate the other. Ralph may wish to testify that the whole caper was really Ruth's idea. Ruth may want to testify that Ralph drove over the state line over her objections. One or the other may want to plead guilty in exchange for a lesser sentence. One or the other may not want either of them to testify at all. These are all reflections of the irreconcilable conflict between them and of their adverse interests.

On these facts, it should be clear to Edward that conflicts of interest are likely to arise in dual representation. If he ignores the standard wisdom and agrees to interview both Ruth or Ralph, he risks having to withdraw from representing *either*. His interviews with both teenagers may disclose substantial discrepancies in their stories and put him in possession of confidential information about one that is detrimental to the other. The only way to resolve this dilemma ethically is to refuse to represent either at the outset or to withdraw from representing both once a conflict is disclosed. MR 1.16(a). On these facts, Edward should not accept the representation of either Ralph or Ruth. Ordinarily, he might be free to choose either one or the other, but, as we shall discuss, the intervention of their mother at this stage of the proceedings, makes this inadvisable.

Linda's Payment of Edward's Legal Fees

A lawyer must not accept compensation for representing a client from one other than the client unless (1) the client consents after consultation; (2) there is no interference with the lawyer's independence of professional judgment or with the client-lawyer relationship; and (3) information relating to representation of the client is protected as required by the duty of confidentiality in MR 1.6. MR 1.8(f).

Linda has assured Edward that she will be responsible to pay all of the legal fees incurred in his defense of Ruth and Ralph. Before accepting her offer, Edward must consult with Ruth and Ralph about the potential risks involved in this arrangement and obtain their consent. Even if Edward obtains their consent, however, he will have difficulty navigating around the hurdles presented by Linda's interference in the defense and by the need to protect the confidences of both Ruth and Ralph and to preserve the attorney-client privilege. Linda has made it clear that she wants to be consulted on all aspects of the case. This is likely to interfere with Edward's independent professional judgment and to jeopardize the attorney-client privilege and the confidences of Ruth and Ralph. Edward should not accept the representation of either Ruth or Ralph under the terms presented by Linda.

Linda's Statement to Edward about Trial Tactics

In a criminal case, a lawyer must abide by the client's decision, after consultation, on three basic issues of criminal advocacy: what plea to enter, whether to waive jury trial, and whether the client will testify. MR 1.2(a). Here, Linda has told Edward that Ruth, not Ralph, should testify at trial and that "the jury will be more sympathetic to a pretty girl." Before Edward has even accepted the case, Linda has, in effect, decided that there will be a jury trial, that there will be no plea bargain, and that only Ruth should testify at trial.

If Edward takes on the representation, he must discuss all three of these issues with Ruth and Ralph, allow them to reach a considered decision, and then abide by their decision. The decision is theirs, not Linda's. Linda has attempted to interfere with the lawyer's independent judgment and also to preempt the process of free and considered decision by her children.

Given all the problems implicit in these facts, Edward will almost certainly breach his duties of confidentiality, diligence, and loyalty to Ralph and Ruth if he chooses to accept their defense under Linda's terms. This would subject him to discipline and also to a claim for malpractice. Under these conditions, Edward should decline representation of both Ruth and Ralph. Or, if he wishes, he may represent only one of the children, provided: 1) that child agrees to the representation after consultation; 2) Linda promises not to influence or to interfere with any of the child's decisions; and 3) Edward insists on interviewing only his client and not the other child. Also, Edward should advise that other child to seek independent counsel immediately.

Answer to Question 12

The rules of professional conduct help insure, among other things, that a government lawyer shall not exploit his position as a public officer for his own private gain or for the benefit of a private client after he leaves the government. This fact pattern poses several conflict of interest problems related to an attorney who was formerly a government lawyer. I will discuss the various issues presented.

Acceptance of Employment at Logaway

Except as the law may otherwise expressly permit, a lawyer serving as a public officer or employee shall not negotiate for private employment with any person who is involved as a party in a matter in which the lawyer is participating personally and substantially (with certain exceptions which do not apply here). The term "matter" includes any judicial or other proceeding, application, request for ruling or other determination, contract, claim, controversy, investigation, charge, accusation, arrest or other particular matter involving a specific party or parties; and any other matter covered by the conflict of interest rules of the appropriate government agency. MR 1.11(2).

Immediately prior to his employment by Logoway, Jerry was an attorney with the Department of Justice. He participated in the investigation of environmental violations by logging companies in the Pacific Northwest. He accepted an offer to become general counsel of Logaway at the close of the investigation.

It's clear that Jerry participated personally and substantially in the federal investigation of Logaway's operations and then accepted employment from the same company immediately after. His employment by Logaway was necessarily preceded by negotiations between Jerry and Logaway. Although the Department did not find any violation by Logaway, its investigation into that company's practices would constitute a "matter" as defined by the Model Rules. Jerry is subject to discipline for negotiating with Logaway during the investigation and for accepting employment by Logaway.

Representing Logaway in a Complaint by the Department of Justice

Except as the law may otherwise expressly permit, a lawyer shall not represent a private client in connection with a matter in which the lawyer participated personally and substantially as a public officer or employee, unless the appropriate government agency consents after consultation. MR 1.11(a). Immediately before his employment by Logaway, Jerry participated personally and substantially in an investigation of alleged environmental violations by various logging companies, including Logaway. Although the original investigation into Logaway did not turn up any violations, the current suit may well involve some of the evidence from the former inquiry. In any event, because the substance of the complaint grows out of the same or similar activities by Logaway, Jerry will not be permitted to represent Logaway in the criminal action brought by the Department of Justice against the company, unless the agency consents to his representation of the company after consultation. The agency may be prevented from giving its consent in a particular case by an existing statute or regulation.

If the Department of Justice does not consent to Jerry's representation of Logaway in this matter, it may be possible for another attorney in his office to handle the matter, but only if Jerry is completely screened from the matter. MR 1.11(a)(1). Of course, the company may also engage outside counsel to handle the complaint.

Representation of Logaway in Civil Lawsuit Against Woodchuck

Except as the law may otherwise expressly permit, a lawyer who has information that the lawyer knows is confidential government information about a person or entity acquired when the lawyer was a public officer or employee, may not represent a private client whose interests are adverse to that person or entity in a matter in which the information could be used to the material disadvantage of that person or entity. MR 1.11(b). While Jerry was a lawyer for the Department of Justice, a Woodchuck vice president provided him with inside information regarding Woodchuck's operations. This information was not available to the public; it was confidential government information used by the Department to further its investigation of Woodchuck. Logaway and Woodchuck are now involved in a lawsuit over the title to land for the building of a new plant. Logaway's interests are as adverse to Woodchuck's as it's possible to imagine. Although the litigation between the two companies is not directly related to envirnmental issues, Jerry may be able to use the information he has about Woodchuck to that company's material disadvantage during the litigation. This is precisely the kind of situation Model Rule 1.11 was intended to control. Jerry will have to be completely screened from the case by the attorneys for Logaway.

Answer to Question 13

Margie's Defense of Henry's Lawsuit Against Sweetums

A lawyer has a duty to represent her client with reasonable diligence. MR 1.3. She is required to abide by her client's decision concerning the objectives of the representation and to consult with her client about the means for achieving these objectives. MR 1.2. At the same time, she must not bring or defend any proceeding, or assert or controvert any issue therein, unless the basis for doing so is not frivolous MR 3.1. However, "the filing of an action or defense... is not frivolous merely because the facts have not first been fully substantiated or because the lawyer expects to develop vital evidence only by discovery. Such action is not frivolous even though the lawyer believes that the client's position ultimately will not prevail. "The action is frivolous, however, if the client desires to take the action primarily for the purpose of harassing or maliciously injuring a person... ." MR 3.1, Comment [2].

As general counsel for Sweetums, Margie has a duty to represent the corporation and to defend it competently and diligently against Henry's lawsuit. Frank, Sweetums' Vice President, has asked Margie to do three things: (1) assert the defense of contributory negligence, (2) bombard Henry with massive and numerous discovery requests, and (3) investigate every possible witness with respect to Henry's action in the BVF store. After giving the matter some thought, Margie chose to do none of these things. If she failed in her duty to represent Sweetums competently and diligently, Margie will be subject to discipline.

The decision whether or not to assert an affirmative defense which may or may not prevail will certainly affect the client's substantive rights. If there is any basis for the defense which is not clearly frivolous, the lawyer has a duty to assert it, especially when the client specifically instructs him to do so. Here, it's not clear whether Henry was negligent in rushing to grab the wrong box and eat the candies when he couldn't devote all his attention to what he was doing, or whether Sweetums was negligent in packing the candies in the wrong box. Clearly, regardless of her sympathies for Henry, her duty was to assert, protect, investigate and develop the facts proving contributory negligence. Margie should have asserted the contributory negligence defense.

With respect to the scope and frequency of discovery, Margie's duty was to conduct all the proceedings necessary to the full development of all the facts. She was not obligated to respect or follow Frank's instructions to conduct numerous and massive discovery solely to force Henry into submission. On the contrary, she was required not to make a frivolous discovery request. MR 3.4(d). A competent lawyer is expected to walk the fine line between harassment and purposeful investigation of the facts. Here, Margie conducted one discovery. Whether that was sufficient is a matter for reasonable analysis of all the facts. If

Margie limited the scope and number of discoveries out of concern for Henry, that was improper. If she came to the reasonable conclusion that other discovery would be unproductive, her actions would be proper.

Margie was wrong not to hire investigators to look for other witnesses to Henry's trip to the BVF store. These other witnesses might have been able to confirm that Henry acted carelessly by rushing to grab the box and by eating the candies when his attention was on the check-out counter.

Margie's Meeting with Ellen

A lawyer who is employed or retained by an organization represents the organization, not the constituents. MR 1.13(a). In dealing with an organization's directors, officers, employees, members and shareholders, a lawyer must explain that her client is the organization, not the constituent, whenever it appears that the organization's interests are adverse to the constituent. Whenever a conflict is threatened, the lawyer should advise the constituent that a conflict or potential conflict exists, that the lawyer cannot represent the constituent under the circumstances, and that the constituent should retain independent counsel. The attorney for the organization should also take care to explain to the individual(s) involved that any discussions between the individual and the attorney may not be privileged. MR 1.13.

Margie properly explained to Ellen that, as corporate counsel, she represented the Sweetums Corporation, not Ellen, and that her conversations with Ellen were not privileged. Margie then advised Ellen to seek the advice of independent counsel, which Ellen refused. Ellen threatened that she or others on the assembly line would remove the company's equipment if conditions did not immediately improve. Margie reported her conversation with Ellen to the Sweetums assembly line manager, who responded to the threat the next morning by placing armed guards throughout the assembly line plant to protect the equipment.

Margie took the steps necessary to protect the interests of the company by informing the appropriate officer about the threats. Confronted by Ellen's threat to commit an unlawful action which would also constitute a violation of Ellen's legal oblgation to the company, Margie's obligation was to proceed "as reasonably necessary to the best interests of the organization." MR 1.13(b). In view of the seriousness of Ellen's threat and the need for speed to avoid the theft of company property, Margie was justified reporting the threat without waiting to ask Ellen to reconsider the matter.

Answer to Question 14

Tony's Initial Discussions With Hilly

In general, a lawyer cannot communicate directly with a party represented by another lawyer concerning the subject matter of the representation unless the other lawyer has consented. MR 4.2. This rule has a two-fold purpose: to prevent interference with the lawyer's representation of his client; and to discourage "invasion" by other lawyers after the attorney-client relationship has been established. The rule is called the "no-contact" rule. The rule does not apply, however, when a client approaches another lawyer to investigate a possible change of counsel. Here, because Hilly was dissatisfied with Sally and asked Tony to represent her, Tony did not violate the no-contact rule.

Tony's Agreement with Hilly

Before the representation is concluded, a lawyer shall not negotiate or enter into an agreement with the client that gives the lawyer literary or media rights to a portrayal or account of the client's life based in substantial part on information relating to the representation. MR 1.8(d). This rule helps prevent an impermissible conflict between the interests of the lawyer (who may, for example, prefer a sensational trial for the value it adds to the client's story) and the interests of the client (who may, for example, be better off entering into a run-of-the-mill plea bargain). This conflict is manifested here. Tony discouraged Hilly from accepting a plea bargain in his anxiety to get a "big" win. By suggesting the agreement to Hilly as a solution for her indigence and by negotiating the agreement with Hilly, Tony has violated MR 1.8(d) and will be subject to discipline.

Tony further compounded his ethical trangression by drafting the agreement himself and giving it to Hilly to sign — without suggesting that she have independent counsel first review it. An attorney cannot enter into a business transaction with a client unless the transaction is objectively fair, the terms are fully disclosed to the client, the client is given the opportunity to seek the advice of independent counsel, and the client consents in writing. MR 1.8(a). Tony should have urged Hilly to have the agreement reviewed by independent counsel before he allowed her to sign it. His failure to do so could subject him to discipline as well.

Tony's Violation of the Advocate-Witness Rule

An attorney should not accept the role of trial advocate if it is likely that he may be called as a necessary witness at the trial. MR 3.7. Tony was one of Hilly's most ardent clients. He has knowledge of her professional activities and is privy to information that may be useful to the prosecution. He should have anticipated that he might be called as a witness. He should not have accepted Hilly's case and will be subject to discipline for doing so.

Tony's Handling of the Prosecution's Plea Bargain Offer

A lawyer must keep his client informed about the status of her case and answer all her reasonable questions. MR 1.4(a). His explanations should be clear and accurate enough to enable the client to make informed decisions about the representation. MR 1.4(b). In a criminal case, some decisions must be made by the client, not the lawyer. These include the following decisions: what plea shall I enter; shall I ask for or waive a jury trial; and shall I testify. MR 1.2(a). Obviously, these decisions cannot be made intelligently unless the client is informed about all the consequences. Here, after the prosecutor told Tony that she was willing to negotiate a plea bargain agreement with Hilly, Tony communicated this to Hilly "in passing" and, without any discussion, advised her instead that her best interests would be served by winning a "big" acquittal at trial. Tony had an obligation to discuss the plea bargain option much more thoroughly with Hilly, including a discussion of the risks involved in pressing forward with the trial. His failure to do so stemmed from his interest in maximizing the value of his media rights, rather than from any legitimate concern for his client. Tony will be subject to discipline for violating his duty of zealous advocacy, his duty to communicate appropriately with Hilly about a significant development in her case, and his duty to allow his client to make an informed decision about the prosecutor's plea bargain offer.

Tony's Misconduct

It is professional misconduct for a lawyer to commit a criminal act that reflects adversely on his honesty, trustworthiness or fitness as a lawyer in other respects. MR 8.4(b). In this day of freer sexual expression, the act of patronizing prostitutes may not be considered a sufficient transgression to warrant lawyer discipline. (One should reflect, however, on the occasional police incentive which culminates in the round-up of male patrons and on the resulting publicity.) Tony committed a criminal act by patronizing Hilly's illegal business. It's questionable whether this one act alone will subject Tony to discipline, however. Every jurisdiction has its own threshold for this type of misconduct by a lawyer.

The Prosecution's Motion to Disqualify Tony

As noted above, an attorney should not act as an advocate in a case in which his testimony as witness is likely to be necessary. MR 3.7. As an advocate, the lawyer's duty is to *argue* his client's case by presenting the evidence in its best light. As a witness, the lawyer must testify truthfully as to his own knowledge. Further, he subjects himself to rigorous cross-examination. It will be difficult for the trier of fact to distinguish between the two roles and for the lawyer to preserve the integrity of his evidence. Furthermore, if the lawyer's testimony is regarded by the trier of fact as prejudicial to the client, it creates an impossible burden for the lawyer to overcome through other testimony and unfairly impinges upon the client's right to a fair trial.

Under the facts, Tony is a former client of Hilly's and therefore someone with first-hand knowledge of at least some of her key activities. The prosecution has moved to disqualify Tony from representing Hilly on the grounds that he is a potential witness. The motion should be granted because the potential for conflict is too great. The stakes are particularly high in a criminal case where a failure to disqualify an attorney at the trial level could result in an overturned conviction on appeal based on a subsequent "ineffective assistance of counsel" argument.

Answer to Question 15

1. Reggie's Representation of Fred

A lawyer owes his client both a duty of loyalty and a duty of confidentiality. These duties form the backbone of the rules controlling conflicts of interest. How the rules are applied depends in part upon whether the client is a current one or a former one. The rule for former clients (Milton falls into this category because he was a client but is now dead) is: A lawyer who has formerly represented a client in a matter shall not thereafter represent another person in the same or a substantially related matter in which that person's interests are materially adverse to the interests of the former client, unless the former client consents after consultation. MR 1.9(a). This duty to a former client continues indefinitely so long as the matter itself is the same or substantially related; on these facts it will even survive death.

Here, Reggie represented Milt in drafting his will fifteen years ago. The will would still represent Milt's wishes for the disposition of his property on death. Now, six months after Milt's death, Milt's son Fred wishes to retain Reggie in order to attack the very will that Reggie prepared. This would represent an impermissible conflict of interest: Fred's interests are materially adverse to Milt's as expressed in his will. Fred's proposed action would be "substantially related" to the matter in that it would challenge the provisions of the will. And the consent of the client can no longer be obtained because he is dead. Reggie cannot ethically represent Fred in this matter. He must advise him to retain independent counsel.

Reggie's representation of Fred would also violate the lawyer as advocate vs. lawyer as witness rule. Under that rule, an attorney should not act as an advocate in a case in which his testimony is likely to be necessary. MR 3.7 (with certain exceptions which are not applicable here). Reggie was the attorney who drafted Milt's will. He will undoubtedly be called to testify at trial regarding Milt's state of mind and the events surrounding the creation of the will. Reggie would have to refuse Fred's case even if the "former client" conflict did not exist because he cannot at the same time represent Fred as a diligent advocate and testify as a witness in support of Milt's will.

You may have asked how Reggie could testify about his services in preparing the will without violating the attorney-client privilege (the privilege prevents the lawyer from testifying at trial to disclose any evidence communicated to him by the client; only the client may waive the privilege). The answer is that the privilege is not applied with respect to testimony by a lawyer who has drafted a will concerning the state of mind of the decedent at the time the will was drafted. Reggie might very well be called as witness in the trial of Fred's complaint.

2. What Reggie Should Have Said to Fred

Reggie would be precluded from accepting Fred's case under both the "former client" conflict of interest rules and the advocate-witness conflict of interest rule. As soon as Reggie realized why Fred had come to see him, he should have cut off further discussion by explaining that he was *Milt's* former attorney and that conflict of interest rules would now prevent him from representing Fred in any matter based on a challenge of his father's will. In addition, Reggie should have rejected any communication from Fred which might be treated as a confidence. Reggie should have taken care not to reveal any of Milt's confidences, e.g., in response to questions by Fred about his father's reasons for preferring Fred's brother.

3. Larry's Possible Representation of Fred

If a lawyer is required to decline representation under one of the Model Rules, including the rule controlling conflicts of interest (MR 1.9) no partner or lawyer associated with him or his firm may accept such employment. MR 1.10. This is known as the imputed disqualification rule. Because it would be a violation of this rule and the advocate-witness rule for Reggie to accept Fred's case, his partner Larry is prohibited from doing so as well. There's nothing wrong with Larry's lunch offer to Fred, and lunch itself would be OK. But Larry must take special care to avoid any discussion of Fred's grievances against his father or his siblings or any of Fred's comments about his case. At the beginning of lunch, he should say, "Let's talk about about old times, but, please no mention of the will. I'll have to cut you off. And, remember, I can't say anything at all about it either."

4. Reggie's Consultation Fee

Reggie's fee would ordinarily be regarded as fair and reasonable, thus satisfying the requirement of MR 1.5: "A lawyer's fee shall be reasonable." However, the fee is completely improper here. Reggie did not perform any legal services for Fred. On the contrary, it was improper for him to do so or to suggest that a lawyer-client relationship had been established between them. Reggie will be subject to discipline for billing Fred for his visit. He should correct his error by voiding his invoice and by advising Fred in writing of the reasons for his rejection of the representation.

Answer to Question 16

A lawyer has a duty to represent her client with diligence. MR 1.3. This duty is not unlimited, however, as Tonya's actions demonstrate. Tonya's conduct has strayed beyond the limits set by the rules of professional conduct on several counts.

Tonya's Production of Documents

Lawyers owe a duty of fairness to the opposing party and opposing counsel. Under that duty, a lawyer shall not unlawfully obstruct another party's access to evidence or unlawfully alter, destroy or conceal a document or other material having evidentiary value. MR 3.4(a). Here, Dr. Hackem's lawyer had a right to conduct discovery on behalf of his client and Tonya was obligated to produce all relevant documents in response to his demand. But in her response, she withheld documents unfavorable to her case and produced illegible copies of others. Tonya defeated her opponent's legitimate right to relevant information. This is a serious offense and Tonya is subject to discipline.

Tonya's Letter to Dr. Hackem

In representing a client, a lawyer shall not communicate with another represented person concerning the subject matter of the representation without the prior consent of the party's counsel. MR 4.2. Here, Tonya wrote a letter directly to Dr. Hackem at a time when she knew that he was already represented by counsel. (She had previously responded to counsel's demand for discovery.) There is no indication that Hackem's lawyer was consulted or that he consented to Tonya's direct communication with his client. Tonya will be subject to discipline for corresponding directly with Dr. Hackem.

(Note that MR 4.2 prohibits communication with *persons* represented by counsel, not *parties* alone. The MR draftsmen mean to extend the rule to include all persons who might have an interest in a matter, including witnesses, and who are represented by counsel. In some states, the rule is limited to represented *parties* only.)

Tonya's Threat of Criminal Prosecution

Under the old Model Code of Professional Responsibility, a lawyer was specifically instructed not to "present...or threaten to present criminal charges solely to obtain an advantage in a civil matter." This specific prohibition was not carried over into the Model Rules. However, virtually all states have statutes defining the crime of coercion as including conduct which induces a person to give up a legal right by putting him in fear that criminal charges will be brought against him. (*See*, New York Penal Law, Section 135.60.) These statutes apply to all citizens, including lawyers. Tonya has committed criminal coercion by threatening criminal action to encourage Dr. Hackem to settle. She is subject to discipline under MR 8.4, which defines as professional misconduct both criminal acts reflecting adversely on the lawyer's honesty, trustworthiness, or fitness as a lawyer in other respects and any conduct involving dishonesty, fraud or deceit. Tonya is subject to discipline once again. In some states, she will be automatically disbarred for committing the crime of coercion.

Closing Arguments

During the trial of a matter, a lawyer must not assert her personal opinion as to the justness of her case, the credibility of a witness, or the culpability of a civil litigant. MR 3.4(e). A trial is an exposition of relevant facts and evidence to the jury and judge. The attorney's opinion is unsworn testimony and therefore inadmissible as proof. The attorney who expresses her opinion is placed in the untenable position of acting both as advocate and as witness. The lawyer's job is to present and characterize the evidence in a way most favorable to her client and to guide the jury in drawing the most helpful inferences from the evidence. In presenting her case, a lawyer shall not engage in conduct intended to disrupt a tribunal. MR 3.5.

During closing arguments, Tonya used excessively sensational and inflammatory language when she characterized Dr. Hackem as a "butcher." This language, designed to inflame the passions of the jury, probably violates both Model Rule 3.4(e) and 3.5(c)—the former by alluding to matter not supported by admissible evidence and by commenting on the culpability of a litigant, and the latter by engaging in conduct capable of disrupting the trial. Tonya also declared her personal opinion that Hackem should never be allowed to practice medicine again and that he had "destroyed" George's life. This violated Model Rule 3.4(e). Tonya's tactics may have won her and her client an impressive verdict, but the price is almost certainly a complaint by opposing counsel or the judge to Tonya's grievance committee reciting her many violations of the Rules.

Answer to Question 17

Judge Stern's Night at the Opera

In general, a judge cannot accept a gift, bequest, favor or loan from anyone. CJC Canon 4, Section D(5). The purpose of this rule is to avoid undue influence and the appearance of impropriety — these gifts can be looked upon as influence buying. There are several exceptions to the rule, all in recognition of the fact that no judge can be expected to live in a sealed cocoon. One exception is ordinary social hospitality. Canon 4, Section D(5)(c). Ordinarily, social contact between a judge and a lawyer is not proscribed. Consider these facts, however: Larson, an attorney set to appear before Judge Stern shortly in a hotly contested dispute, suddenly calls the judge to invite him to an expensive evening at the opera, and especially to a performance by a great star for which tickets are unavailable. Larson's intent is clear. After minimal social contact over a period of many years, Larson calls the judge on the eve of an important trial in which she has a vested interest. The only inference to be drawn from Larson's spontaneous invitation is that she is seeking to curry favor with the judge before the trial. Under these circumstances, it was improper for the judge to accept the invitation — even though he was careful not to discuss the case with Larson. His evening out with Domingo, Wagner and Larson will subject him to discipline.

Does the judge's night at the opera now require him to recuse himself from the case? A judge shall disqualify himself in any proceeding in which his impartiality might reasonably be questioned, including instances where the judge has personal bias or prejudice concerning a party or a party's lawyer. CJC Canon 3 Section E(1)(a). We are told that Judge Stern and Larson were law school classmates and that they have run into each other at bar committee meetings. All of these encounters were minimal and incidental to their general activities and would not ordinarily raise any issue requiring or suggesting disqualification. Their evening together on the eve of trial is a more serious matter. Participating in a round of golf with three lawyers or in a poker game with lawyers who are regular friends—even if one is to appear before the judge—is one thing; an evening with one lawyer alone at the opera—especially one who will be lead counsel in an important trial—is another thing all together. Judge Stern would be well advised to recuse himself before the other side moves to disqualify on an affidavit by someone who saw the Judge and Larson together at the opera.

Lisa Larson's Invitation to Judge Stern

If it was improper for the judge to accept Larson's offer of a night at the opera, it was also wrong for Larson to extend the invitation in the first place. It is professional misconduct for a lawyer to engage in conduct that is prejudicial to the administration of justice (MR 8.4(d)) or to knowingly assist a judge in conduct that violates the rules of judicial conduct or other law. MR 8.4(f).

Larson is charged with knowing that the judge could not accept her offer without creating at least an appearance of impropriety under the circumstances. She should never have extended the invitation in the first place. Because she did so, she will be subject to discipline.

Judge Stern's Membership in Club Anglo

Judge Stern belongs to a club called Anglo which is apparently limited to males. We are not told that this is the case, but if use of the name "Anglo" indicates an actual bias on account of race or national origin, Judge Stern's membership in the club is forbidden. A judge cannot be a member of any club or organization that practices invidious discrimination on the basis of race, sex, religion or national origin. CJC Canon 2, Section C. This rule was established to help judges avoid even the appearance of impropriety. In addition to apparent discrimination on the basis of national origin, it would appear that the club systematically excludes women. Though there may be no club rule or policy which excludes women by its terms, discriminatory treatment may be established by practice over a period of time. Given the fact that the club has 250 members, all male, we may reasonably conclude that women are being excluded deliberately and systematically. The judge should not associate himself with the club and will be subject to discipline for doing so.

Judge Stern's Encounter With the Traffic Cop

A judge shall not lend the prestige of judicial office to advance his own or another's private interests. CJC Canon 2, Section B. Judge Stern made a point of telling the officer who stopped him for speeding that he was a state court judge, that his name was *Judge* Stern, and that the officer was likely to appear before him. His remarks were a crude attempt to influence the officer not to issue a ticket. This behavior is improper and will subject him to discipline — even though the officer refused to take the bait.

Judge Stern's Comments to the Reporter

The Code of Judicial Conduct contains several rules designed to ensure that judges not engage in inappropriate political activity. These rules help to immunize a judge from attacks on his impartiality and integrity. Thus, when he is a candidate for re-election, he shall not make any public comments or statements that commit or appear to commit him to a position with respect to cases, controversies or issues likely to come before him . CJC Canon 5, Section A(3)(d)(ii). Judge Stern clearly and unequivocally stated his opposition to the death penalty to a reporter during his campaign for re-election. He thus stated his bias on an issue likely to come before him as a state court judge, contrary to the CJC. He will be subject to discipline for his remarks.

Similarly, a judge shall not publicly endorse or publicly oppose another candidate for public office. Canon 5, Section A(1)(b). As an excepion to this general rule, judges may publicly endorse or oppose candidates running *for the same judicial office for which the judge himself is running*. Canon 5, Section C(1)(b)(iv). Here, Judge Stern has indicated his preference for one candidate for city council. This public endorsement is improper and will subject him to discipline.

Answer to Question 18

1. Joanne's Conduct

In general, a judge shall not accept a gift, bequest, favor or loan from anyone, though there are several exceptions to this rule. CJC Canon 4, Section D(5). A judicial candidate shall not personally solicit or accept campaign contributions or publicly stated support, but she is permitted to establish committees to conduct a campaign in her behalf. These committees are permitted to solicit and accept reasonable campaign contributions. Canon 5, Section C(2). Judicial campaign committees can accept contributions from attorneys, provided the contributions adhere to the standard of "reasonableness."

On the other hand, it is professional misconduct for an attorney to knowingly assist a judge or judicial candidate in conduct that violates the rules of judicial conduct or other law. MR 8.4(f). Thus, a lawyer is expected to know and follow the CJC insofar as it defines acceptable conduct between lawyer and judge. Because a judge may not accept a gift, favor or loan from anyone directly, a lawyer may not offer or make such a gift or loan. On the other hand, because a judge's campaign committee is permitted to solicit and accept reasonable contributions, a lawyer may make such a contribution.

According to these facts, Joanne made a $5,000 campaign contribution to the campaign committee of her friend Mary. The committee was properly established to accept contributions. Although generous, a $5,000 contribution is not so great as to be considered unreasonable, especially from one friend to another. There is nothing here to indicate that Joanne acted improperly in making her contribution.

The facts do not state whether Joanne and Mary intend to continue their tradition of exchanging generous family Christmas gifts now that Mary has become a judge. Even if they do, an exchange of once-a-year gifts among the two families would probably not be considered improper. Gifts from relatives or friends for special occasions such as birthdays (and, presumably, holidays) which are fairly commensurate with the occasion and the relationship are excepted from the general rule prohibiting gifts to judges. CJC Canon 4, Section D(5)(d). Here, Mary's and Joanne's families have already established a long history of exchanging gifts at Christmas. Continuing in this tradition is not likely to create an appearance of impropriety.

2. Mary's Conduct as a Judicial Candidate
A. Campaign Contributions

A candidate for judicial office subject to public election shall not personally solicit or accept campaign contributions or personally solicit publicly stated support. However, a candidate may establish a committee of responsible persons to conduct her campaign, and the *committee* is permitted to solicit and accept reasonable campaign contributions, manage the expenditure of funds for the candidate's campaign and obtain public statements of support for her candidacy. Campaign committees are not prohibited from soliciting and accepting reasonable campaign contributions and public support from lawyers. CJC Canon 5, Section C(2).

Mary has properly established a campaign committee to run her campaign. This committee may accept campaign contributions from people like Joanne, and the committee may spend those funds to further her candidacy.

Mary has apparently paid from her own funds for a number of TV and radio ads. Self-promotion is not prohibited by the CJC. Only the personal solicitation of funds from others by the candidate herself is prohibited. Solicitation must be done by a duly constituted campaign committee.

B. Mary's Campaign Publicity

The range of political activities permitted to a candidate for election to a judicial office is described in Canon 5, Section C. The candidate may appear in newspaper, television and other media advertisements *supporting her own candidacy*; identify herself as a member of a political party; purchase tickets for and attend political gatherings; and speak at political gatherings *on her own behalf.* Canon 5, Section C (1)(b)(i). However, she is extremely limited in what she can say as part of her campaign publicity: she may not, for example, make any pledges or promises about her conduct once elected, other than the pledge to faithfully and impartially perform the duties of office. Similarly, she may not make any statements that commit or appear to commit her with respect to cases or issues that are likely to come before her as judge. Canon 5, Section A(3)(d)(i), (ii).

During the course of her campaign, Mary appeared in various television and radio advertisements and spoke on her own behalf at several Democratic Party gatherings. If Mary limited her comments — in both her ads and speaking engagements — to discussions of her qualifications and steered clear of any campaign promises or pledges (other than a commitment to fulfilling the duties of office impartially and faithfully), then Mary has acted properly. If she allowed herself to make campaign promises or state any positions on issues or controversies likely to come before her, she will be subject to discipline.

3. Joanne's Appearance Before Mary At Trial

A judge must disqualify herself in a proceeding in which the judge's impartiality may reasonably be questioned, including but not limited to those instances in which the judge has a personal bias or prejudice concerning a party or a party's lawyer. CJC Canon 3, Section E(1)(a).

In one of Mary's first cases as a judge, she has been assigned a case in which her friend Joanne is counsel for one of the parties. Mary may honestly feel that she will be able to preside over the trial involving Joanne's client in a completely unbiased and impartial manner. However, their long history of close and personal friendship makes it reasonable for an objective observer to question Mary's ability to remain impartial under these circumstances. As the more prudent measure, Mary should disqualify herself from the case. (Note that if Mary does disqualify herself from any case in which Joanne appears, there will no longer be any reason at all to curtail the exchange of gifts between Mary and Joanne. The theory behind the rule forbidding gifts—to avoid the appearance of improper influence—will no longer be applicable.)

4. Mary's Supreme Court case

A judge must not practice law. Canon 4, Section G. This is an absolute rule and completely closes the door on any work by Mary on her appeal to the U.S. Supreme Court. The lack of compensation is irrelevant. The problem is a that a judge must be impartial in all matters; she must forego the spirit of advocacy which controls the work of lawyers. Mary will have to withdraw from the case and turn it over to another lawyer, or she will risk facing disciplinary measures.

Answer to Question 19

Mueller's Solicitation of Simpson

A lawyer shall not, either by in-person or live telephone contact, solicit professional employment from a prospective client with whom the lawyer has no family or prior professional relationship when a significant motive for the lawyer's doing so is the lawyer's pecuniary gain. MR 7.3(a). The reason for this prohibition is that the potential for abuse under these circumstances is too great. The facts in our example typify the problem: The prospective client feels overwhelmed by the very circumstances which create his need for legal services. He needs time and perspective in order to evaluate his alternatives. At a time of crisis, he should not be subjected to the wiles of a trained advocate who persists in being retained immediately. "The situation is fraught with the possibility of undue influence, intimidation, and overreaching." MR 7.3, Comment [1].

Despite this time-honored and unequivocal prohibition against in-person solicitation, Mueller went straight up to Simpson, victim of a car accident who had not even made it into the ambulance, and handed him his card. Mueller had no prior family or professional connection with Simpson. Despite his expression of concern for Simpson, his actions were motivated solely by his own potential monetary gain. Mueller has violated one of the prime rules of lawyer professional conduct and will be subject to discipline.

Mueller compounded his problems by making a "sales pitch" which was both misleading and coercive. A lawyer shall not make a false or misleading statement about his services. A statement is considered misleading if it is likely to create an unjustified expectation about the results the lawyer can achieve. MR 7.1(b). Here, Mueller boasted to Simpson about a $3 million verdict he had just received for another client. The implication was that he could expect to get a similar result for Simpson. He did this without knowing a single thing about Simpson's accident or, especially, the extent of his injuries. He happened upon the scene after the accident had occurred and had not yet talked with anyone.

Further, "a lawyer shall not solicit professional employment from a prospective client...by in-person or telephone contact...if the solicitation involves coercion, duress or harassment." MR 7.3(b)(2). Confronted by a lawyer who had just rushed at him card in hand immediately following an accident which was obviously painful and traumatic, Simpson would surely have defined the confrontation as coercive.

Mueller will be subject to discipline not only because he violated the rule against unwanted in-person solicitation but because his statements to Simpson were misleading and coercive.

Mueller's Pre-trial Publicity of Simpson's Case

A lawyer who is participating in a case shall not make statements about the case outside the courtroom if a reasonable person would expect the statements to be disseminated by means of public communication and if the lawyer knows (or reasonably should know) that the statements will have a substantial likelihood of materially prejudicing an adjudicative proceeding in the case. MR 3.6(a).

With knowledge that the other driver was a famous music star and that the public would relish news about him, Mueller made a phone call to a friend he knew to be a newspaper reporter and disclosed a number of facts which he knew the reporter would be quick to report. Specifically, he disclosed the existence of photographic evidence, the fact that Padrona had refused to submit to drug and alcohol testing, and his belief that Padrona was under the influence at the time of the accident. Each of these statements was highly prejudicial to Padrona and almost certain to affect his case at trial. Comment [5] to Model Rule 3.6 identifies subjects which are more likely than not to have a material prejudicial effect on the trial of a matter. These include:

(1) the character, credibility, reputation...of a party;

(3) the performance or results of any examination or test or the refusal or failure of a person to submit to an examination or test;

(5) information that a lawyer knows or reasonably should know is likely to be inadmissible at trial and that would, if disclosed, create a substantial risk of prejudicing an impartial trial.

Mueller's statements to the reporter all fall within these parameters and will subject Mueller to discipline.

Mueller's Opening Statement

A lawyer shall not falsify evidence. MR 3.4(b). Further, during a trial, a lawyer shall not allude to "any matter that the lawyer does not reasonably believe is relevant or that will not be supported by admissible evidence, [or] assert personal knowledge of facts in issue except when testifying as a witness..." MR 3.4(e). In Mueller's opening statement, he refers to Padrona as a "drugged out rock and roll star." He has no evidence whatsoever to support this statement, knows that he doesn't, and doesn't intend to present any. Mueller has violated the rules of professional conduct by introducing Padrona's alleged drug use when he has no intention of backing his statement up with any proof. He will be subject to discipline.

Answer to Question 20

Quack's Store Front Sign Constitutes a False and Misleading Communication

We will discuss these facts from the viewpoint of a lawyers' grievance committee construing the conduct of a lawyer as defined by the Model Rules. We express no opinion on the viewpoint of a medical board reviewing Quack's conduct as a doctor.

Quack is licensed as a lawyer in State A but carries on all his professional activities in State B. Because he is a lawyer only in A, his conduct will be reviewed by the grievance committee in that state. However, his conduct in State B will be treated for purposes of the rules as though it were committed in State A.

A lawyer shall not make a false or misleading communication about his services. A communication is false or misleading if it contains a material misrepresentation of fact or law or if it omits a fact necessary to make the statement as a whole not misleading. MR 7.1(a). It is false or misleading also if it is likely to create an unjustified expectation about results the lawyer can achieve or implies that the lawyer can achieve results by means that violate the rules of professional conduct or other law. MR 7.1(b).

Lawyer Quack has opened up a store-front clinic in State B under the name "Quack's Quick Clinic for Victims of Personal Injury." There is no indication that he lists his full name or identifies his profession. Because the word "clinic" is used interchangeably by the public to refer both to legal clinics and medical clinics, the sign is misleading and deceptive. It omits an essential fact necessary to make the sign not misleading—the sign should read either "Quack's Quick *LEGAL* Clinic..." or "Quack's Quick *MEDICAL Clinic...*"

If his intent is to function as a doctor, Quack deceives his patients by offering neither medical treatment nor consultation. His true purpose is solely to determine the extent of their injuries and to inquire into the circumstances which caused them. This is a clever ruse to deceive victims who expect medical evaluation and treatment into becoming prey to his skills as a lawyer. The only advice he provides falls entirely within the practice of law. His clinic is therefore a front for recruiting accident victims for the purpose of promoting their legal claims. Quack is in violation of MR 7.1 and also of MR 7.3, which proscribes in-person solicitation of prospective clients with whom the lawyer has no family or prior professional relationship when the lawyer's motive is pecuniary gain.

Quack is not immune from discipline as a lawyer because he is not licensed to practice law in State B, where his conduct occurs. As we shall discuss, he is subject to discipline in State A by virtue of his conduct in State B.

(In addition to the violations noted above, Quack may also be subject to discipline for using a trade name to identify a law practice. This is a matter for determination under the laws of the local jurisdiction)

Quack's Legal Advice to Clinic Clients

An attorney shall not practice law in a state in which he is not licensed or authorized to do so; nor may he assist a person who is unlicensed as a lawyer to perform activities that would constitute the practice of law. MR 5.5. A person not licensed to practice in a state may represent *herself*— that is not considered the unauthorized practice of law. Not all jurisdictions agree on the activities which fall within the term "the practice of law", but it's generally agreed that a person who offers legal advice to another person is engaged in the practice of law.

Quack's "How To" Book

Quack has written a book entitled "How to File Your Own Personal Injury Lawsuit." Although he is not licensed to practice law in State B, he instructs his receptionist to hand these books out to clients in that state. The states are split on whether or not "How To" books on legal subjects ("How to Write a Will; How to File a Patent Application", etc.) fall within the definition of the practice of law. Most, however, say they do not. They point out the books provide no individualized legal advice and are designed solely to help people to help themselves. Assuming the information Quack provides in his book is accurate and is limited to the forms and process by which an individual may bring a claim *pro se*, he will most likely not be subject to discipline for providing the book to clinic clients. Of course, the book in its author's credits must describe Quack accurately as a lawyer admitted only in State A.

Quack's Examination of Clinic Clients

After conducting a brief medical exam for the purpose only of determining the extent of injury, Quack interviews his patients to determine whether or not they have a valid legal claim. He then provides individualized legal advice on how the patients can proceed *pro se*, including an offer to help the clients fill out the necessary court forms. There can be no question that these actions constitute the practice of law, *and in a state where Quack is not authorized to practice law*. The fact that he is helping his patients to represent themselves will not save him from this violation of the rules of professional conduct. In contrast to the generalized advice provided in his book, Quack's consultations involve specific, targeted legal advice: what court to proceed in (raising questions of jurisdictional amount; residential requirements, etc); what amount to sue for; what facts to allege; what parties to join, etc. Quack is engaging in the unauthorized practice of law by providing legal advice to clients in a state where he is not licensed to practice law. He will be subject to discipline for doing so.

Quack's Clinic Fees

A lawyer's fee must be reasonable. MR 1.5. Quack charges his clinic clients $500 for their initial visit, or 50% of the amount the clients eventually recover on their suits. Measured as compensation for service by a lawyer, either of these fees would be excessive under the circumstances. Any value we assign to Quack's medical services (recording medical history, performing a short physical exam to determine the extent of injuries) would be minimal. The bulk of the fee would therefore be assigned to Quack's services as lawyer. By this measure, the fee is clearly excessive, especially if the contingency formula is applied. Even if the client selects the fixed fee of $500, we are left with the mental picture of a mill through which clients parade with the sole consequence of generating excessive income for Quack.

Furthermore, because Quack was not licensed in State B, he was not entitled to any legal fees all. The collection of fees for legal services by a non-lawyer is a no-no defined as a crime in most states.

Quack compounds his problems by offering a contingent fee option of 50% of a client's recovery, and this for no services whatsoever except a few minutes' instructions on litigation forms. First, all contingent fee agreements must be in writing. MR 1.5(c). There is no evidence that Quack complied with this requirement. Second, contingent fee agreements must be reasonable. In personal injury matters, the standard contingent fee percentage is one-third of recovery — for a lawyer who represents the client through all the trials and perils of litigation. Quack's formula here is to take advantage of indigent victims who cannot afford a $500 fee by forcing them into the 50% contingency. Either way, Quack has developed a perfect win-win formula. The problem for him is that he's not authorized to practice law in State B and that he's violated the rules applied to lawyers in State A. Doctor-lawyer Quack is clearly subject to discipline.

Where Quack Will Be Subject to Discipline

A lawyer is subject to discipline in any jurisdiction in which he is admitted to practice, regardless of where the lawyer's conduct occurs. MR 8.5(a). Quack is licensed to practice law in State A. Although all of the conduct which will subject him to discipline appears to have taken place in State B, the authorities in State A will construe the conduct and provide the discipline. State B has no jurisdiction over Quack as lawyer. However, State B should be able to discipline Quack as doctor and may be able to prosecute Quack for commission of several statutory crimes.

Multiple-Choice Questions

1. Rambeau Ramrod is the County Prosecutor for Principis County in the State of Enterprise. He dispatches his chief investigator to investigate a drive-by shooting in the town of East Lenox. The investigator talks to a witness who identifies Larry Hilliard as the driver of the car. Six other witnesses insist that Larry could not be the driver because Larry is black and the driver was white. Larry swears that he was in West Lenox at the time and has witnesses to prove it. Anxious for an indictment, Rambeau refuses to talk to Larry's witnesses and has Larry arrested and charged. Rambeau's investigators confirm that Larry was indeed in West Lenox at the time of the shooting. Rambeau ignores this information and causes a subpoena to be served on Larry requiring his appearance before the grand jury. He fails to tell Larry that he may be entitled to consult with counsel before he appears.

   Rambeau is:

   I. Subject to discipline for instituting a criminal proceeding against Larry without probable cause.
   II. Subject to discipline for failing to notify Larry of evidence which tended to negate his guilt.
   III. Subject to discipline for failing to advise Larry of his right to obtain counsel when he was subpoenaed before the grand jury.

   (A) I and II.
   (B) I, II and III.
   (C) I only.
   (D) III only.

2. Michael Messinger, an attorney admitted to practice in both Upper Dakota and West Dakota with an office only in Upper Dakota, is negotiating an employment contract for client Dennis with Hexon, Inc., a manufacturer with its plant in the state of East Dakota. In the process of negotiating the contract, Michael visits the Hexon plant, where he lies to and threatens Hexon's manager, George. George complains to the grievance committee of West Dakota. The Committee will apply the rules of professional conduct of:

   (A) Upper Dakota.
   (B) West Dakota.
   (C) East Dakota.
   (D) Both Upper and West Dakota.

3. David Waters, an attorney, belongs to the Musclebuilder Spa and loves to bathe in its hot tub. One afternoon, he is in the hot tub when Janet enters the tub. No one else is in the hot tub at the time. David tells Janet that he specializes in tort claims. Janet says in response, "What luck. I've got a little

problem—I was teasing my neighbor's dog last week when the dog bit me." She proceeds to expand on all the details. Finally, she says, "Do I have a case against my neighbor, and will you represent me?" David offers Janet no legal advice and tells her that he cannot represent her because he is busy with other matters. David is subpoenaed to testify against Janet in the trial of her $25,000 claim against the owner of the dog. David refuses to testify. What result?

(A) David must testify because he heard Janet admit that she teased the dog.

(B) David must testify because there was never an attorney-client relationship with Janet.

(C) David may not testify because the attorney-client evidentiary privilege has attached.

(D) David may not testify because Janet spoke to him in confidence.

Questions 4-5 are based on the following fact situation:

Helen Holmes has been practicing law for two years. As her first malpractice case, she undertakes to represent Don in a medical malpractice suit against Dr. Killjoy. She spends almost no time preparing the case and her research and trial work fall far below reasonably prevailing norms for lawyers in her area. The jury finds against Don. Don subsequently initiates a disciplinary proceeding against Helen and also sues her for legal malpractice.

4. In the disciplinary proceeding against Helen, Don will likely:

(A) Prevail, because Helen represented Don in a manner which did not meet the prevailing local norms for general practitioners.

(B) Prevail, provided Don proves that his doctor was in fact guilty of malpractice.

(C) Prevail, provided Don proves that but for Helen's incompetence, he would have won his medical malpractice case.

(D) Not prevail, if Helen can show that her level of competence was at least equal to that of other attorneys in the area with only two years of experience.

5. In Don's malpractice suit against her, Helen refuses to answer questions concerning confidential communications with Don during the suit against Dr. Killjoy; she relies upon the attorney-client evidentiary privilege. Her refusal is:

(A) Proper, if necessary to her defense in the malpractice action.

(B) Proper, because an attorney can always assert the attorney-client privilege.

(C) Improper, because the attorney-client relationship ended when the original suit against Dr. Killjoy was terminated.

(D) Improper, because the attorney-client privilege was waived by Don by bringing the suit against Helen.

6. Attorney Nero Mozell is a zealous litigator who is well known for his aggressive trial advocacy. He agrees to represent author Francis Fabricant in a copyright infringement action against author Tony Telltale. Telltale's attorney introduces samples of writing by both authors. Mozell has possession of a number of letters from Francis to her publisher acknowledging her use of text borrowed from Tony. Nero does not offer the letters in evidence nor does he disclose their existence to Tony's attorney. Nero is:

(A) Not subject to discipline because his first duty is to maintain the confidences of his client.

(B) Not subject to discipline if his actions did not affect Tony adversely.

(C) Subject to discipline for concealing relevant documents and obstructing Tony's access to evidence.

(D) Not subject to discipline because a lawyer's responsibility is to represent his client competently and zealously.

7. Joe Novitae has just been admitted to practice in the State of Anxiety. His very first client needs advice regarding a complex corporate tax problem. Joe did not take a course in corporate taxation in law school and knows virtually nothing about it. Desperate for income, Joe takes the case. He remembers his course in Professional Responsibility well enough to know that he has to take some precautions to escape discipline for taking on a matter he is not competent to handle.

Which of the following may Joe properly do to avoid discipline?

I. Associate himself with an expert in corporate taxation after receiving the client's consent to do so.
II. Purchase a manual on corporate taxation and review it until he feels confident to render an opinion.
III. Offer to withdraw from the case after the first conference with the client.
IV. Deal with each issue raised by the client as it arises, to the best of his ability.

(A) I only.
(B) II and III.
(C) I and III.

(D) IV only.

8. Henry Harris is an attorney licensed in the State of East Carolina. His client, Dan, provides business management services to small companies. At lunch one day, Dan confesses to Henry that he has been embezzling funds from his clients on a regular basis. Henry convinces Dan to stop committing any further crimes immediately. Together, they discuss how Dan can conceal his thefts to avoid detection for the crimes and how he should respond if his crimes are discovered. Dan takes Henry's advice and stops his embezzlements. Henry congratulates himself for saving Dan from jail and submits a substantial invoice. One year later, a routine audit at one of Dan's clients discloses his original embezzlement. Henry is subject to discipline because:

   (A) He should have withdrawn from representing Dan immediately upon learning that Dan had committed a crime.
   (B) He advised Dan how to avoid detection for his crimes.
   (C) He had a duty to report Dan's crimes to the police.
   (D) He failed to advise Dan's clients that they were being victimized by Dan's crimes.

Questions 9-10 are based upon the following fact situation:

Attorney represents Jack Bienstock, who has a long criminal record and is now being prosecuted for the crime of false pretenses. Attorney advises Jack that a jury will probably find him unsympathetic because of his "sleazy" mannerisms and uncouth speech, and counsels him to waive jury trial and not to take the stand in his own defense. However, Jack insists on a jury trial and informs Attorney that he wishes to testify. Against Jack's wishes, Attorney waives jury trial and does not call on Jack to testify. Jack is found not guilty.

9. Which of the following is correct?

   (A) Attorney is subject to discipline because he did not call Jack to testify.
   (B) Attorney is subject to discipline because matters of trial strategy should be determined by the client.
   (C) Attorney is not subject to discipline because he was entitled to control the trial strategy.
   (D) Attorney is not subject to discipline because Jack was found "not guilty."

10. Assume that Jack is found guilty. Which of the following is now correct?

    (A) Attorney is subject to discipline because he ignored Jack's request for a jury trial.
    (B) Attorney is subject to discipline because he imposed his decisions on trial strategy on his client.
    (C) Attorney is not subject to discipline because he reasonably believed the jury would be hostile to Jack.
    (D) Attorney is subject to discipline because Jack was convicted, *i.e.*, his decisions were harmful to his client.

11. Fred tells Beth Bethune, his attorney, to settle his insurance claim if Insurer offers $10,000. Insurer offers $15,000 but Beth does not reveal the offer to Fred and does not settle because she believes that Insurer will increase its offer. After a few more efforts at negotiation, the Insurer closes the door on further talks. The case goes to trial and Fred wins a $100,000 award. Beth is:

    (A) Subject to discipline for taking the case to trial.
    (B) Subject to discipline for not obeying Fred's instructions as to settlement.
    (C) Not subject to discipline because Fred gained much more money than the original offer.
    (D) Not subject to discipline because Beth, as the attorney, had the discretion to determine the value of Fred's claim and to hold out for the best result.

12. Attorney Trustworthy creates a trust for his client, Bart. When the trust is completed and executed, he sends Bart an invoice marked, "Final Billing." Bart responds with a check in full marked "final payment." Two years later, the trust laws change dramatically and several critical provisions of the trust are no longer effective. Bart has had no further contact with Trustworthy since his payment of the invoice. Trustworthy is:

    (A) Subject to discipline if he does not contact Bart and tell him about the changes in the law.
    (B) Subject to discipline only if Bart suffers a loss as a result of ignoring the changes in the law.
    (C) Subject to discipline for improper solicitation if he calls Bart and offers to revise the trust document.
    (D) Not subject to discipline even if he makes no effort to find Bart to tell him about the changes in the law.

13. Dave, Attorney's old college classmate, contacts Attorney for the first time in twenty years and tells Attorney that he has had a mid-life change in direction and has just graduated from law school after a career in architecture. He asks

Attorney for a letter recommending his admission to the bar. He tells Attorney that over the previous summer he worked for Paul Barkum, Attorney's former law partner. Attorney was close to Dave in college but lost all contact with him after graduation. He knows nothing about his work as an architect except for an occasional technical reference to him in the newspapers and magazines. Dave assures him that he has never been sued for malpractice or been disciplined by the architects' licensing board.

Which of the following represent(s) proper conduct for Attorney?

I. To write the letter in reliance on Dave's assurances about his professional integrity.
II. To write the letter in reliance on Dave's assurances, but only after checking with his former partner Paul.
III. To make his own independent investigation and write the letter only if Attorney is thoroughly satisfied that Dave is qualified.

(A) III only.
(B) I and II but not III.
(C) I and III, but not II.
(D) I, II, and III.

Questions 14-16 are based on the following fact situation:

Frick retains Attorney Susan Strick to institute an action against Frack for breach of contract. The retainer agreement provides for a retainer fee of $1,000, which Frick pays, and a charge of $50 per hour for Strick's services. Strick spends eight hours reviewing Frick's files, making an independent investigation of some facts in Frick's case, and preparing a complaint. After undertaking the preliminary investigation, Strick concludes that Frick's recollection of the facts is faulty and that Frick cannot prevail in a lawsuit. The statute of limitations will run on Frick's claim in one week. Strick wishes to withdraw without filing suit. Frick insists that Strick at least file the complaint before withdrawing, to give him time to find another lawyer.

14. Is Strick subject to discipline if she files the complaint for Frick?

(A) Yes, because Strick believes that Frick cannot prevail in the lawsuit.
(B) Yes, if the Judge later finds no factual basis for the suit and grants summary judgment to Frack.
(C) Yes, if Frick admits to Strick after consultation that he knows his claims have no merit but that is bringing the suit just "to make life difficult for Frack."

MULTIPLE-CHOICE QUESTIONS

(D) No, because Strick had accepted a retainer and was therefore bound to proceed in the matter.

15. Is it proper for Strick to withdraw without filing the complaint?

   (A) Yes, if Strick reasonably believes that there is no factual basis for Frick's lawsuit.
   (B) Yes, because the matter is not yet pending before a tribunal.
   (C) No, because Strick has accepted a retainer to represent Frick.
   (D) No, unless Strick first takes steps to insure that Frick's rights are adequately protected before the statute runs.

16. Assume that, after Strick has spent eight hours on Frick's case and challenges Frick's story, Frick admits that his story is untrue and Strick withdraws with Frick's consent. Which of the following should Strick do?

   (A) Keep the entire $1,000—if $1,000 was a reasonable retainer under the circumstances.
   (B) Keep no more than the $400 she earned for the eight hours spent in Frick's service.
   (C) Return the entire retainer because Strick was the one who insisted on terminating the representation.
   (D) Return the entire retainer because Strick did not obtain any results for Frick.

Questions 17-20 are based upon the following fact situation:

Little Tim is charged with first degree murder and Jane Dooright is his criminal defense attorney. One afternoon, Tim walks into Jane's office and throws a gun on her desk. Tim says, "This is the murder weapon." He then tells Jane that he removed some of the murder victim's belongings from the scene of the homicide and that he lied to the police when he told them he was at the movies at the time of the murder. "I'm telling you this because you're my lawyer and I know you can't tell anyone else, but I'll deny it to anyone else until my dying day." Before leaving, Tim says, "As for Alice, I'm going to get her if it's the last thing I do." Jane knows that Alice may have witnessed the murder.

After Tim leaves, Jane puts the gun in her office safe and never mentions its existence to anyone.

17. If Jane informs the police about Tim's threat of harm to Alice, Jane will be:

   (A) Subject to discipline because she has breached her duty of confidentiality to Tim.

(B) Subject to discipline if she informs the police without first investigating whether Tim is lying.

(C) Not subject to discipline because she was acting to prevent the commission of a crime involving bodily harm.

(D) Not subject to discipline because she is Tim's attorney only with respect to the murder of which he is charged, not with respect to the threats against Alice.

18. Jane's suppression of the gun was:

(A) Proper because Tim was her client.
(B) Proper because the attorney-client evidentiary privilege had attached.
(C) Proper because the gun was given to her for safekeeping.
(D) Not proper.

19. Jane was under a duty to tell the prosecution that Tim had removed evidence from the scene of the crime.

(A) True, because the evidence was probative.
(B) False, because Jane's knowledge was obtained under the attorney-client privilege.
(C) True, because Tim's removal of evidence was an independent crime which could be separated from his statements to Jane about the murder.
(D) False, because the evidence was prejudicial to her client.

20. If Tim insists on taking the stand in his own defense at trial after telling Jane that he will testify that he was at the movies, can Jane question Tim about his whereabouts at the time of the murder?

(A) Yes, because Tim has a constitutional right to tell his version of the facts.
(B) Yes, if this line of questioning is necessary to a zealous defense.
(C) No, because she cannot offer false evidence.
(D) No, even when Tim offers Jane the corroborating evidence of his friend Irma.

21. Frank and Stein, attorneys, prepare a stock subscription agreement for Success, Inc. Many months later, the lawyers learn that the subscription agreement is riddled with fraudulent statements by Success and its accountants. The law firm insists that Success issue a notice revealing the facts to all persons who have subscribed. When Success refuses to do so, the lawyers distribute their own notice to subscribers setting forth the true facts. This action by Frank and Stein was:

(A) Required.

(B) Permissible.

(C) Impermissible.

(D) None of the above.

Questions 22-25 are based upon the following facts:

Deanne Demonio, an attorney, is handling a high stakes insurance case for Joey Jumbo. The contingent fee contract, signed only two months ago, provides that Demonio will receive one-third of the recovery after reimbursement of expenses. Fearing a large verdict and anxious to settle, the insurance company offers Demonio $6 million dollars. After consultation with Joey, she accepts and soon receives a check for the full amount. After talking with his friends, one of whom is still in law school, Joey is unhappy that Demonio will receive so much money for so little work, and he challenges Demonio's fee. After depositing the check in her trust account, Demonio issues a check to Joey for $4 million and transfers the balance to her office account. Demonio brings an action against Joey to fix her fee. She takes the stand and testifies about the difficulty of the case, the hours she spent working on it, and that, because Joey has a severe drug and alcohol problem, her work was made unusually difficult. Upon objection by Joey's new counsel, the court rules Demonio's testimony relevant and admissible.

22. Demonio is subject to discipline for:

   I. Charging an excessive fee.
   II. Suing Joey for her fee.
   III. Refusing to revise her fee on Joey's request.
   IV. Basing her fee on a contingency.

   (A) I only.
   (B) II only.
   (C) III and IV only.
   (D) None of the above.

23. Demonio is subject to discipline for:

   I. Testifying about Joey's drug and alcohol problems.
   II. Initiating the law suit instead of waiting for Joey to sue.
   III. Transferring $2 million dollars to her office account before the outcome of her lawsuit.

   (A) I only.
   (B) II only.
   (C) III only.

(D) None of the above.

24. If Demonio had paid $4 million to Joey and retained the balance in her client trust account, her actions would have been:

    (A) Proper, because the balance represented the contested amount.
    (B) Proper, because under the circumstances, this was her legitimate fee.
    (C) Proper, because she had a right to retain all $6 million pending the outcome of the law suit, and she was exercising less than her full right.
    (D) Not proper.

25. Assume for this question that the disciplinary rules for Attorney Demonio's jurisdiction require an attorney to submit all fee disputes first to the disciplinary committee and then to binding arbitration. Under these circumstances, Demonio's actions were:

    I. Improper, because she failed to comply with the local rule.
    II. Improper, because lawyers are not supposed to sue their clients in any event.
    III. Proper, because local disciplinary rules do not preempt the general standards for propriety contained in the Model Rules of Professional Conduct.

    (A) I only.
    (B) II only.
    (C) I and II only.
    (D) III only.

26. Lucy Lexos, an experienced employment lawyer, is a solo practitioner. Charlie comes to her for help with a small wrongful termination claim. Lucy immediately determines that Charlie has another year before the statute of limitations will run on his claim. Shortly after Charlie signs a retainer agreement, Linus comes to Lucy with a case that could be worth several million dollars. Lucy agrees to take Linus's case and immediately gets to work on it. It requires almost all of her work time. After nine months, she settles Linus's case for $2.5 million. The following month (ten months after Charlie first met with Lucy), Lucy begins to work on Charlies' file. She files Charlie's complaint before the statute runs and shortly thereafter settles his case for a sum greater than Charlie anticipated. Has Lucy properly handled Charlie's case?

    (A) Yes, because the amount of Charlie's recovery was not affected by her delay.

MULTIPLE-CHOICE QUESTIONS 119

    (B) Yes, a lawyer may juggle the cases she handles so long as the results are reasonable.

    (C) No, Lucy has violated her duty of diligence to Charlie.

    (D) No, Lucy should have filed Charlie's complaint before accepting Linus' case.

27. Judge Thoroughbred is a civic-minded citizen who participates in many law-related activities. She teaches, speaks and writes on legal topics. The Judge also appears at legislative hearings on legal issues. In addition, she serves as chairman of an organization devoted to penal reform; she manages the funds of this organization. Recently, she has taken part in the organization's "Teach Them to Be Good" fund drive.

    Which of the following is correct?

    (A) All of the activities conducted by the judge are permitted.

    (B) None of the activities conducted by the judge is permitted.

    (C) All of the activities described are permitted except participation in the fund-raising drive.

    (D) All of the activities described are permitted except management of the organization's funds.

28. Sammy Speedwell is arrested for exceeding the local speed limit by 25 miles and hires Attorney Steadfast to defend him. Sammy tells Steadfast that he was speeding because he was rushing his wife to the hospital. In preparation for the hearing, Steadfast interviews Sammy's friend Lanny, who tells him that he is often a passenger in Sammy's car and that Sammy "never observes the speed limit." Steadfast asks you as his law partner to advise him which of the following is a correct statement.

    I. Both Sammy's admission and Lanny's statements are covered by the attorney-client privilege.

    II. Sammy's communication to Steadfast is covered by the attorney-client privilege.

    III. Lanny's communication to Steadfast is covered by the rule of confidentiality.

    IV. Steadfast has a duty to decline to represent Sammy after he hears the statements of Sammy and Lanny.

    (A) I only.
    (B) II only.
    (C) II and III.
    (D) III and IV.

29. Fred Foresight, an attorney, represents Burnham Oil, Inc., a large conglomerate. The company has embarked on a broad-based campaign to defeat a tax proposal that is pending in the state legislature. Forsesight believes the tax proposal is sound and fair and wants to support it by speaking at a rally by its main supporters. If you were advising Foresight, you would tell him:

   (A) You must abstain from taking a public position contrary to that of your client.
   (B) You must first obtain your client's permission before publicly expressing views that are in opposition to its views.
   (C) You may take a public position in opposition to your client's only if you make it clear that you are speaking for yourself and not for your client.
   (D) You may take a public position contrary to your client's, but only if you take every precaution not to prejudice your client's position with respect to the proposal.

30. Fletcher Flaunty spends ten years working as copywriter at the Show'nTell ad agency, then attends law school and is admitted to practice in a state which follows the Model Rules. He begins to specialize in negligence and criminal matters. Using his advertising background, he places conspicuous ads in the local paper and begins to prosper. One day, there is an extensive fire at a local plant and many are killed or injured. The police announce that the fire was set by a disgruntled former employee who gained admission to the plant when the two plant guards were asleep at their posts. The police arrest the employee and one of the guards.

    Fletcher writes and mails two letters: one to the victims of the fire and/or their surviving families, the other to the employee and the guard. In both letters, he offers his immediate services. Both letters are mailed in envelopes labelled "Advertising Material."Fletcher is subject to discipline:

    (A) For writing the letter to the victims and/or their families, but not the letter to the employee and the guard.
    (B) For writing the letter to the employee and the guards, but not the letter to the victims and/or their families.
    (C) For neither letter.
    (D) For both letters.

31. During the course of a complex trial, Helen, one of the jurors, is confused about a crucial point of law. She hesitates to ask the judge because he has treated other jurors with irritation and sarcasm. During an evening recess, Helen phones her brother, a lawyer with a major local firm, and questions him about the point of law that perplexed her.

MULTIPLE-CHOICE QUESTIONS   121

If Helen's brother knows that Helen is a juror but answers her questions about the case anyway, is he subject to discipline?

(A) Yes, Helen's brother must refuse to discuss the matter with her.
(B) No. Although Helen's brother should not answer her question, this proscription is aspirational only. He will not be subject to discipline for violating it.
(C) No, because the conversation falls within the attorney-client privilege.
(D) No, because he is not involved in the case and only lawyers connected with the case must refrain from communication with a member of the jury during the trial.

32. Citizens United for Justice in Arizona, a nonpartisan organization, invites Blackwell Raven, a federal district court judge, to travel to Arizona from his California district, to speak on the issue of court reform.

Which of the following statements is/are correct?

I. Judge Raven may give the speech, but should decline to be paid anything by the organization.
II. Judge Raven may give the speech, and may accept a speaker's fee in the amount which is normally paid by the organization to other judges.
III. Judge Raven may be reimbursed by the organization for his actual travel, lodging and meal expenses.
IV. Judge Raven must issue a public report of the amount and source of his compensation.

(A) I only.
(B) I and III.
(C) II and III.
(D) III and IV.

33. Beau Johnson is a well known art dealer, as well as an attorney. He keeps both businesses separate by maintaining two different offices and two different sets of records. One day, while completing the sale of a painting in his gallery, he defrauds McNamara by misrepresenting the name of the artist. Attorney Heller, who has been counseling Johnson in his capacity as chairman of the county's lawyer assistance program and who is familiar with the painting and the artist, enters the gallery to speak with Johnson, hears the misrepresentation and confronts Johnson. Johnson admits that he lied to make the sale. During their earlier counseling sessions, Johnson has admitted to Heller that he is often incapacitated by his use of alcohol.

Which of the following is the proper basis for a report by Heller to the local disciplinary committee?

I. That Johnson was running an art gallery at the same time as an active law practice.
II. That Johnson was guilty of fraud and misrepresentation in a business dealing.
III. That Johnson is often incapacitated by his use of drugs.
IV. All of the above.

(A) I only.
(B) II only.
(C) II and III.
(D) IV only.

34. Professor Tom Tombs, a law school professor and lawyer who often argues cases before the Supreme Court, is grading his finals in Accounting for Lawyers. In the process, he finds that his favorite student, Hannah Holiday, has obviously cheated on several questions. Tombs calls Hannah to his office and asks her to explain. Hannah tells him that she has never cheated before and that she has been under a terrible emotional strain brought on by her mother's serious illness. Tombs believes Hannah will not cheat again but gives her a warning and a minimally passing grade. Hannah graduates tenth in her class and passes the bar exam. Tombs receives an official request to comment on Hannah's qualifications for the bar.

Which of the following is correct?

(A) Tombs is required to disclose his knowledge of Hannah's cheating.
(B) Tombs is not required to disclose the cheating if he believes she will not cheat again.
(C) Tombs may recommend her admission provided he also discloses her cheating.
(D) Tombs may ignore the request and make no comment.

35. Abner Abernathy works as a partner in a landscaping firm by day and attends Old State Law School at night. After he graduates, he has a bitter battle with his landscaping partner and they agree to separate. Abner consults Tess Trueheart, a local attorney, about his rights. His partner's lawyer tells Tess that the partner suspects Abner of cooking the books and of pocketing cash receipts. In his first conference with Tess, Abner confesses these misdeeds and several others. Tess concludes the negotiations between the partners as well as she can under the circumstances, and the partnership

is dissolved. Two months later, Abner graduates from Old State, passes the Old State bar exam and submits Tess' name to the authorities as a character reference on his application for admission to the bar. Tess is obligated to:

I. Disclose all the conduct confessed to her by Abner.
II. Withhold all information about Abner's conduct.
III. Reveal only those acts which in her judgment reflect adversely on Abner's character.
IV. Conduct and report her own independent investigation into Abner's character and general reputation.

(A) I only.
(B) II only.
(C) III only.
(D) III and IV.

36. Attorney Rudy Russell represents Val in a personal injury action on a 25% contingent-fee basis, with expenses to be advanced by Russell and then deducted from Val's percentage of recovery. Russell advances $300 in court costs and receives a check payable to Russell as attorney in the amount of $2,000 in settlement of Val's personal injury claim:

(A) Russell must promptly return the check and obtain two checks, one payable to Val for $1,200 and the other to Russell for $800.
(B) Russell must first deposit the entire $2,000 in his client trust account, then send Val her $1,200 with a written explanation of his calculation of fees and disbursements.
(C) Russell must promptly deposit the check in his client trust account, and remit $1,200 to Val, but he need not explain his calculations in writing.
(D) Russell may deposit the entire amount in his personal account, but must immediately send a check to Val in the amount of $1,200.

37. Betty Boop and Sam Snoop are both passengers in the car of a friend who becomes involved in an automobile accident. Both are injured. Forelock Holmes, an attorney, represents Boop in her subsequent personal injury suit. Holmes calls on Snoop to testify as a witness on Boop's behalf. If, after Snopp's testimony and while the jury is still deliberating, Holmes discovers that Snoop perjured himself in a way that is certain to influence the jury improperly, which of the following actions should he take?

(A) Immediately reveal the perjury to the judge.
(B) Confront Boop immediately in an effort to remedy the effect of the perjured testimony.

(C) Remain silent.

(D) Obtain Snoop's consent before revealing the perjury.

38. Six-year-old Penny is in a coma following an automobile crash which killed both of her parents. A guardian ad litem is appointed for Penny.

    The guardian retains Wendell Willie, an attorney, to bring a wrongful death and personal injury action on Penny's behalf. After extensive negotiation, the defendant's insurance company proposes a settlement offer of $500,000, which is far less than Wendell believes he can recover. Which of the following statements is correct?

    (A) Wendell must convey any settlement offer to Penny's guardian and accept the offer if the guardian directs him to.

    (B) Wendell may refuse the settlement offer on his own initiative and notice the case for trial.

    (C) Wendell may accept the offer only after submitting a request to the court and obtaining the court's approval.

    (D) Wendell may withhold any information about the offer and continue to negotiate with the defendant if he believes a larger offer will be made.

39. James, an architect and builder, confidentially informs his attorney, Ford Snelling, that he has contracted to build a shopping center on Mocking Bird Lane, and that he has applied for financing to acquire the neighboring lot. He tells Ford that he plans to build a large public parking structure on the neighboring lot to serve customers to the mall. Smelling a good thing, Snelling purchases the neighboring lot on Mocking Bird Lane himself, before James can do so.

    Is Snelling subject to discipline?

    (A) No, provided he paid fair market value for the property.

    (B) No, because his actions violated an aspirational rule, not a disciplinary one.

    (C) Yes, because he owed James the duty of abstaining from negotiating for the property.

    (D) No, because James can sue to recover damages from Snelling.

40. Client asks Tim Dewey, an attorney, to represent her in a personal injury case resulting from an automobile accident. Dewey agrees to accept the case on a 33% contingent fee arrangement and to advance all litigation-related expenses. The agreement provides that Client will reimburse Dewey for his expenses. Dewey advances $750 on Client's matter. After extensive trial preparation and failed negotiations, but before the case goes to trial, Client

fires Dewey and retains another attorney, Anne Howe, who eventually loses the case at trial after a spiritless and incompetent performance.

What amount is Dewey entitled to recover from Client for his services?

(A) The reasonable value of his services rendered up to the time of the discharge as determined by the standards of the local bar.
(B) Nothing.
(C) 33% of the sum which Client would have recovered if the trial had been handled competently by Anne.
(D) Reimbursement for the expenses advanced by him.

41. Sally Sharp, an attorney, successfully defended Retail, Inc., after it was sued for misrepresentation. During the course of the representation, several officers of Retail told Sharp in confidence about the company's internal policies regarding sales and warranties. Two years later, Jones asks Sharp to represent him in a lawsuit against Retail. During their first meeting, Sharp realizes that the suit may involve details of Retail's internal policies regarding sales and warranties. Sharp has not provided any legal services to Retail for more than 18 months. Under what circumstances may Sharp accept this case?

(A) Sharp must first consult with Retail, Inc. and obtain Retail's informed consent.
(B) Sharp must first reveal to Jones her prior representation of Retail and obtain Jones' informed consent.
(C) Both Retail and Jones must give their consent.
(D) Sharp cannot accept the case under any circumstances.

42. Attorney Albert Landon represents plaintiff in a personal injury lawsuit which is about to go to trial. Landon plans to call Dr. Swift, an expert witness from a distant city, to testify as to the extent and lasting effects of the plaintiff's injuries.

Which of the following is Landon able to pay to Dr. Swift?

I. Dr. Swift's reasonable expenses in attending the trial, including travel, hotel and meals.
II. A reasonable fee for Dr. Swift's services in pre-trial preparation and in testifying at trial.
III. A fee contingent upon the amount recovered by plaintiff.
IV. Only a sum equal to Dr. Swift's regular hourly fees multiplied by the number of hours expended by Dr. Swift on a portal-to-portal basis.

(A) I only.
(B) I and II.
(C) II and III.
(D) IV only.

43. Judge Beasely Yearly is campaigning for re-election as a judge of the Superior Court. Attorney Ambrose Ambitious is on the ballet running against Judge Yearly. Which of the following may *both* Yearly the judge and Ambitious the lawyer do during the campaign?

    I. Attend all political gatherings.
    II. Speak at political gatherings in support of their respective candidacies.
    III. Identify themselves as members of a political party.
    IV. Solicit funds in support of their respective candidacies.

    (A) All of the above.
    (B) II only.
    (C) II and III.
    (D) I, II, and IV.

44. Sherman Melville, a personal injury attorney with no experience in commercial matters makes an oral agreement with Client to prepare a complicated contract for a fee of $500 per hour. The customary hourly fee for similar work by experienced local lawyers is $350. Sherman spends 4 hours on the contract but sends an invoice for $2,500. Which of the following subject(s) Melville to discipline?

    I. He failed to reduce the fee arrangement to a writing.
    II. His fee is greater than the customary local hourly fee for more experienced lawyers.
    III. His invoice exceeded the fee agreed upon.
    IV. As an inexperienced lawyer, he should have agreed to a fee of less than $350 per hour.

    (A) I only.
    (B) I, II and IV.
    (C) II, III and IV.
    (D) II only.

45. Attorney Mack Smart learns that his Uncle Ted has been in a serious automobile accident. Smart visits Ted at the hospital and, after a few greetings, immediately offers him legal advice, including advice about customary fees and tactics. When Ted is released from the hospital, he asks

Mack to represent him. Is Mack subject to discipline if he agrees to represent Ted?

I. Yes, for improper solicitation.
II. No, if Ted was a previous client.
III. Yes, because Ted is not a member of his immediate family.
IV. No, because Ted is a relative.

(A) I only.
(B) II and III.
(C) III and IV.
(D) II and IV.

46. Flint Matlick, a solo general practitioner, attends a lavish cocktail party where he meets Lester Highpocket, an accountant who specializes in employee benefit plans. In the course of his practice, Lester meets many individuals. Lester and Flint become good friends and often meet for lunch. Over time, Flint realizes that Lester's contacts could serve as an appreciable source of new clients.

In an expansive moment during one of their lunches, Flint suggests to Lester that Lester refer all his clients who need legal advice to Flint. In exchange, Flint agrees to represent them at a reduced hourly rate.

Is Flint subject to discipline for proposing this arrangement?

(A) Yes, because Flint proposed a referral arrangement from a non-lawyer.
(B) Yes, because he has proposed a fee which is less than his usual fee.
(C) No, if Lester will not be compensated in any way for referring cases to Flint.
(D) No, if Lester's clients are fully informed of his relationship with Flint and are given an opportunity to consult with other lawyers before choosing to retain Flint.

47. Simon Splendid, an attorney, successfully defends an accused rapist in a highly publicized and controversial trial. He receives a great deal of publicity in the months after his client is acquitted. Which of the following constitute(s) proper conduct on the part of Splendid?

I. To write and publish an article in a legal journal in which he identifies himself both by name and by his involvement in the rape trial.
II. To appear as a guest on a national television program to discuss penal reform and the judicial system.

III. To speak before a convention of women who sponsor the death penalty for all rapists.

(A) I and II.
(B) I, II and III.
(C) II only.
(D) II and III.

48. Attorney Hannah Hanson joins many groups and societies to promote her practice and makes many friends. Her friends begin to ask her for advice and help. Which of the following may Attorney Hanson do without subjecting herself to discipline?

   I. Advise a friend who is drafting his own will.
   II. Assist a friend who is drafting a will for his uncle.
   III. Provide a real estate broker with the text of a statute that will help him prepare a sales contract.
   IV. Advise a friend who plans to appear for himself in small claims court.

   (A) I and II.
   (B) I and III.
   (C) III only.
   (D) I and IV.

49. The Rough and Ready Agency engages in many illegal collection practices, including the harassment of debtors in violation of local statutes. One of the debtors, Harry Hapless retains Jerry Sturdy, to protect him against actions threatened by Rough and Ready. Which of the following actions may Sturdy take against the Rough and Ready Agency without discipline.

   I. Contact the local district attorney and request that criminal charges be filed against Rough and Ready.
   II. Write to Rough and Ready Agency and advise it that he is preparing a civil complaint for damages and injunctive relief.
   III. File a civil complaint and, in the ensuing negotiations, threaten to initiate criminal charges if Rough and Ready does not offer a satisfactory settlement.

   (A) I only.
   (B) I and II.
   (C) II only.
   (D) All of the above.

50. Attorney Santos Santori represents both Jack and his estranged wife Jill. They believe they can resolve their differences and ask Santos to help them. He advises them that he cannot proceed without their joint consent, but that he believes he can mediate their differences without adversely affecting their relationship. Jack and Jill initially believe that they can easily work out an equitable settlement and sign a letter authorizing Santori to proceed. However, their negotiations eventually break down, and it becomes clear that they will have to litigate. Santori informs the parties that he cannot represent both in the litigation. He offers to represent Jill, and because she has no funds, he agrees to a contingent fee to be calculated at 30% of her property settlement. Santori's conduct is improper in that he:

   I. Initially agreed to represent both sides of a dispute.
   II. Agreed to represent Jill alone after representing both parties.
   III. Agreed to represent Jill on a contingency basis.
   IV. Did not continue to mediate in an effort to avoid litigation.

   (A) I only.
   (B) I and II only.
   (C) II and III only.
   (D) III and IV only.

51. Doug Douglas, an attorney, represents Michael. In support of Michael's case, Douglas has to argue to a trial court judge that a provision of the state's laws is unconstitutional. Douglas also represents Julia in a totally unrelated matter. In support of Julia's case, Douglas has to argue to another trial court judge in the same jurisdiction that the same statute which is at issue in Michael's case is constitutional. Douglas' actions are:

   (A) Impermissible because no lawyer can competently argue contradictory positions on the same legal issue.
   (B) Impermissible because a lawyer may not be of record at the same time in two cases relying on contradictory positions.
   (C) Proper.
   (D) Proper only if Douglas first informs both judges that he is advocating two completely contradictory positions.

52. David is arrested on a charge of computer fraud. He is 16 years old. David's father, an attorney, retains another lawyer, Tammy Corcoran, to handle David's case. David's father writes a long and detailed memo instructing Tammy what witnesses to call and how to handle the case. Tammy agrees with some of his comments but believes that others will seriously hurt David's defense. Tammy should:

(A) Refuse the case because the father's interference will probably prevent her from effective representation of David.
(B) Accept payment from David's father if David's father can be prevented from interfering with her independent judgment.
(C) Cooperate with David's father because he is an attorney.
(D) Refuse payment of her fees from David's father.

53. Felix Friendly, an attorney, is managing partner in a very busy law firm that is known for charging fees much lower than the local standard. Friendly is able to afford these fees by advertising daily on radio and TV and by requiring all of his prospective clients to sign a contract waiving all possible malpractice claims. Relying on these contracts, Friendly does not carry malpractice insurance.

    Friendly is subject to discipline because:

    I. He advertises excessively.
    II. He requires a waiver of liability from all his clients.
    III. His fees are lower than the local standard.
    IV. He does not carry malpractice insurance.

    (A) I and II only.
    (B) I and III only.
    (C) I and IV only.
    (D) II only.

54. Sharon Simple has just been charged with the crime of battery. Sharon consults with Karen Kingsley, a celebrated criminal defense attorney. Karen mentions to Sharon in passing that Marion Bingsley, the prosecuting attorney in charge of Sharon's case, is Karen's sister and then says, "But that won't affect our defense at all. We no longer see or talk to one another. Just tell me what happened." Karen proceeds to prepare for Sharon's trial. She is:

    (A) Not subject to discipline if she believes she can represent Sharon without any conflict of interest.
    (B) Subject to discipline because Karen and Marion were sisters.
    (C) Not subject to discipline because Karen informed Sharon that Marion was her sister.
    (D) Not subject to discipline because there was no continuing contact between Karen and Marion.

55. Ben, an attorney, is licensed to practice law in State Alpha. He has taken the examination for admission to the bar in State Delta several times, but has

failed each time. Ben serves as general counsel for Bigtown Manufacturing Co., a company with its principal offices in Alpha and several subsidiary offices in Delta. Ben represents Bigtown in several litigation matters. An important suit is brought by a plaintiff in Delta and Ben enters an appearance as attorney for Bigtown and appears before the Delta court to argue for dismissal of the lawsuit. Ben is:

I. Subject to discipline in Delta for the unauthorized practice of law.
II. Subject to discipline in Alpha for the unauthorized practice of law in Delta.
III. Not subject to discipline because an attorney may follow the interests of his client wherever they lead.

(A) I only.
(B) I and II.
(C) II only.
(D) III only.

56. Jerry Faxwell is general counsel for Franco, Inc., a large corporation. One morning, Dean, one of Franco's executives and a good friend of Jerry, walks into Jerry's office and says, "Jerry, I have a serious problem and it's affecting my work." Jerry nods and Dean then continues, "I've developed a terrible drug problem. I can't think straight and I've made a couple of bad decisions for the company. What should I do?" Jerry offers a few words of innocuous consolation. When Dean leaves in despair, Jerry immediately advises Dean's superior that Dean has bcome a serious liability to Franco, and that the company should strongly consider letting him go. Jerry is:

(A) Subject to discipline for divulging Dean's confidence.
(B) Subject to discipline for failing to advise Dean to obtain independent counsel.
(C) Not subject to discipline because Jerry's first and only obligation is to his client, Franco.
(D) Subject to discipline because Dean is his good friend.

57. Mary Mushball has been general counsel over many years for the Rancheros, a minor league baseball team, and she's done a bang-up job. The Rancheros are sold without notice and the new owner fires Mary because "Women don't belong in the baseball business." Mary refuses to leave her office and insists on writing and submitting memos to management on grievances referred to her by the ballplayers, who like and respect Mary. At the same time, Mary brings an action against the Rancheros for breach of contract, unlawful discharge, and employment discrimination. Mary is:

(A) Subject to discipline for continuing to perform legal services by writing and submitting memos on grievances referred to her by the ballplayers.
(B) Subject to discipline for commencing a law suit against the Rancheros.
(C) Not subject to discipline because her refusal to accept discharge was reasonable under the circumstances.
(D) Not subject to discipline because the action of the new owner was clearly prompted by employment discrimination.

58. Johnny Sourseed is representing Rocko Roccocco in an appeal from a criminal conviction in the State of Alpha. While doing research for the appeal, Johnny finds four cases on point that are contrary to Rocko's position. One case is from a lower court in Alpha, another is from Alpha's highest court, the third case is from the adjoining state of Beta, and the fourth is from a federal circuit court of appeals in another district. Johnny prepares for his appeals by "sizing up" the judges on the panel. He concludes that the judges who will hear Rocko's appeal are incompetent, quick to jump to judgment and careless about their research. Therefore, after discussing the matter with Rocko, he decides not to cite any of the four cases. He is relieved when the state's attorney fails to cite any of them as well.

Johnny is subject to discipline for:

(A) Not citing the federal circuit court case.
(B) Not citing the case in alph's highest court.
(C) Not citing the Beta case.
(D) None of the above.

59. The trial of Brutus Brutum for aggravated assault and rape has been long and bitter. In his closing argument, Prosecutor Wendell Washington continually refers to Brutus as the "Rabid Rapist" and the "Brutus the Brute". He closes by saying, "In my thirty years as a prosecutor, I've never encountered a more despicable or savage criminal." Defense counsel fails to object and the judge does not intercede. Brutus is acquitted. Washington is:

(A) Not subject to discipline because Brutus was acquitted.
(B) Not subject to discipline because no objection was made and the court failed to warn or admonish him after his first reference to Brutus as the "rabid rapist".
(C) Not subject to discipline if Washington believed his statements were true.
(D) Subject to discipline for expressing his personal opinions to the jury.

MULTIPLE-CHOICE QUESTIONS

Questions 60-61 are based on the following fact situation:

Defendant Larry is arrested on a charge of aggravated sexual assault against Michelle. Medical tests reveal that Michelle's fingernail scrapings match Larry's skin and blood-type.

Philip Phillips is the state's prosecutor against Larry. Immediately after Larry's arrest, Philip is interviewed by the press and makes a formal statement as follows: "On June 17, at 3:00 AM, Larry was arrested on a charge of sexual assault against a 17-year old woman. The woman will be a witness for the prosecution. We have a great deal of evidence against Larry. We've matched the blood of the assailant to Larry's blood. Larry has been arrested many times and we believe that the public is much safer now that Larry is in custody. I expect that our evidence will be more than sufficient to convict Larry. Indeed, we are expecting a confession at any moment. However, we are continuing our investigation, and if anyone, including any other victims, has any information related to Larry or the crime, please contact this office."

In response to a question by Reporter Gaggle, Philip responded, "Yes, I'm confident that we will be able to convince the jury beyond a reasonable doubt in this case."

60. Philip is subject to discipline for:

   I. Stating that a confession is expected.
   II. Revealing his own opinion as to Larry's guilt.
   III. Revealing Larry's past criminal record.

   (A) I only.
   (B) I and II only.
   (C) I, II, and III.
   (D) All of the above.

61. Philip is subject to discipline for:

   I. Discussing the evidence against Larry.
   II. Asking the public for information related to the crime.
   III. Speaking with the press before the state's investigation is concluded.

   (A) I only.
   (B) II only.
   (C) I, II, and III.
   (D) None of the above.

62. Adam Adams, professor of law at Hyndham Law and a nationally recognized expert on criminal appeals, is asked to coordinate the appeal of Senator Hector Huxtable from a conviction for tax fraud. The Senator's face and voice are known throughout the country and Adams knows that the appeal will result in a great deal of public exposure, including, almost certainly, several books and a movie. Adams wants to participate in the rewards. He tells Huxtable that he will handle the appeal only if Huxtable signs an agreement assigning to Adams 20% of all future income from any book, movie, TV program or other public display or expression about the appeal. Huxtable agrees. Adams wins the appeal and Huxtable is vindicated and goes on to become a candidate for President.

Which of the following apply(ies) to these facts?

(A) Adams is not subject to discipline because he succeeded in his appeal.
(B) Adams is not subject to discipline because an attorney may insist on any compensation commensurate with the results.
(C) Adams is subject to discipline for making an agreement giving him an interest in media rights arising from the matter at issue.
(D) Adams is not subject to discipline because Senator Huxtable was free to engage another attorney.

63. Attorney Francine Franco is a member of the California bar. However, she does not practice law and few people know that she's admitted. Instead she produces movies, sometimes for her own account and sometimes on behalf of Central Goldman Meyer studios. Over the years, she has accumulated a stable of promoters who will put money into her movies, but only if she herself has a sizeable investment in the production. Francine is asked by the CGM Studio to produce a new version of Mutiny on the Bounty. She thinks the movie is too risky for her own money, but she does agree to act as nominal producer for CGM. CGM knows Francine's name will attract other investors if they think she has an investor's interest in the movie. CGM and Francine announce that they will co-produce the movie as equal investors. Irving Investor, a good friend of Francine, has often put substantial sums in her movies and inquires about the new one. He says to Francine, "If you've got your money in it, then I'm in, too." Francine assures Investor that she has put a substantial sum of her own money in the production. Is Francine subject to discipline by the California bar?

(A) No, because Investor was relying on statements made, so far as he knew, by a non-lawyer.
(B) Yes, because Francine's failure to disclose her role in the venture was a misrepresentation of the facts.

(C) No, because Investor did not consult Francine in her position as an attorney.

(D) No, because Francine does not practice law.

64. Attorney Jack B. Nimble, a veteran practitioner, has argued many motions and tried many cases before Judge Ozzie Brand, a judge of declining patience and increasing irritability. Jack genuinely believes that the Judge has neither the temperament nor the knowledge to decide cases. When the Judge becomes a candidate for re-election, Jack makes a careful study of all the other candidates and decides that Attorney Abner Smith would make the best choice. Jack decides to assist Smith in getting elected.

Which of the following may Jack do?

I. Give $5,000 to Smith personally "to be used for your campaign."
II. Give his time and efforts to Smith's campaign by calling voters, writing letters to other lawyers, addressing envelopes, and composing advertising copy.
III. Announce his support of Smith during a speech before the local bar association.
IV. Donate $5,000 to a committee formed to further Smith's election.

(A) I, II and III.
(B) I and IV.
(C) III and IV.
(D) II, III and IV.

Questions 65-67 are based on the following fact situation:

Attorney Alma Alison is a new associate in a large law firm in Big City. Alison's work is supervised by senior partner Zelda Zabar. In reviewing their list of clients and matters, Zelda tells Alison, "Heads up when you bill your hours on ABC's matters. They have a healthy legal budget and they never check our bills. Their general counsel used to work here. With the help of your paralegal, I am sure you can bill 70 hours every week. Don't forget, we look for lawyers who know how to bill. I like you and I'd like to see you become a partner one day."

Alison was soon overwhelmed by her workload and began to delegate all of her work for ABC to her paralegal, including reviewing contracts, drafting settlement letters, and drafting an answer to an employment discrimination complaint. The paralegal, an experienced hand at covering for young associates, did excellent work barely distinguishable from the work of young lawyers. Alison scanned most of the paralegal's output before mailing it to ABC Corp. Alison billed ABC Corporation for 70 hours of her own time every week for several months. While filling out her time-sheet one week, Alison bragged about her creative billing efforts to Charlie, a fellow associate at the firm. Shortly thereafter, Charlie informed the chairman of the firm's disciplinary committee about Alison's actions.

65. Alison is:

(A) Subject to discipline for misrepresenting her time.
(B) Not subject to discipline because she was acting under Zelda's guidance and instructions.
(C) Not subject to discipline if she would have spent 70 hours herself doing the work submitted by the paralegal.
(D) Subject to reprimand only, not discipline, because this was not a major infraction of the Rules.

66. Zelda is:

I. Subject to discipline for permitting a paralegal to practice law without a license.
II. Subject to discipline for instructing Alison to misrepresent her work hours.
III. Not subject to discipline if her conduct corresponded with the firm's work ethic and standards.
IV. Not subject to discipline if ABC's general counsel approved and condoned the firm's billing practices.

(A) I only.
(B) I and II.
(C) III only.
(D) I, III and IV.

67. In informing the chairman of the firm's disciplinary committee, Charlie:

I. Violated his duty of confidentiality.
II. Violated his duty of loyalty to Alison.
III. Acted properly.

(A) I only.
(B) II only.
(C) III only.
(D) I and II only.

MULTIPLE-CHOICE QUESTIONS

68. Naomi Neophyte has been practicing law for three years, handling a variety of matters, including a few criminal cases. She is outspoken and takes many controversial public positions, including participation in a campaign to apply the death penalty in connection with all crimes committed with a gun. A criminal court judge has just appointed Neophyte to represent George, an indigent defendant, in a prosecution for armed robbery. Neophyte is reluctant to handle the case because of her declared prejudice against criminals who resort to the use of deadly weapons. Which of the following steps may Naomi take:

I. Accept the appointment and represent George as competently as she is able.
II. Ask the judge to relieve her of the appointment because it is repugnant to her to represent a criminal charged with armed robbery.
III. Ask the grievance committee of the local bar association whether she may take the case under the circumstances.

(A) I only.
(B) II only.
(C) II and III only.
(D) III only.

69. Attorney Snader Shnazz ("the Shnazz") runs a television advertising spot directed at securing new clients. He appears on camera in a three-piece suit and tie (which he never wears ordinarily), surrounds himself with law books (which he rarely consults), and proceeds to give the following 10 second announcement:

> "My name is Shnazz. Everyone calls me 'the Shnazz.' I'm a licensed attorney in your state. My fees are the lowest around. My clients are always satisfied with my work. Just call anytime and meet the Shnazz."

In fact, Shnazz's fees are lower than most and Shnazz regularly distributes client questionnaires, all of which confirm client satisfaction with Shnazz's work. Shnazz's advertisement:

I. Violates general ethical standards by creating an unjustified expectation about the results Shnazz can realistically achieve.
II. Violates general ethical standards by using a huckster's techniques.
III. Does not violate prevailing general standards because media advertising by lawyers is unrestricted.
IV. Falls within general ethical standards if nothing in the ad is in fact false or misleading.

(A) I only.
(B) II only.
(C) III only.
(D) IV only.

70. Clara, an attorney, is an expert in the law relating to new securities issues. She has represented Apco Corporation for several years. Each time Apco is involved in a new securities issue, Clara writes an opinion letter stating whether the new issue satisfies the rules and requirements of the Securities and Exchange Commission. Clara is asked to write an opinion letter for a new Apco debenture issue of $100 million, the largest issue Apco has ever done. Clara spends approximately forty-five minutes checking to make sure that the law has not changed since her last opinion letter and fifteen minutes dictating to her secretary some minor changes from her last opinion letter. Clara's normal hourly billing rate for drafting opinion letters is $400 per hour, which is also the hourly rate usually charged in her locality for general legal services not involving specialization. Increasingly annoyed that Apco's business is growing and that each issue is larger than the last, but that her fees have not grown commensurately, Clara considers charging a fee of $5,000 for the opinion letter. Clara may properly rely on the following factors in fixing her fee:

   I. Lawyers in the area who handle securities issues generally consider the amount of the issue in fixing their fees.
   II. The broker who introduced Apco to the securities underwriter which arranged the issue was paid $50,000.
   III. Clara has represented Apco in similar matters for a long period of time and has become increasingly expert in SEC regulations relating to securities issues.

   (A) I only.
   (B) I and II.
   (C) I and III.
   (D) None of the above.

71. Frances Farmer is an attorney in Meccatown, a large city with many practitioners. The jurisdiction follows the Model Rules and has no regulatory authority granting certification in legal specialties. Frances takes out an ad in the Yellow Pages which reads in part, "Frances Farmer, attorney with experience in commercial and corporate litigation; I specialize in patent litigation...." In reality, Frances has had many commercial and corporate clients, but her experience in patent litigation is limited to

assisting Patent Attorneys in trial preparation. Frances is subject to discipline for:

(A) Describing herself as a specialist in patent litigation.
(B) Describing herself as experienced in commercial and corporate law.
(C) Listing any special qualifications other than her status as an attorney.
(D) None of the above.

72. Attorney Raymond Rembo is a leading member of the bar of Franklinia. He is chairman of many committees and serves as managing partner of his law firm, but he rarely sets foot in a courtroom. Frustrated by many adverse decisions by bankruptcy Judge Noitall, the law firm's principal client, Pre-Eminent Insurance, insists that Rembo appear personally to argue a number of motions before the Judge. The Judge angrily denies all of Rembo's motions, citing authority which is clearly incorrect. Rembo asks the Judge to recuse himself, stating that the Judge is obviously biased and prejudiced against his client. The Judge tells Rembo to "sit down and get on with it." Rembo says, "Your Honor is not fit to decide this case, nor, I suspect, any other case. You are a disgrace to the judiciary." Rembo is:

I. Subject to discipline for insulting a Judge.
II. Subject to discipline if he does not report the Judge to the appropriate authorities.
III. Not subject to discipline if he reasonably believes Judge Noitall is unqualified.
IV. Subject to discipline if he reports the Judge to the appropriate authorities.

(A) I only.
(B) I and II.
(C) I and IV.
(D) IV only.

73. Julia Juliana is head of the 150-lawyer prosecutor's office of Poston City. She is famous for her courtroom histrionics. In one famous case, she got down on her knees to plead to the jury for conviction of a notorious murderer. For the last several weeks, the Poston papers have been filled with stories about the arrest and trial of Brad and Tad, serial rapists. Julia decides to try the case herself. On a motion by the defendants, trial of the two is separated to avoid prejudice. Brad is tried first. The trial is difficult and emotional. Before the closing arguments, the judge carefully instructs the lawyers to avoid inflammatory language and personal opinions. In her closing argument, Julia appeals for conviction. Carried away by her own arguments, Julia

begins to sob uncontrollably. She cries out, "You can't ignore the evidence. I've never seen a more heinous crime. His victims cry out for revenge. Put an end to this scourge. Put this fiend away." The jury convicts. The trial judge should

I. Report Julia's conduct to the local disciplinary authorities.
II. Direct Julia not to act as trial prosecutor in the trial of Tad.
III. Discipline Julia himself.

(A) I only.
(B) II only.
(C) I and III only.
(D) III only.

74. Mishna retains Attorney Greg Gregson to prepare and file a license application before the local Taxi Commission. The agreed upon fee for the representation is $200 per hour. Gregson receives a check for $1,200 from Mishna. $700 is a deposit against payment of Gregson's fee and $500 is to pay the license fee required by the Commission if and when the license is granted.

Gregson maintains two office bank accounts: a "Fee Account," in which all fees are deposited and from which all office expenses are paid, and a "Clients' Fund Account." Gregson deposits the entire $1,200 in the "Clients' Fund Account" the week before the license hearing. Gregson expends three hours of time preparing for and attending the license hearing. However, Gregson's attempt to obtain the license is unsuccessful. Mishna immediately demands the return of the entire $1,200, arguing that Gregson's application was defective and that Gregson came to the license hearing unprepared.

Until their dispute is resolved, Gregson may properly:

(A) Transfer the entire $1,200 to his "Fee Account."
(B) Transfer $600 to the "Fee Account" and leave $600 in the "Clients' Fund Account".
(C) Transfer $600 to the "Fee Account" and send Mishna a $600 check on the "Clients' Fund Account."
(D) Send Mishna a $600 check and leave $600 in the "Clients' Fund Account."

75. Attorney Jeff Jeffries recently inherited 10,000 shares of stock in Macronext, a computer software giant. Jeff's interest in the company represents a very small percentage of total outstanding shares. Client, a former manager at Macronext, retains Jeff to sue Macronext for breach of contract. Jeff does not

inform Client that he owns stock in the computer company and proceeds with the law suit.

Is Jeff subject to discipline for representing Client in her breach of contract suit against Macronext?

(A) No, because Jeff is not the attorney for Macronext.
(B) No, because Jeff does not own a material interest in Macronext.
(C) Yes, if Jeff suspects that his stock interest may adversely affect his representation and he fails to get Clients' consent to the representation.
(D) No, because the outcome of the suit is not likely to affect the value of the company's shares.

Questions 76-77 are based on the following fact situation:

Attorney Hendricks Henderson represents Butch Hennessy, a defendant on trial for the gunshot murder of his girlfriend, Sharon. Butch insists that he is innocent and pleads not guilty to all charges. The police arrested Butch because of a history of past arrests following violent fights between Butch and Sharon. Sharon's neighbor testifies at trial that he heard the sound of a gunshot followed by a scream coming from Sharon's apartment on the night she was killed, and that he then saw someone who looked like Butch leave Sharon's apartment. Butch testifies that, on the evening of the murder, he was on a driving range 50 miles away from Sharon's apartment, practicing his golf swing.

76. Before the conclusion of the trial, the Prosecutor learns from a reliable source that Sharon's neighbor was actually at a friend's house on the night of the murder and saw nothing. She must:

   I. Proceed with the trial but omit any reference to the neighbor's testimony in her closing arguments.
   II. Drop the charges against Butch.
   III. Inform defense counsel and the court that the neighbor's testimony was perjurious.

   (A) I only.
   (B) II only.
   (C) III only.
   (D) All of the above.

77. The case goes to the jury and Butch is acquitted. Several months later, he runs into Henderson and says, "Now that the whole mess is behind us, I just need to get something off my chest. I really did kill Sharon." Henderson should:

(A) Reveal Butch's perjury to the court.
(B) Write a memo to his files recording Butch's remarks to him.
(C) Notify the Prosecutor's Office in writing that Butch was lying.
(D) Do nothing.

78. Lance Lancelot, an attorney, represents Greater Neck Hospital, a large institution in Metropolis. The Hospital treats thousands of patients each year and is often sued for malpractice. As soon as a case is threatened, and, in most cases, as soon as the Hospital suspects that a claim may arise, all relevant files are transferred to Lance and his partners at Lancelot & Camelot. Over many years, Lance accumulates thousands of files, many of which never result in lawsuits. After a time, Lance begins to suspect that the Hospital is systematically transferring to him all evidence of negligence on the part of any or all of its employees and doctors, with the deliberate intent to bring them within the coverage of the attorney/client privilege and the duty of confidentiality. The Metropolis Board of Health begins an investigation into the Hospital's practices after several patients die suddenly in its geriatric wards. The Department subpoenas all the Hospital's records, including all records held by Lancelot & Camelot. The Hospital directs Lance not to comply with the subpoena, asserting both the attorney-client privilege and the duty of confidentiality.

Lance should do which of the following:

(A) Comply with the Hospitals instructions and refuse to turn over any files.
(B) Turn over all the files covered by the subpoena.
(C) Carefully examine all the files and turn over to the Department only those on which Lancelot & Camelot have performed no legal services.
(D) Retain and refuse to turn over only those files on which Lancelot & Camelo performed legal services and return all other files to the Hospital.

79. Judge Horace Thomas is a trial judge in the state of Delta. Judge Thomas is currently hearing a case involving copyright infringement. Both sides present several expert witnesses who testify with respect to the contents of two best-selling books. The plaintiff alleges that the defendant has appropriated large portions of his text and plot. Testimony is limited to the two books at issue. At the close of testimony, Judge Thomas decides that he needs more facts. He goes to the local library and reads every book written by the plaintiff and every book written by the defendant. He concludes that the defendant has been stealing from the plaintiff for a long time. He returns to court and decides in favor of the plaintiff.

Was Judge Thomas justified in conducting his own investigation of the facts?

(A) Yes, as an officer of the court, Judge Thomas was simply fulfilling his obligation to discover the truth.
(B) Yes, if he suspected that defendant was guilty of perjury.
(C) No, a judge must make his decision only on the basis of the facts developed during the trial.
(D) Yes, provided he first advised the attorneys for both sides that he would conduct his own investigation.

80. You advise other lawyers on ethics issues. The firm of Cassidy, Harraday & Farraday has been in existence for forty years. Lately, many disputes have developed among the fifty partners and the firm has agreed to break up. Some of the partners are going to other firms; some are opening their own offices; and some will retire. The firm has thousands of files, spread among its three regional offices and a large warehouse. The files represent the work product of many lawyers over many years, some working alone and some working in large lawyer teams, including contract draftsman, negotiators, and litigators. The partners cannot agree on the disposition of these files and they ask you to advise them. Your best advice is:

(A) The firm itself has no responsibility under the circumstances and should arrange with each partner to take the files of his or her clients.
(B) The firm as a continuing entity must make arrangements to designate a partner or a successor firm to act as custodian of its records.
(C) The firm should write to each client, past and present, and ask the client to choose one or another partner as custodian of the client's records.
(D) The firm should return each file to the client identified in the file.

81. Tennessee Wilson is founder, chairman, and chief stockholder of Mountain Music Corp. The long-term attorney for Mountain Music is Dolly Sparton. After a lengthy negotiation, Mountain Music is purchased by and merged into the Dibney Corporation, a large conglomerate. Dibney discovers that Tennessee grossly overstated the income and profits of Mountain Music and sues Tennessee personally for fraud. Tennessee asks Dolly, his long-time friend and advisor, to represent him personally in the law suit. Dolly:

(A) may represent Tennessee without the consent of Dibney.
(B) may represent Tennessee only after getting the consent of Dibney.
(C) may not represent Tennessee because she owes a duty to Dibney.
(D) may represent Tennessee only if she formally severs all relationships with both Mountain Music and Dibney.

Question 82 is based on the following fact situation:

The firm of Abner & Doubleday specializes in representing plaintiffs in complex torts claims arising from accidents in large condominiums. The firm of Yanks & Dodger is often retained by Resistance Insurance to defend against these claims. After many years of studying the incredible disparities in jury verdicts between one case and another, the two firms agree to urge their clients to enter into a "high-low" agreements. Under these agreements, no matter what the jury may award, the plaintiff agrees in advance to a recovery with prescribed upper and lower limits, and so does the defendant. Several owners in the ABC Condo retain the Abner firm in a suit against Resistance for storm damage to their units. Abner and Yanks agree between themselves in advance of trial that, regardless of the verdict, the plaintiffs will receive no less than $1,000,000 but no more than $5,000,000. The jury returns a verdict for 25 million dollars.

82. The "high-low" agreement between the firms is:

    (A) Proper.
    (B) Proper only if both clients approved the agreement in writing.
    (C) Proper only if the court approves the agreement in writing.
    (D) Improper.

83. Roger Williams has been a solo general practitioner in the Town of Winthrop, State of Buena Vista for more than thirty years. Over the years, he has represented clients in a variety of general transactions. Five years ago, he was asked to represent a client in a claim against a major drug company. Since then, at least thirty clients with similar claims have retained his services. Roger's good friend, Ted Phillips, is another solo practitioner in the same town. Roger offers to sell all his practice except the drug claims to Ted. Ted agrees and they fix a price of $250,000. Ted pays $100,000 in cash and agrees to pay the balance in three annual installments of $50,000 each. Ted writes to all of Roger's clients except the drug-claim clients advising them that he has purchased Roger's practice. Roger writes to all his drug-claim clients to advise them that he will now be able to concentrate more effectively on their matters. Are Roger and Ted subject to discipline.

    (A) No, because lawyers are free to sell all or any part of a law practice.
    (B) No, because all the clients have been advised of the sale in writing by either Ted or Roger.
    (C) Yes, because a law practice must be sold in its entirety.
    (D) No, if the price paid by Ted is fair and reasonable.

Questions 84-85 are based on the following fact situation:

Judge Noble Speaker is a long-standing and well respected member of his state's judiciary. He has a very compelling personality and is often asked to speak before groups of lawyers and judges. Reporters on various newspapers and TV programs begin to call him to ask for his comments on trials in the news. Local TV Station WYYY asks the judge to sign a contract to appear for 15 minutes each night and comment publicly on one or another trial taking place within the State. The program is sponsored by Food Delites, which offers to pay the judge $1,000 per broadcast. The judge agrees.

After one of his broadcasts, the Judge meets John Beaver, an old friend and former client who has become a famous novelist. John asks him to look at a contract that's been offered to him by his publisher. The Judge reviews the contract and writes a memo recommending many changes. John signs the contract, which now incorporates many of the Judge's suggestions. Delighted with the results, John sends the Judge a check for $15,000, which the judge deposits.

84. Is Judge Speaker subject to discipline for appearing regularly on WYYY?

 (A) Yes, because a Judge may not have any source of income except his salary.
 (B) Yes, because a Judge may not lend the prestige of his office to a commercial enterprise.
 (C) No, because a Judge has as much right to freedom of speech as any other citizen.
 (D) No, because a Judge may speak freely on any aspect of the judicial system or the practice of law.

85. The Judge's conduct with respect to the contract of John Beaver is:

 (A) Proper because the Judge did nothing more than review the contract and write a memorandum.
 (B) Proper because John was an old friend and former client.
 (C) Improper because a judge may not engage in the practice of law.
 (D) Proper because $15,000 was not an unreasonable fee under the circumstances.

86. Cleopatra owns the Bayou jewelry store. She hires Attorney Marcus Anthony to represent her in a breach of contract action against one of her diamond suppliers. A year after the case is concluded, Cleopatra runs a red light and hits a car driven by Niles. Niles asks Anthony to represent him in his personal injury action against Cleopatra. Should Anthony represent Niles?

(A) No, because it would violate Anthony's duty of loyalty to Cleopatra.

(B) No, it would violate Anthony's duty of confidentiality to Cleopatra.

(C) Yes, because the new matter is neither the same nor substantially related to Cleopatra's breach of contract action.

(D) Yes, but only if Cleopatra consents after consultation.

87. Angela Sainsbury, a part-time adjunct law professor at Podunk Law and an active practitioner, has been misusing her client fund account for many years. Several complaints are submitted to the Committee on Discipline, which finds that Angela has misappropriated more than $500,000 in client funds. Which of the following actions may the Committee not take?

(A) Suspend Angela from practice for a period of months or years.

(B) Order the disbarment of Angela for a period of seven years, with leave to apply for readmission at that time.

(C) Disbar Angela for life.

(D) Order her to resign from her appointment at Podunk Law.

Questions 88-89 are based on the following fact situation:

Attorney Haven Adam is general counsel for HCN Corporation, the largest software distributor in the state. He has a staff of ninety lawyers. His own time is spent in assigning files to his staff, referring complex matters to outside counsel and sitting in on meeting of directors and committees. At these meetings, he acts only as recording secretary, in which role he simply drafts the minutes. If any legal matter comes up at the meetings, it is referred to outside counsel. The Corporation is accused by the State's Attorney General of collusive price fixing and consumer fraud. The investigating attorney subpoenas Adam's attorney files, as well as all minutes of the board of directors and the HCN Committee on Sales and Marketing.

88. What action may Adam properly take with respect to his attorney files?

(A) Refuse to turn them over in reliance on the attorney-client privilege.

(B) Refuse to turn them over because they are in his possession.

(C) Respect the subpoena and turn the files over.

(D) Turn over only those portions of the files which are relevant to the State's investigation.

89. What action may Adam properly take with respect to the minutes:

(A) Refuse to turn them over in reliance on the attorney-client privilege.

(B) Refuse to turn them over because to do so would violate Adam's duty of confidentiality to HCN.

(C) Turn them over because they were not kept by Adam in his role as attorney and are not covered by the attorney-client privilege.

(D) Turn them over only if the Board of HCN formally resolves to authorize it.

90. Attorney Woppinger Biddle runs a small office with one associate and two paralegals. Most of his cases involve simple real estate closings of private homes and small taxpayer properties. He represents John and Mary Alpinoff in the purchase of their home. John is impressed with Biddle and asks him to handle the foreclosure of a mortgage on a large commercial property. The mortgage is held by the firm of which John is CEO. Biddle has never conducted a foreclosure proceeding and runs into problems from the start. When the mortgagor files for bankruptcy, things go from bad to worse. Biddle is suddenly in the middle of a complex bankruptcy proceeding. He works as hard as he can, but he falls farther and farther behind. His staff is overwhelmed. Motions are filed late. Files are misplaced. Court dates are ignored. Biddle fails to return John's phone calls. A critical motion in the bankruptcy proceeding is decided against the mortgagee because of inadequate prepration by Biddle. Alpinoff write to the grievance committee. Under these facts, the committee is likely to charge the following violations:

(A) That Biddle failed to act with reasonable diligence.
(B) That Biddle failed to provide competent representation.
(C) That Biddle failed to keep his client reasonably informed.
(D) All of the above.

91. The firm of Havath, Haines & Stores, 500-partner strong, is asked to represent the government of Surumbu before the International Court of Justice. Surumbu has a long and volatile history of civil rights abuses and genocide. It is considered a pariah among nations. Many of the Havath partners object to the representation and insist that the partners conduct a secret ballot to decide whether the firm should accept Surumbu as a client. The partners vote 252-248 to accept. The Surumbu case is assigned to Drew Ballenshine, who voted in favor of the representation. Drew's staff consists of five associates, all of whom refuse his instructions to work on the Surumbu matter. Are the associates subject to discipline?

(A) Yes, for refusing to abide by the vote of the partners.
(B) Yes, for refusing to accept the orders of the partner in charge.
(C) No, because no lawyer can be required to perform services for a client which is personally repugnant to him.
(D) Yes, because all clients are entitled to diligent representation regardless of their reputation or notoriety.

92. Laura Lindsey is the attorney for the Hi Y Utility Company. The company is charged with monopolistic trade practices by the State's Commissioner of Investigations. The Commissioner brings an action to enjoin the company's practices and to fine it $5 million dollars. Laura undertakes an intensive investigation of the Commissioner and his staff, and she begins to suspect that a high-ranking member of the Commissioner's staff is on the payroll of the Slo Bo Utility, a direct competitor of Hi Y. One day, Laura's secretary hands her a fax and says, "get a load of this". The fax is from a vice-president of Slo Bo to the Commissioner's staff member. It says, "Your help has been invaluable to us. You're worth every penny." Laura says nothing. She waits for the right moment and blows the trial open when she introduces the fax. Slo Bo's VP and the commission staff member are indicted. Laura is:

(A) Subject to discipline for introducing the fax.
(B) Subject to discipline for withholding the fax until the trial.
(C) Not subject to discipline because her first duty is to her client.
(D) Not subject to discipline because the error in transmission was caused by the negligence of Slo Bo's VP.

Questions 93-94 are based on the following fact situation:

Judge Thorndike Thornwood is a judge of the Criminal Court of the State of Enterprise. He is known among lawyers as "Ornery Thornery." He is imperious, ill-tempered and thin-skinned. He is driving home from a political dinner and meeting when he is stopped for weaving and speeding by a motorcycle trooper. The trooper asks the Judge to get of the car and submit to a breathalizer test. The Judge refuses and says, "Do you know who I am, officer? I've been known to skin people like you. You'll be sorry if you ever appear before me." The Judge shows his judge's badge. The trooper says simply. "Get out of here as fast as you can". Later, at the station house, the trooper tells his sergeant about the incident. The sergeant says, "No way, we've got to stop that guy once and for all. I'm going to report him to the Judicial Inquiry Board." The sergeant proceeds to make good on his threat.

93. Is the Judge subject to discipline?

(A) No, because he was not acting in his judicial capacity.
(B) No, because the Judge's conduct is not specifically covered by any provision of the Code of Judicial Conduct.
(C) No, because the Judge's conduct was a minor infraction of the Code.
(D) Yes, because the Judge violated several provisions of the Code of Judicial Conduct.

MULTIPLE-CHOICE QUESTIONS　　149

94. The Inquiry Board has the power to take which of the following actions?

   I. Reprimand the Judge.
   II. Suspend the Judge for a stated period.
   III. Disbar the Judge.
   IV. Remove the Judge from Office.

   (A) I only.
   (B) I and II.
   (C) I, II and IV.
   (D) All of the above.

95. Criminal defense attorney Randy Hamilton is involved in the murder trial of his client, Marter, who insists on his innocence. The prosecutor presents the testimony of Abe Arby, who claims to have witnessed the crime. Marter takes the stand and testifies that he spent the night with his girlfriend. She backs up his story, as do three other witnesses who testify that they saw Marter enter his girlfriend's apartment. When the jury returns a guilty verdict, Randy is appalled and disbelieving. He approaches three of the jurors after the judge discharges them and says, "I don't understand you people. How could you convict on these facts? I'd love to know what went on in that jury room." Are Randy's comments to the jurors proper?

   (A) Yes, provided opposing counsel is present and has an equal opportunity to interview the jurors.
   (B) Yes, since the trial was over and the judge had discharged the jurors.
   (C) No, in most jurisdictions, because Randy's remarks tended to harass or embarrass the jurors.
   (D) No, because Randy did not have the court's permission to interrogate the jury.

96. Client Lenore Lenape enters into a written contract with Gerard Bros. to sell them an apartment building she owns. The contract calls for the buyers to pay Lenore $100,000 per year for three years. The buyers pay Lenore $100,000 in the first year, but breach the contract by paying $50,000 in the second year, and nothing in the third year. Lenore retains attorney Whitney Wheaton to represent her in a breach of contract suit against the buyers. Wheaton procrastinates and files the lawsuit after the statute of limitations has run.

   When Lenore discovers that Wheaton has allowed the statute to run, she sends him an angry letter threatening to file suit for malpractice. Wheaton responds, without admitting liability, by offering to pay her $75,000 in exchange for a general release. Wheaton's liability carrier had previously threatened to cut off his malpractice insurance.

Is Wheaton subject to discipline for offering to settle Lenore's lawsuit against him in this manner?

(A) No, because Lenore's letter terminated the attorney-client relationship and Wheaton was free to bargain with her.
(B) Yes, because Wheaton did not first advise Lenore in writing that she should seek independent counsel to resolve their dispute.
(C) No, because attorneys should be encouraged to settle malpractice actions as expeditiously and economically as possible.
(D) No, if Lenore consents to the settlement.

97. Stephen Stevens is a prominent criminal defense attorney. One afternoon, Defendant makes an appointment to see him. Defendant, out on bail, is charged with sexual assault on two teen-age females. Defendant tells Stevens that he videotaped the attacks and that the tapes are hidden in a closet in his apartment. At defendant's request, Stevens goes to the apartment, takes the tapes and deposits them in his office safe. The defendant is acquitted. After the trial, Stevens removes the tapes from the safe and leaves them openly on his desk. The tapes are discovered and Stevens receives a letter from counsel to the grievance committee requesting an explanation of the matter.

Is Stevens subject to discipline?

(A) Yes, because he secreted evidence and allowed his office to be used in violation of the law.
(B) No, because he owed the duty of confidentiality to his client.
(C) No, because he was observing the attorney-client privilege.
(D) No, because the tapes were not the instrumentalities of the crime itself.

98. Attorney Blair Blumberg has been an associate at Leadbettor & Higgenbottom for seven years. When he first joined the firm, he was required to sign an agreement which provided, in part, that if he left the firm for any reason, he would not join any firm within 250 miles of the Higgenbottom office for five years after his departure. The agreement was a standard condition of employment with Higgenbottom. Blumberg has just been passed over for partner and gets an offer from the firm of Snare & Beatom, located ten blocks from the Higgenbottom office. He accepts the offer.

The Higgenbottom firm sues to enjoin Blumberg. Is the firm subject to discipline?

(A) No, because it is enforcing a valid agreement.
(B) No, if it can show that Blumberg's clients have agreed to follow him to Snare & Beatom.
(C) Yes, because the employment agreement was an improper restriction on Blumberg's right to pursue his profession.
(D) Yes, because it is improper to impose conditions on a lawyer's employment.

99. Frank Fosdick has been a single practitioner all his life. He no longer feels the old spark and decides to retire. As he looks around his office, he wonders what to do with the piles of files he has accumulated over the years. His records tell him that he's represented at least 12,500 clients and been involved in thousands of trials and transactions. Overwhelmed by the task before him, he decides to discard all his files as quickly and painlessly as possible. Every day for several weeks, Frank puts as many files as he can in his office trash bins and they are carted off by the garbagemen. One day, a number of papers fall out of a garbage bag and land on a public walk outside Frank's office building. The papers concern a former divorce client whom Frank represented three years before. The papers find their way to the client. Incensed that her private affairs have been made public, the client initiates a grievance proceeding against Frank. Frank is subject to discipline for:

I. Failing to contact his clients to request instructions on the disposition of their files.
II. Failing to preserve those records created over the previous seven years.
III. Failing to shred or otherwise destroy his clients' private papers.
IV. Failing to deliver the papers to another attorney to hold as custodian.

(A) I and II.
(B) IV only.
(C) I only.
(D) All of the above.

100. Attorneys Brenda Berlingham and Brian Butterworth are partners in an active negligence practice. They employ two investigators who interview witnesses and perform other trial preparation duties. Brenda and Brian have an office in East Upper Platte in the State of Iroquois. One day there is a major mining accident in West Lower Platte, which is across the river in Sioux State. Many miners are injured. Brenda and Brian send both investigators into Sioux State with instructions to visit as many victims as possible and "sign them up." They fail to get anyone to sign a retainer agreement. Brenda and Brian are admitted to practice in Iroquois but not in Sioux.

Brenda and Brian are:

(A) Subject to discipline for solicitation in Iroquois, but not in Sioux.
(B) Subject to discipline in Sioux, but not in Iroquois.
(C) Subject to discipline in both Sioux and Iroquois.
(D) Not subject to discipline because no one signed a retainer agreement.

Multiple-Choice Answers

MULTIPLE-CHOICE ANSWERS

1. A A public prosecutor may not institute criminal proceedings without probable cause and must promptly disclose to defendant's counsel any evidence which tends to negate guilt or mitigate the degree of the offense. MR 3.8. A prosecutor is a minister of justice, not merely an advocate. His responsibility is to help find the truth, not to "win." The correct answer is **A**. Statements I and II correctly identify two of the situations in which a public prosecutor or other government lawyer is subject to discipline. Choice **B** is incorrect because it includes Statement III, which is wrong. A prosecutor is not subject to discipline for failing to advise a suspect of his right to counsel when he is summoned to appear before a grand jury. Choice **C** is incorrect because, although it correctly identifies Statement I, it does not also include Statement II, which is also correct. Finally, Choice **D** is incorrect. The obligation of police officers and police officials to advise an accused of his right to counsel before and during an interrogation (*Miranda v. Arizona*, 384 U.S. 436(1966)) does not extend to a prosecutor's subpoenas to grand jury witnesses. However, a prosecutor *may* grant immunity to a grand jury witness if he wishes. A witness who is granted immunity may not plead the Fifth Amendment.

2. A A lawyer must conduct himself at all times so as to avoid discredit upon himself and the profession. Michael's conduct in lying to and threatening Hexon's manager is improper and subjects him to discipline. MR 4.1(a) and 4.4. It is professional misconduct for a lawyer to violate one of the Rules of Professional Conduct or to engage in conduct that is prejudicial to the administration of justice. MR 8.4. In determining what rules will apply to the disciplinary proceeding, we look to MR 8.5. Under these facts, Michael is subject to discipline in the two states in which he is admitted to practice—Upper Dakota and West Dakota—but not in East Dakota, because he is not admitted there. Choice **C** is therefore incorrect. Because Michael maintains an office in Upper Dakota and, therefore, presumably, practices there principally, the rules of Upper Dakota will apply. MR 8.5(2)(ii). If Michael's conduct in lying and threatening the Hexon manager had occurred in West Dakota, however, then the rules of that state would apply because the effect of Michael's conduct would be felt predominantly there. Choices **B, C** and **D** are all incorrect for the reasons cited. Choice **A** is the correct answer.

3. D Even though the attorney-client relationship may not result, an attorney owes any person who consults him in his professional capacity the duty of confidentiality. Under these facts, Janet clearly revealed to David information which she intended to keep confidential. Because

David identified himself as a tort specialist and did not interrupt or discourage her while she spoke, he induced Janet to assume that she was speaking to him in his role as attorney and that her statements would be treated with confidence. Choice **D** is the correct answer. MR 1.6(a). Choice **A** is incorrect for the very reason that **D** is correct. An attorney may not reveal information given to him by a client or potential client in confidence, whether or not the information is detrimental to the client's interests. Choice **B** is incorrect. The attorney-client privilege and the duty of confidentiality are two facets of the same basic obligation to protect a client's confidences. MR 1.6 Comment [5]. However, there are subtle differences between the attorney-client privilege and the general duty of confidentiality. The attorney-client privilege is a rule of evidence which prevents a lawyer from testifying at trial about matters revealed by his client. The general duty of confidentiality applies in all circumstances to all client confidences and secrets. The attorney-client privilege attaches only when the relationship of lawyer-client begins. That relationship did not develop here because David refused the representation; however, Janet's disclosures to David are protected by the other facet of the obligation—the general duty of confidentiality. Choice **C** is incorrect because the attorney-client relationship had not attached.

4. **A** The standards which apply to disciplinary proceedings are not the same as those which prevail in malpractice cases. A lawyer may violate a Rule of Professional Responsibility and not be guilty of malpractice. On the other hand, a lawyer may commit malpractice without violating a disciplinary rule. The requirements of competent representation are imposed by MR 1.1. Generally, the Rule requires that an attorney have the proficiency of a general practitioner in a particular matter. Choice **A** is the right answer because it tells us that Helen's work did not meet the standards of a general practitioner in her area. Choice **B** is incorrect because it's not necessary in a disciplinary proceeding over a lawyer's incompetence to prove that the attorney should have prevailed in the matter he handled. It's enough to show that the attorney did not handle the matter with the proficiency of a general practitioner. Choice **C** is also incorrect. Don does not have to show that he would have won his malpractice suit. He needs to show only that Helen did not perform as competently as a general practitioner. Lawyers are not guarantors of results; but they are required to show reasonable knowledge and skill. Choice **D** is incorrect because it does not accurately state the standards for measuring competence in a matter. Helen's competence is not measured by comparing her to lawyers with two years of experience. Experience and the length of practice are only

two of the tests of competence. Helen is expected to measure up to the level of the average general practitioner. "A newly admitted lawyer can be as competent as a practitioner with long experience." MR 1.1 Comment [2].

5. **A** The attorney-client evidentiary privilege (which protects against attorney disclosure of client confidences in judicial proceedings) belongs to the client and not the attorney. MR Preamble, Scope [7]: "The attorney-client privilege is that of the client and not of the lawyer." However, a lawyer may use information imparted by a client to establish a claim or defense in a dispute with the client or to respond to allegations in a proceeding concerning the lawyer's representation of the client. The correct answer is **A**. Helen is permitted to disclose the client's communications if they are reasonably necessary to her defense in the malpractice action; the right to disclose would include the right not to disclose. MR 1.6(b)(2). Choice **B** is incorrect because it misstates the attorney-client privilege. A lawyer may not always assert the privilege. First of all, it is not his to assert, but the client's. Secondly, there are many circumstances under which a lawyer may not assert the privilege, e.g., when the client has waived it. Choice **C** is incorrect because the attorney-client privilege does not end when the action or proceeding to which it relates ends. It continues even after the client-lawyer relationship has terminated. MR 1.6 Comment [22]. Choice **D** is incorrect because a client does not waive the attorney-client privilege by bringing a malpractice action against the attorney to whom the matter was disclosed. The contrary result would act as a deterrent to claims for malpractice by clients against lawyers. The lawyer may use the client's information to the extent she may need to defend herself against the claim of malpractice, but the privilege itself is not waived and may be asserted by the client in another proceeding.

6. **C** An attorney is often faced with difficult and seemingly irreconcilable alternatives and conflicts. Torn between his obligations to his client and his duty to maintain the integrity of the judicial system, he is adrift in the seas between Scylla and Charybdis. Here, the correct answer is **C**. However great his obligations to his client, a lawyer may not conceal evidence or obstruct his adversary's access to evidence. MR 3.4(a). A contrary rule would destroy the very foundations of our adversary trial system. Choice **A** is incorrect because it overstates a lawyer's obligation to his client. There are circumstances in which a lawyer has a greater duty than to maintain the confidence of his client. Choice **B** is incorrect because it's immaterial whether Nero's conduct disadvantaged his adversary. He has an affirmative duty to disclose rel-

evant testimony in order to satisfy the search for truth. Choice **D** is incorrect. It states a valid general principle of lawyer-client relationships, but the principle must give way to the more compelling duty to protect the integrity of the judicial process.

7. **C** A lawyer should not accept a case unless he is competent to handle it. MR 1.1. The correct answer is **C**. Competence requires "the legal knowledge, skill, thoroughness and preparation" reasonably necessary to the representation. In complex corporate tax matters, the competence required is that of a tax specialist, not a general practitioner. This would be especially true in the case of a lawyer who was only recently admitted. MR 1.1 Comment [1], [2]. When an attorney does not have the skills and knowledge necessary to provide competent representation, he has three choices: (1) he can turn down the case (or withdraw if the case has already been accepted), (2) he can study to become proficient in the area of law in question, but he cannot charge his client unreasonably for this time and he must actually become proficient as a result, and (3) he can associate with an attorney who is competent to provide the representation, as long as he obtains client consent to do so. Choice **C** correctly identifies two of these three options—Statements I and III. Joe could associate with a tax expert or he could offer to withdraw. Choice **B** is incorrect because it offers only one of the two valid Statements. Statement II, that Joe could rely on his purchase and study of a manual, could not reasonably be expected to give him the knowledge he needed; nor is it enough that he feel "confident" to give an opinion. The test is objective, not subjective. He must *be* competent, not *feel* competent. Choice **A** is incorrect because it relies on only one of the two valid Statements. Choice **D** is wrong because it relies on Statement IV, which is wrong. It would be improper for Joe to proceed in reliance on his own existing ability, especially without continuing and serious efforts to acquire the specialized knowledge he needs to serve the client competently.

8. **B** A lawyer may not assist his client in conduct that the lawyer knows to be criminal. MR 1.2(d). The correct answer is **B**. The facts tell us Henry advised Dan how to avoid detection and prosecution. In giving this advice, Henry was helping Dan to avoid the consequences of his crimes. "...the lawyer is required to avoid furthering the purpose, for example, for suggesting how it might be concealed." MR 1.2(d) Comment [7]. Choice **A** is incorrect. Everyone, including a confessed criminal, is entitled to competent representation. MR 1.2(d) Comments [6]-[9]. Choice **C** is also incorrect. A lawyer representing a client who confesses the admission of a crime to him has no obligation to report

the crime to the police. On the contrary, his duty is to preserve the client's confidences. MR 1.6 Comment [11]. Choice **D** is also incorrect because the duty of confidentiality mandates that attorneys generally not reveal the crimes of their clients to anyone, including their victims. MR 1.6(a).

9. A In a criminal case, a lawyer must ask for and abide by a client's decision with respect to certain primary rights—to determine what plea to enter; whether or not to waive a jury trial; and whether or not to testify in his own defense. MR 1.2(a). The correct answer is **A**. Although an attorney can and should make reasonable strategic choices throughout the trial, the decision whether or not to testify is so fundamental to an accused's defense that an attorney cannot disregard his wishes. The contrary rule would impinge too severely on the client's autonomy— one of the values our adversary system was designed to protect. Attorney Harris is subject to discipline for ignoring Jack's request to testify at trial in his own defense. Under these facts, he would also be subject to discipline for disregarding Jack's request for a jury trial. Choice **B** is incorrect because it misstates the principles governing trial strategy— as a general rule, the attorney should decide issues of trial strategy. But the rights affected here are rights fundamental to a client's defense— not matters of trial strategy. Choice **C** is incorrect because, although an attorney can and should choose the trial strategy, he is not allowed to decide whether or not the client will testify, but must respect the client's decision. Of course, the attorney may, if he wishes, advise the client that he thinks the client would hurt his cause by testifying. Choice **D** is incorrect because a lawyer's responsibility to the prevailing rules is measured not by the results he achieves but by the nature of his conduct. Any other view would encourage lawyers to think only of the ends and not the means.

10. A In a criminal case, an attorney must abide by his client's decision whether or not to waive a jury trial. MR 1.2(a). The correct answer is **A**. Although Attorney may have correctly assessed the jury's reaction to Jack's appearance and personality and although he did properly discharge his duty to advise Jack of his assessment, he was not entitled to ignore Jack's request and waive the jury trial. The decision whether or not to waive a jury trial is not a decision involving trial strategy only, but one involving the client's basic legal rights. Choice **B** is incorrect because it implies that an attorney may not impose some decisions on trial strategy; indeed, in a criminal case, he may make all decisions involving trial strategy except the three which involve a client's substantive rights—the right to a jury trial, the right to testify in his own defense, and the right to decide how to plead. Choice **C** is incorrect because Attorney's reasonable belief is immaterial except as something to communicate to his client; the ultimate decision must be left to the client. Choice **D** is incorrect because it is irrelevant whether Jack won or lost. The issue is not the verdict itself but the attorney's failure to comply with the standards of trial advocacy in a criminal trial.

11. **B** An attorney is not the master of all decision-making in the representation of her client. In a civil case, she must abide by her client's decision and instructions regarding settlement. MR 1.2. The correct answer is **B**. The decision whether or not to settle is solely up to the client. Here, Beth completely ignored Fred's instructions regarding settlement. The failure is even more grievous because she failed to communicate an offer which was even greater than Fred's target. Choice **A** is not a good answer because it ignores the central issue—Beth's failure to communicate an offer of settlement. A lawyer is supposed to take a claim to trial if the case cannot be settled satisfactorily. Choice **C** is not correct. A lawyer is judged not only by the results she achieves but also by the means she utilizes. A breach of duty is not cured by a successful outcome. Choice **D** is incorrect because it misstates the applicable rule. The lawyer may indeed be the better judge of a claim's value, but his function is to communicate his assessment to the client to enable the client to make an informed decision; he may not substitute his judgment for the client's. The final decision whether to accept an offer of settlement is the client's alone to make.

12. **D** Once an attorney-client relationship has ended, the attorney's obligation to provide legal advice ends as well. He does have an obligation to return unearned fees and to surrender the client's papers and records, but not to advise hum. MR 1.16. The correct answer is **D**. Trustworthy effectively terminated the attorney-client relationship when the trust was executed and he sent Bart an invoice which read, "Final Billing." His obligation to provide legal advice ended when the relationship did. If the rules were otherwise, an attorney would have a perpetual duty to keep a continuing database of clients and their affairs and legal interests—an impossible task. Attorneys should clearly communicate—preferably in writing—the point at which representation in any matter is over, so that the client does not mistakenly believe the attorney is continuing to look out for her legal interests. **A** is incorrect for the same reason that **D** is correct: once the attorney-client relationship was terminated, Trustworthy had no continuing duty to tell the client of changes in the law. Although it adds a new dimension—loss to the client—**B** is incorrect for the same reason that **A** is incorrect. Once a

matter is ended, an attorney has no continuing duty to protect the interests of a former client. **C** is incorrect because there is an exception to the in-person solicitation prohibition which allows solicitation of former clients. Comment [4] to MR 7.3(a) supplies the rational for this exception: "There is far less likelihood that a lawyer would engage in abusive practices against an individual with whom the lawyer has a prior personal or professional relationship....").

13. **A** An attorney should not write a letter recommending an applicant's admission to the bar if the attorney has no personal knowledge of the applicant's fitness to practice law. A statement attesting to the applicant's fitness by a lawyer who had no personal knowledge of his fitness would constitute a knowingly false statement of a material fact. MR 8.1.The correct answer is choice **A,** because it relies only on Statement III. To help maintain the integrity of the bar, an attorney may not recommend anyone for admission unless the attorney has **personal knowledge** of that person's character, integrity and intellectual abilities. Anything less would be considered a misrepresentation of the facts. Attorney may not rely solely on the unsubstantiated recommendation of his old classmate, nor even on the additional comments of Paul Barkum. Attorney must conduct an independent investigation adequate to convince himself personally of Dave's qualifications and fitness. Statements I and II are incorrect because they depend on the knowledge and assessments of others, not Attorney's. Choices **B**, **C**, and **D** are therefore incorrect because they all include Statements I and/or II.

14. **C** So long as the complaint is not frivolous, an attorney may ethically file a complaint even if she herself believes her client will not prevail. MR 3.1 Comment [2]. The correct answer under these facts is **C**. A lawyer may not file a complaint if the sole purpose is to harass and intimidate the opposition. Frick's admission of his purpose justified Strick in concluding that the complaint was frivolous. Choice **A** is wrong because Strick's belief is not conclusive. So long as a complaint is not frivolous, the lawyer has a duty to proceed. MR 3.1 Comment [2]. Choice **B** is incorrect because it states the wrong measure for determining whether a complaint should be filed. A judge's decision to grant summary judgment dismissing the complaint is not in and of itself proof that the complaint was frivolous. The attorney who must decide whether to file a complaint cannot possibly know in advance how a judge will react to the facts. Choice **D** is also incorrect. It doesn't matter that Strick had accepted a retainer. An Attorney's first duty is to practice according to the rules of professional conduct. An attorney is

not bound to proceed in a matter merely because she has accepted a retainer. If circumstances warrant, she may always withdraw. MR 1.16(a)(1).

15. **D** An attorney may not withdraw from representing a client unless withdrawal can be accomplished "without material adverse effect on the interests of the client." MR 1.16. The correct answer is **D**. Before withdrawing, Strick must take all reasonable steps to mitigate the consequences to Frick. Among these steps are allowing sufficient time for employment of other counsel and returning the client's files. Under these facts, Strick must take special steps to ensure that Frick's claim will not be foreclosed by the expiration of the statute of limitations in one week. It would be improper for Strick to withdraw without first filing the complaint because it is unlikely that Frick's rights could otherwise be protected in the time involved. **A** is incorrect. Frick is entitled to have the court determine whether or not his version of the facts is correct. Strick's beliefs are not controlling. Whatever her beliefs, she must pursue her client's interests diligently. **B** is incorrect. Strick has an obligation to protect Frick's interests during the entire course of the representation, not just when the matter is before a tribunal. **C** is incorrect. An attorney cannot be held "hostage" by a client because she accepted a retainer. Where necessary and proper, an attorney may withdraw. She may, however, have an obligation, if she has not earned it all, to return a portion of the retainer.

16. **B** A lawyer's fees must be reasonable when measured under all the circumstances. MR 1.5(a). The correct answer is **B**. A lawyer may require advance payment of a fee, but is obligated to return any part of the advance which is unearned. MR 1.5(a) Comment [2]; MR 1.16(d). Here, Strick and Frick entered into a fee agreement under which Strick was entitled to bill $50 per hour. Because she has expended eight hours of time on Frick's claim, she is entitled to a fee of $400 for this time—even though in hindsight the time was spent without result. Frick can keep the $400 she has earned but must refund the balance of the $1,000 retainer to Frick. **A** is incorrect. The fact that $1,000 may have been a reasonable fee under all the circumstances is immaterial. Strick is stuck with her bargain. **C** is also incorrect. A lawyer is entitled to withdraw from a case when the circumstances warrant. Because Frick's claims were untrue and, therefore, baseless and frivolous, Strick was required to withdraw. She is entitled to compensation for the time spent on Frick's claims. **D** is incorrect. An attorney is not generally required to obtain results for a client before she is entitled to collect a

fee, unless the fee agreement is a contingent one. Here, Frick agreed to pay Attorney on an hourly basis. Attorney is entitled to be compensated for the time she expended on Frick's behalf.

17. **C** As an exception to the general duty of confidentiality, an attorney may reveal a confidence when reasonably necessary to prevent a crime which may result in imminent death or substantial bodily harm. MR 1.6(b)(1). Here, the threat against Alice by Little Tim would clearly satisfy this Rule. **C** is therefore the right answer. Jane would not be subject to discipline for revealing the threats to kill Alice. Jane is not ***required*** to disclose the threats, she is ***permitted*** to do so without breaching her ethical duties. **A** is incorrect because the rules recognize an exception to the general duty of confidentiality in the case of threatened future crimes. **B** is incorrect because Jane has no obligation to verify independently that Little Tim's threats are real. The investigation of crimes is the responsibility of the police, not a lawyer. A lawyer is entitled to believe and act upon the threats of her client. **D** is incorrect because it states the wrong basis for relieving Jane of the duty of confidentiality. A lawyer may not avoid the issue of deciding whether or not to reveal threats of a future crime by arguing that her representation is limited to the present crime. She may decide in her discretion not to reveal the threat of a future crime but she must confront the issue, not ignore it.

18. **D** Jane may not conceal the gun. Material physical evidence which comes into the attorney's possession must be surrendered to the prosecution. MR 3.4(a) Comment [2]; MR 1.6 Comments [1]-[5]. The correct answer is **D**. Most courts have recognized that criminal defense attorneys have a duty to turn over to the prosecution physical evidence of the crime if the evidence comes into their possession. This duty generally applies to evidence that is either a product of the crime (e.g., stolen property) or the instrumentality of the crime (e.g., a weapon). Upon receipt of Tim's gun, Jane had a duty to turn the weapon over to the authorities. **A** is an excessively broad statement of the principles governing confidentiality. Jane could not properly suppress the gun merely because Tim was her client. **B,** although narrower in scope, incorrectly applies the privilege to these facts. Physical evidence arising from or related to the crime is not protected by the privilege. Keep in mind that the attorney-client privilege relates essentially to the right of the lawyer not to testify during trial. **C** is incorrect. A defendant cannot "protect" evidence by giving it to his attorney for safekeeping.

19. B Communications to an attorney from her client during the course of the attorney-client relationship are confidential and should not be revealed. MR 1.6(a) Comments [1]-[5]. The correct answer is **B**. The American adversarial system is designed to promote candor between attorney and client. This goal would be impossible if lawyers were permitted to reveal the confidences of their clients. It would be improper for Jane to tell the prosecution that Tim had removed evidence from the scene of the crime because the source of this information was a confidential statement from Little Tim. In her discretion, Jane was free to advise Tim to turn in the evidence. **A** is incorrect because the issue is Jane's duty of confidentiality, not whether the evidence was probative. The privilege becomes critical only when and because evidence is probative. **C** is incorrect because it is both illogical and immaterial. The act of removing the evidence cannot logically be separated from the crime. Inevitably, it is the commission of a crime which prompts the effort to secrete evidence of the crime. The answer is immaterial because whether or not the removal of evidence could be separated from the commission of the crime, it was protected by Jane's duty of confidentiality. Choice **D** is incorrect because it is irrelevant whether or not the evidence was prejudicial. The duty attaches to all confidences, prejudicial or not.

20. B This question poses some of the most difficult ethical questions faced by the lawyer for a criminal defendant. The issues are discussed in detail in the Comments to MR 3.3. The basic conflict is between the lawyer's obligation to offer the client the best defense available and his duty of candor to the tribunal. The best answer is **B**. Clearly, the lawyer defending a criminally accused will often be privy to potentially perjurious testimony. His first duty is to ask the client to refrain from offering the testimony. MR 3.3 Comment [7]. Failing that, he can withdraw. Often, however, the client will insist on taking the stand at the last moment, when it's too late for the lawyer to withdraw. Comment [8]. Under these facts, for example, Little Tim insisted on testifying and on repeating his alibi. Because Jane had no independent means for determining whether Tim was lying, she had no choice but to let him offer the testimony and let the jury decide. His testimony was necessary to a zealous defense. Choice **A** is not the best answer. Although Tim had a constitutional right to testify, that right did not control Jane's conduct when confronted by his possibly perjurious testimony. Choice **C** is wrong because it begs the issue. Under the prevailing view, Jane must permit the client to testify in his defense even if she believes personally that he may be lying. Choice **D** is wrong for the same reason as **C**. Although obviously helpful to Tim's case, Irma's testimony was not material to Jane's dilemma except to add weight to the wisdom of letting the jury hear all the evidence.

21. **B** These facts raise the issue of a lawyer's dilemma when he discovers that he may have become innocently involved in a client's fraud. To whom does he owe the greatest duty? The client, under the general requirement to protect the client's confidences? The victims of the fraud? Or to himself and his own reputation for integrity. Obviously, there is a tension among these interests which is difficult to resolve. The Model Rules require that a lawyer preserve his client's confidences except in the case of prospective criminal conduct which is likely to result in imminent death or substantial bodily harm. MR 1.6 Comment [12]. But they also recognize that the lawyer may be put in a position which requires protection of his own self-interest. Here, the client and his accountant have used the lawyer to commit a fraud. It's clear that a lawyer may disclose a client's confidence to establish a defense to a criminal charge or a civil claim against him arising from the client's fraud. MR 1.6(b)(2). Reasoning from this principle, the lawyer should be free to disclose a client's fraud in order to forestall or prevent a charge or claim against him. Under these facts, the best answer is **B**. Frank and Stein were faced with a difficult choice, and, so long as they resolved it reasonably and intelligently, they are not subject to criticism. They were entitled in their discretion to consider several factors, including their responsibility to those who would be injured, and, especially, their own involvement in the continuing fraud of their client. When Success refused to reveal the true facts, their best course was to reveal the facts themselves. Choice **A** is wrong under the Model Rules because they were not *required* to reveal the fraud; but they were, in their reasonable discretion, ***permitted*** to do so. Choice **C** is wrong because it is contrary to the best answer. Choice **D** is obviously incorrect. It negates all possible choices, including the best one.

22. **D** Although a lawyer's fee must be reasonable (MR 1.5), contingent fees are expressly permitted except where prohibited by law. The prohibitions against contingencies usually apply to matrimonial and criminal cases. MR 1.5(c). The correct answer is **D,** because none of the listed alternatives applies. A contingent fee is not excessive merely because it is large. Choice **A** is therefore incorrect. Choice **C** is incorrect because it relies on Statements III and IV, both of which are incorrect. Demonio was not required to reduce her fee on Joey's request and was entitled to base her fee on the contingency agreement with Joey. Choice **B** is wrong because Demonio was entitled to sue for her fee. If a jurisdic-

tion requires that lawyer-client fee disputes be resolved by arbitration or mediation, the attorney must submit the dispute to the alternative procedure. In the absence of such a procedure, she may sue to determine and recover her fee. MR 1.5 Comment [5]. It should be noted that contingent fee agreements must almost always be in writing and that the contingency percentages are limited in many jurisdictions. In this case, the agreement was in writing and there is no indication that 33 1/3% was considered excessive in this jurisdiction.

23. C An attorney may reveal client confidences to the extent necessary to resolve a controversy with the client, including a controversy over fees. MR 1.6(b)(2). However, the attorney should limit her disclosures only to the information necessary to prove her claim. The lawsuit must not turn into a threat to "tell all" in an effort to force the client to accede to the lawyer's demands. Here, Demonio's testimony about Joey's drug and alcohol problems was proper to show that she was required to spend more time on the matter than would have been required in the absence of Joey's habit. Choice **A**, which relies on Statement I, is therefore incorrect. **B** (which identifies Statement II) is incorrect because an attorney may sue a client for her fee, although many states compel the use of arbitration or mediation instead. When a suit is permitted, the attorney may initiate it and does not have to wait for action by the client. Choice **D** is incorrect because Choice **C** is correct. Choice **C** is correct because a lawyer may not transfer to her personal use any funds in which the client may have an interest if there is any dispute between them. Instead, the money must continue to be held in the lawyer's client account until the dispute is resolved. MR 1.15(c) Comment [2].

24. A An attorney must maintain a client trust account separate from his own and must deposit and hold in that account all funds in which the client or any third party has any interest MR 1.15(a). The correct answer is **A**. Demonio's actions were quite proper. She paid the undisputed part ($4 million) to Joey and kept the disputed part, untouched, in her client trust account pending resolution of the dispute. This is exactly what was required of her. **B** is incorrect; it states the wrong reason for supporting Demonio's actions. So long as a dispute over fees remains unresolved, it cannot be said with certainty that the fee is rightful. Choice **C** is incorrect because a lawyer must promptly remit to her client any funds belonging to the client over which there is no dispute. MR 1.15(b) Comment [2]. Any other rule would enable the lawyer to hold the client's fund's hostage to the resolution of the dispute between the lawyer and the client. Choice **D** is incorrect for the same reason that **A** is correct.

25. A The states have adopted rules and codes of their own to govern and guide attorneys in the discharge of their duties and responsibilities. The rules and code of each jurisdiction control the conduct of lawyers in that jurisdiction. Many of them are modelled after the Model Rules, but the Model Rules have no independent legislative effect. They serve merely as guides to good practice and professional conduct. MR Preamble and Scope; Model Code Preamble and Preliminary Statement. The correct answer is **A**, because it relies only only Statement I. State rules are binding in state disciplinary proceedings, not the ABA Model Rules of Professional Conduct. Choice **B** is incorrect because it relies on Statement II, which is wrong. There is no general prohibition against suits by lawyers against their clients. In the absence of local requirements for alternative dispute resolution, a lawyer is as free to sue to resolve a dispute as anyone else. Choice **C** is incorrect because it includes Statement II. Choice **D** is incorrect because it relies on Statement III, which misstates the applicable rule. Local disciplinary rules do preempt the Model Rules.

26. C A lawyer must act with reasonable diligence and promptness in representing a client. MR 1.3 Comment [2]. The correct answer is **C**. Even though Charlie ended up with a good settlement, Lexos had an obligation to pursue his matter with diligence from the start. A lawyer cannot take on a client's case and then do nothing for ten months. Lucy will be subject to discipline for unreasonably delaying her work on Charlie's claims. Choice **A** is incorrect because the duty of diligence is not tempered by a successful outcome. Lexos was wrong to ignore Charlie's claim while she pursued Linus' claim. She cannot put one client's needs ahead of another's simply to accommodate her schedule or her own self-interest. It's possible that if she had pursued Charlie's claim sooner, his settlement would have been even larger; furthermore, an earlier recovery would have resulted in interest on the sum recovered and might have supplied Charlie with much-needed funds. Choice **B** is incorrect for the same reasons that **A** is incorrect. The test imposed on a lawyer is not the reasonableness of her results but her own diligence in serving all her clients. Choice **D** is incorrect because it overstates Lexos' obligation. She did not have to complete her preliminary work for Charlie before taking on Linus's case. She simply had to continue to work diligently on Charlie's case while she pursued the Linus matter. If that was impossible, she should either have withdrawn from Charlie's case (if she could do so without unduly prejudicing his rights) or rejected Linus' case.

27. C The facts describe a variety of activities conducted by Judge Thoroughbred. Judges may speak, write, lecture, teach and participate in other extra-judicial activities concerning the law, the legal system and the administration of justice. CJC Canon 4B. They may also appear at public hearings on these same matters. CJC Canon 4C(1). They may also serve as officers or trustees of organizations devoted to the improvement of the law or the judicial system, or, indeed, any charitable or civic organization not conducted for profit. CJC Canon 4C(3). They may even assist in the planning of fund-raising for such an organization and also participate in the management of the organization's funds. CJC Canon 4C(3)(b)(i). However—and this is the dilemma for Judge Thoroughbred—they *are not permitted* to participate in the solicitation of funds or other fund raising activities. The correct answer is therefore **C**. Judge Thoroughbred was permitted all of her activities except the organization's fund drive. Choice **A** is incorrect because it includes the Judge's fund-raising activities. Choice **B** is incorrect because it overstates the scope of the restrictions on the Judge. She was permitted all of her activities except the fund-raising. Choice **D** is incorrect because a Judge is specifically permitted to participate in the management and investment of the funds of a not-for-profit civic organization, but not in soliciting the funds.

28. C A lawyer has an ethical duty not to reveal information related to the representation of a client without the client's consent. MR 1.6 Comment [3]. The Model Rules distinguish between the duty of confidentiality and the attorney-client privilege. MR 1.6 Comment [5]. They suggest that the attorney-client privilege really applies only in the case of judicial and other legal proceedings in which the lawyer is called as a witness or required to produce evidence. The duty of confidentially is more general and applies in all situations, with limited exceptions. The correct answer is **C**, which incorporates Statements II and III. Sammy's communication to his attorney is protected by the evidentiary attorney-client privilege since it was made in the course of an attorney-client relationship and Steadfast may be required to testify. Lanny's communication to Steadfast is covered by the more general duty of confidentiality. It is not covered by the attorney-client privilege because it was not made by the client himself. However, statements which affect the client or are related to the representation and which are made by third parties are protected as confidences (Statement III). MR 1.6 Comment [5]. Choice **A** is incorrect because Lanny's communication to Steadfast is not covered by the attorney-client privilege. Choice **B** is incorrect because it excludes Statement III, which is a necessary part of the correct answer. Choice **D** is incorrect because it includes Statement IV. A lawyer has no duty to withdraw or decline representation even if he is not confident that his client is telling the truth. Sammy was entitled to present his version of the evidence to the court. Under the proper circumstances, a lawyer may withdraw but he would have no *duty* to do so under these facts.

29. B The best answer is **B**. The Model Rules do not address specifically the problem confronted by a lawyer whose political views differ from his client's about an issue on which both have taken positions. But they prohibit a lawyer from representing a client if the lawyer's ability to represent the client will be materially limited by the lawyer's own interests. MR 1.7(b). However, the lawyer may proceed to state his own views if he first obtains the consent of his client after full disclosure. Under these facts, it's fairly clear that Fred will have a difficult time representing his client impartially. He owes the client the duty of making full disclosure of his antagonism to the client's position to enable the client to obtain other counsel if it wishes. Choice **A** is incorrect because it overstates Fred's duty. He doesn't have to hide his views; he must simply disclose them to his client and get his client's consent before stating them publicly. Choice **C** is wrong because it's not sufficient to issue a disclaimer without first consulting your client. Choice **D** is also wrong because it substitutes the lawyer's judgment for the client's, whose views must be respected.

30. C No less an authority than the Supreme Court has spoken on the issue of solicitation of clients by mail. The Model Rules do not prohibit solicitation by mail. They do, however, place a number of restrictions on the practice. A lawyer may not solicit a client who has informed him that he does not wish to be solicited. MR 7.3(b)(1). The solicitation must not involve coercion, duress or harassment. MR 7.3(b)(2). The outside envelope must contain the words "Advertising Material." MR 7.3(c). All attempts to restrict solicitation by mail have been met by the argument that they violate the right of a lawyer to freedom of speech. The issue has been the subject of two major Supreme Court decisions. In *Shapero v. Kentucky Bar Association,* 486 U.S. 466 (1988), the Court held that the states could not impose blanket restrictions on solicitation of prospective clients by mail. The Model Rules were amended to conform to this decision. In *Florida Bar v. Went For It, Inc.,* 515 U.S. 618 (1995), the Court modified its stand by upholding a Florida rule which prohibited lawyers from directing mail to accident victims and their families for thirty days following an accident. Over time, the issue will arise in other circumstances. In the recent case of *Ficker v. Curran,* 119 F.3d 1150 (4th Cir. 1997), the 4th Circuit Court of Appeals held that the 30-day moratorium was invalid when applied to solicitation by mail of criminal defendants. In construing a Maryland statute, the court held that solicitation of criminal defendants was fundamentally different from solicitation of personal-injury plaintiffs because criminal defendants need help and counseling in a greater hurry. The correct answer is therefore **C**. Flaunty is not subject to discipline for either letter. In the absence of a rule like the Florida rule, solicitation by mail is permitted so long as the envelope indicates that the contents are advertising material. No distinction is made in the Model Rules between criminal defendants and personal-injury plaintiffs. Choice **D** is wrong because it relies on the opposite of **C**. Choices **A** and **B** are wrong because each depends on only one of the two correct choices.

31. A A lawyer may not communicate ex parte with a juror or prospective juror. MR 3.5(b). This applies to all lawyers, whether or not they are involved in the matter. The correct answer is **A**. Helen's brother will be subject to discipline because he knows that Helen is a juror. He is not permitted to discuss the case with her at all, let alone advise her on the law. Only the judge is permitted to control the flow of information and instruction about the law to jurors. **B** is incorrect because the prohibition against juror contact is mandatory, not aspirational. "A lawyer shall not...communicate ex parte with [a judge, juror, prospective juror or other official] except as permitted by law." MR 3.5(b). The need to control the jury's access to law and fact is too critical to the judicial process. **C** is incorrect because the attorney-client privilege is not applicable to these facts. Helen and her brother did not have an attorney-client relationship, and, in any event, the relationship is not an umbrella under which a juror may hide or an attorney take refuge. **D** is incorrect because it misstates the rule. All lawyers must refrain from communicating with a member of a jury during the trial concerning the case, including lawyers who are not connected with it.

32. D A judge may receive compensation and reimbursement of expenses for extra-judicial activities such as a public speech on issues of court reform, provided the source of the payments does not raise the appearance of impropriety. CJC Canon 4H(1). The correct answer is **D**, which includes Statements III and IV, both of which are correct. A judge may be reimbursed for ***his actual expenses*** for items such as travel, food and lodging. CJC Canon 4H(1)(b). He must report the date, place and nature of the activity for which he received reimbursement, plus the name of the payor and the amount reimbursed. A judge must make his report at least annually in a public document which he files with the clerk of the court on which he serves. CJC Canon 4H(2). Choice **A** is incorrect because Statement I is incorrect. A judge need not decline compensation so long as it falls within the limits of CJC Canon 4H. CJC Canon 4H commentary. Choice **B** is incorrect because, although it relies on Statement III, it also relies on Statement I, which is, as we have seen, wrong. Choice **C** is wrong because it depends in part on Statement II, which is wrong. A judge may accept a speaker's fee on two conditions: (a) it must be reasonable; (b) it must not exceed the amount *which a person who is* **not** *a judge would receive.* In other words, whether a fee is proper is measured not by what another judge would receive, but what a person *not a judge* would receive. The rationale is that a contrary rule might present a temptation to judges to collude on higher fees than would be available to the public at large.

33. **B** A lawyer with unprivileged knowledge of another attorney's misconduct which raises a substantial question as to his honesty or fitness as a lawyer, is under a duty to report the conduct to the appropriate professional authority. MR 8.3(a). A lawyer is guilty of misconduct if he engages in conduct involving dishonesty, fraud, deceit, or misrepresentation. MR 8.4(c). Johnson violated the rules of professional conduct when he defrauded McNamara in the sale of the painting. Attorney Heller has an obligation to report the fraud to the appropriate attorney disciplinary tribunal. The question raises two important issues: (i) is a lawyer subject to discipline for misconduct unrelated to the practice of law; and (ii) does a lawyer possessing both privileged and unprivileged knowledge of another lawyer's misconduct have a duty to disclose that portion of the information which is unprivileged. The answer to both questions is yes. Johnson is subject to discipline for his fraud, even though the fraud was not related to his law practice. And Heller must disclose the fraud, even though, as we shall see, his knowledge of Johnson's addiction to alcohol was privileged. The correct answer is **B**, which relies only on Statement II. **A** (Statement I) is incorrect because an attorney is not prohibited from owning and participating in other businesses; he must, however, be careful to avoid using the other business either for solicitation of clients or for fee-splitting with non-lawyers. Here, there is nothing to indicate that Johnson failed to keep the businesses separate. **C** and **D** are both incorrect because they rely at least in part on Statement III, which incorrectly states the applicable rule. Under certain circumstances, a lawyer's knowledge of another lawyer's misconduct is privileged and may not be disclosed even to the disciplinary authorities. Heller was counselling Johnson in his capacity as chairman of the county lawyer

assistance program. The information imparted to him by Johnson is therefore privileged to the same extent as if it were communicated subject to the attorney-client privilege. MR 8.3(c).

34. C The best answer is **C**. The requirements of disclosure concerning an applicant for the bar are as extensive and severe as for a practitioner. The rationale is the desire to prevent participation in the profession by persons who are ethically and morally unqualified and who are likely to cause problems after admission. MR 8.1 Comment [1]. Choice **B** is incorrect. Hannah's cheating on an exam was a serious enough infraction to require disclosure, even though there may have been extenuating circumstances and even if Tombs personally believes the conduct will not be repeated. Choice **D** is incorrect because Tombs could not unilaterally decide to withhold the facts about Hannah's cheating; nor could he elect not to answer the inquiry at all. He has an affirmative duty to respond and may be subject to discipline himself if he doesn't. MR 8.1(b). Choice **C** is correct because it satisfies Tombs' duty to disclose but recognizes also that he may express his own opinion about Hannah's problems, her redemption and her commitment to integrity.

35. B An attorney is often forced to pick her way through two conflicting rules. On the one hand, she must not knowingly make a false statement of material fact in connection with a bar admissions application. MR 8.1(a). On the other, she may not disclose a confidence relating to or arising from her representation of a client without the client's consent after consultation. MR 1.6(a). Tess is faced with exactly that dilemma under these facts. Fortunately the Model Rules have resolved the conflict for her. She must elect to protect the Abner confidences. She can accomplish this only by withholding all information about Abner because she acquired it during the course of her representation of him. The correct answer is Choice **B**, which depends on Statement II. "...A lawyer may be obligated or permitted by other provisions of law to give information about a client. Whether another provision of law supersedes Rule 1.6 is a matter of interpretation beyond the scope of these Rules, but a presumption should exist against such supersession." MR 1.6, Comment [21]. Choice **A** is wrong because it depends on Statement I. Under the Model Rules, Tess would be barred from disclosing her knowledge of Abner's misdeeds. Choice **C** is wrong because Tess may not make herself the judge of Abner's deeds or competence. That task is left for the proper authorities. Choice **D** is wrong because it depends on Statement III, but, also, on Statement IV, which is wrong. Tess has no obligation to conduct her own investigation of the facts concerning Abner's qualifications.

MULTIPLE-CHOICE ANSWERS

36. B When an attorney receives funds that belong in part to his client, he must deposit the entire amount in his client trust account before making any disbursements. MR 1.15. The attorney must then promptly notify the client that he has received funds on her behalf and remit those funds to the client. In addition, as soon as it is clear that there is no dispute as to fees and advances, he must promptly withdraw the money due him from the client trust account to avoid commingling his funds with those of his clients. The correct answer is **B**. Russell must first deposit the entire $2,000 in his client trust account. Shortly thereafter, he must deliver to Val her portion of the funds, together with "a written statement stating the outcome of the matter, and, if there is a recovery, showing the remittance to the client and the method of its determination." MR 1.5(c). If there is no dispute as to his calculations, he must withdraw the money due him and deposit it in his own account. The correct answer is **B**. **A** is incorrect. Separate checks would put some of the settlement funds out of the client's reach and make the resolution of fee disputes more difficult. The entire settlement must first be deposited in the lawyer's trust account. **C** is incorrect. MR 1.5 requires that the lawyer send the client a written statement showing how the distribution between lawyer and client was calculated. **D** is incorrect because Russell must not deposit the check into his personal account. This would be an impermissible commingling of funds.

37. B During a trial, a lawyer may become aware that either his client or a crucial witness has committed perjury. His duty then is to "remonstrate with *the client* confidentially." MR 3.3(a)(4) Comment [11]. Although that language is not further amplified in the Comment, the intent is that the attorney shall immediately attempt to negate the effect of the perjury with the cooperation of the client. If that fails, the lawyer shall "seek to withdraw" if that will remedy the matter. If withdrawal will not remedy the situation "or is impossible", the lawyer must make disclosure to the court. The court will then decide what should be done. Choice **B** is the best answer. Choice **A** may appear to be the best answer, but Comment [11] clearly places a burden on the attorney to attempt remedial steps with the help of his client before consulting the judge. Choice **C** is incorrect. An attorney cannot ignore the commission of perjury. He must take steps to remedy the matter. Choice **D** is also wrong. The attorney has no obligation to a witness who commits perjury; his obligation is only to the client and the court.

38. A The lawyer must always remember that in most matters not related to tactics, the power of decision rests with the client. This is especially true in instances of settlement offers in civil matters. The lawyer has an affirmative duty to submit all ***bona fide*** settlement offers to the client for her decision. MR 1.2. In this case, the client is the guardian ad litem appointed by the court to pursue Penny's claim. The correct answer is **A**. Choice **B** is wrong because Willie does not have the right to substitute his judgment for the client's. He must communicate the offer of settlement and abide by the client's decision. Choice **D** is wrong for the same reason as **B**. It implies that the lawyer's judgment is the correct judgment. The lawyer is certainly empowered to discuss the merits of a proposed settlement with the client and to advise against it, but he must ultimately defer to the client's wishes. Choice **C** is wrong because it puts the cart before the horse. In settlement offers involving infants, it may well be necessary to obtain the consent of the court before consummating the settlement, but the application to the court must be made by the gaurdian ad liem *after* the guardian has been told of the offer and has determined that it justifies an application to the court.

39. C In the course of representing a client, a lawyer will often be exposed to information and disclosures which may tempt the lawyer to exploit the circumstances for his own benefit. Under the Model Rules, he must not use this information to the client's disadvantage. The facts recited here are almost exactly those covered by the Rule. MR 1.8(b) Comment [1]. Snelling learned from James confidentially that James intended to buy the adjoining lot as part of his shopping center. Snelling hoped to benefit by inflating the price of the lot; this was certainly to James' disadvantage and a clear misuse of his trust. Choice **C** is the correct answer. Choice **A** is incorrect. The prohibition against misuse of the client's confidence is absolute; it's immaterial that Snelling paid a fair price. Choice **B** is wrong because the language of the MR 1.8(b) is clearly compulsory and not aspirational (the Rule begins "A lawyer shall not..."). Choice **D** is incorrect. Snelling's conduct is not excused because James may have a remedy for damages. The Rules do not substitute remedy for propriety.

40. D Contingent fee agreements are permissible in most civil cases. Most states have enacted rules or statutes controlling these agreements. Generally, the attorney who gambles on a contingency is not entitled to his fees unless and until the client obtains a recovery. MR 1.5(c). The attorney assumes the risk that there will be no recovery—and thus no fee. Dewey took Client's case knowing that his fees were contingent on a successful outcome. When Client exercised her absolute and unilateral right to discharge Dewey (MR 1.16(a)(3) Comment [4]), control of the case passed to Anne Howe and Dewey remained subject to the contingency. Choice C is wrong for the reasons cited. Dewey was never entitled to any compensation unless there was recovery. Choice A is wrong; Dewey is not entitled to any measure of compensation except the measure anticipated and provided for in the contingency agreement. Choice B would be the correct answer in the absence of a provision in the contingency agreement providing for reimbursement to Dewey of his advances for court costs and expenses. Because the facts tell us that the agreement between Dewey and Client did provide for reimbursement of expenses and Dewey had advanced $750 in the Client's behalf, Choice B is wrong and Choice D is the correct answer. MR 1.8(e)(1).

41. A The facts tell us that Sharp has information obtained in confidence during her prior representation of Retail and that her representation of Jones will require her to use this information in a suit adverse to Retail. Under these circumstances, she may not accept the representation of Jones unless she first obtains Retail's consent "after consultation". MR 1.9(a), (c)(1). The correct answer is A. B is incorrect because there is no requirement that Sharp obtain the consent of her new client. Under these facts, however, it would be prudent for Sharp to inform Jones of her prior representation of Retail and of her possession of confidential information from Retail. Jones may not wish to retain Sharp after he learns of her prior relationship with Retail, and he is entitled to information necessary for "an informed decision" MR 1.4(b). (See also MR 1.16(a)(1) Comment [1].) Choice C is incorrect because, as we have seen, there is no requirement that Sharp obtain the consent of Jones. Choice D is incorrect because Sharp can accept the case if she obtains the prior consent of Retail.

42. B The only reference to the reimbursement or compensation of expert witnesses in the Rules is in Model Rule 3.4(b), which prohibits a lawyer from offering an inducement to a witness "that is prohibited by law." Comment [3] to this provision tells us that it is not improper to pay a "witness's expenses" or to compensate an expert witness on terms permitted by law. The comment also tells us that the common law prohibits the payment of contingent fees to expert witnesses. The best answer is Choice B, which incorporates Statements I and II. In most jurisdictions, Landon would be permitted to advance Dr. Swift's reasonable expenses as well as pay him a reasonable fee for his preparation and appearance. Choice A is not the best answer because it excludes Statement II. Choice **C** is not the best answer because, as we have seen, the compensation of an expert witness may not be contingent upon the outcome of the trial. Choice **D** is incorrect because it implies a lack of flexibility on the part of Landon in negotiating a reasonable fee for Swift's appearance. Dr. Swift's regular hourly fees may not be reasonable under the circumstances.

43. C The activities of a judge who campaigns for reelection are circumscribed by Canon 5 of the Code of Judicial Conduct. Judge Yearly is permitted to identify himself as a member of a political party (CJC Canon 5C(1)(a)(ii)) and to speak to gatherings on his own behalf (CJC Canon 5C(1)(b)(i)). However, he is not permitted to solicit funds in his own behalf. CJC Canon 5C(2). Also, he may not attend political gatherings at which he is not scheduled to speak in his own behalf. CJC Canon 5A(1)(d). As a candidate for the same judgeship as Yearly, Lawyer Ambitious is subject to the same limitations. MR 8.2(b). "When a lawyer seeks judicial office, the lawyer shall be bound by applicable limitations on judicial activity." Comment [2]. The correct answer is therefore **C**, which depends on Statements II and III. Choice **A** is wrong because Statements I and IV are wrong. A candidate for election to judicial office may not indiscriminately attend all political gatherings. And he may not solicit funds himself, even in his own campaign. Choice **B** is wrong because it identifies only Statement II, instead of both II and III. Choice **D** is wrong because it includes Statements I and IV, both of which are wrong.

44. C A lawyer must not charge or collect an unreasonable, illegal, or clearly excessive fee. MR 1.5(a). While it is prudent to put all fee agreements in writing, an attorney will not be subject to discipline for failing to do so unless the fee agreement is a contingent one. MR 1.5(c). Rule 1.5 sets forth specific criteria which help determine whether a fee is reasonable. One of these is the relative experience and ability of the lawyer. Another is the fee customarily charged in the locality for similar legal services. MR 1.5(a). Here, Melville was relatively inexperienced and nevertheless charged a fee in excess of the fee customarily charged by more experienced lawyers in the area. If anything, he should have asked for a fee less than $350 an hour. In addition, he sent an invoice for an amount larger than he had agreed to charge. He is subject to discipline for all the reasons set forth in Statements II, III and IV. The correct answer is therefore Choice **C**. Choice **A** is wrong because it relies only on Statement I. An agreement concerning services and fees need not be in writing unless it involves a contingent fee. Choice **B** is wrong because it depends in part on Statement I. Choice **D** is wrong because it relies only on Statement II.

45. D A lawyer must not by in-person contact solicit employment from persons who have no relationship to him either as relative or client. A lawyer who gives in-person, unsolicited advice to a layperson about obtaining counsel or taking legal action may accept representation from that person only if he is a relative or former client. MR 7.3(a). Attorney Smart, who visits Ted at the hospital and offers him legal advice after his automobile accident, is not subject to discipline if he accepts Ted's case because Ted is a member of his family. The situation falls within one of the exceptions to the rule against in-person solicitation. Another exception is supplied by clients and former clients, who obviously have a degree of relationship with the attorney which justifies contact without fear of abuse. Choice **D** is therefore the correct answer because it relies on Statements II and IV. Choice **A** is incorrect because Mack is not subject to discipline for improper solicitation on these facts. Choice **B** is wrong because it depends in part on Statement III, which is too broad. It is not necessary that the person solicited be a member of the immediate family, only that he be a member of "the family"; an uncle would certainly qualify. Choice **C** is wrong because it includes Statement III.

46. A The Model Rules contain a number of provisions which are intended to prevent any arrangements between lawyers and non-lawyers that have the potential for reducing the lawyer's professional independence. A lawyer may not form a partnership with a non-lawyer if any of the activities of the partnership consist of the practice of law. MR 5.4(b). "A lawyer shall not permit a person who recommends...the lawyer to render legal services for another to direct or regulate the lawyer's professional judgment..." MR 5.4(c). "A lawyer shall not give anything of value to a person for recommending the lawyer's services..." MR 7.2(c). The arrangement suggested by Flint clearly violates the spirit if not the letter of these rules. Because the relationship between Flint and Lester would be a continuing one and because the fine line between legal and accounting problems would be hard to draw, we have something that looks and feels very much like a partnership to practice law. Also, although the facts do not suggest that Flint was agreeing to pay a referral fee, there is an implicit benefit to Lester by availing his clients of Flint's reduced legal fees. The best answer is **A**. Choice **B** is wrong because there is nothing inherently wrong with a reduced legal fee. Choice **C** is wrong because the totality of the circumstances is disciplinable even without a specific agreement to pay a referral fee to Lester. Choice **D** is wrong because the disclosure of the relationship would not cure the basic vice that Flint was proposing a continuing referral commitment from a non-lawyer.

47. B The principal restrictions on the freedom of lawyers to disseminate information about themselves or to take public positions apply either in the course of a trial in which the lawyer is involved or in controls over his advertising of his services. While a lawyer is participating in litigation, he may not make extra-judicial statements if he knows or should know that his statements will have a substantial likelihood of influencing the proceeding. MR 3.6(a). The controls over advertising prevent the dissemination of false or misleading statements about the lawyer's services and control the means of advertising. MR 7.1 and 7.2. Nothing prevents a lawyer from participating in the exchange of ideas about the legal system or from writing or commenting about legal reforms or about society in general. All of the activities described in these facts constitute proper activities for Splendid, and Choice **B** is therefore the correct answer. Splendid may not have been able to speak to the convention of women on the issue of rape while the trial of the rapist was in progress for fear of jeapordizing his client's interests, but that question has been eliminated by the completion of the trial. Choice **A** is incorrect because it does not include Statement III. Choices **C** and **D** are wrong because they both exclude one or both of the correct Statements.

48. D Only a lawyer is entitled to practice the profession of law. It is therefore necessary to define the term "law" and to prevent non-lawyers from engaging in the practice. To complete the circle of controls, it's also necessary to instruct lawyers not to assist in the practice of law by non-lawyers. The Model Rules recognize that it's not always easy to define the practice of law: "The definition of the practice of law is established by law and varies from one jurisdiction to another. Whatever the definition, limiting the practice of law to members of the bar protects the public against rendition of legal services by unqualified persons." MR 5.5 Comment [1]. These facts present four different circumstances in which Hanson is asked to decide whether the practice of law is at issue. In the case of the friend who is drafting his own will, the definition is not infringed. However unwisely, the friend is only representing himself and the Rules permit a lawyer to counsel a non-lawyer who wishes to proceed *pro se*. MR 5.5 Comment [1]. In the case of the friend who is drafting a will for his uncle, we are presented with an activity which clearly falls within the traditional definition of the practice of law.

Hanson is not permitted to advise this friend. She is also wrong to assist the real estate broker in any way in the preparation of a real estate sales contract. While it is true that in some jurisdictions, real estate brokers do as a matter of practice prepare simple real estate contracts (in a few jurisdictions they are even permitted to do so), more generally, the preparation of real estate contracts falls within the definition of the practice of law and is restricted to lawyers. Hanson may advise the friend who intends to appear in small claims court because, here again, we have a *pro se* activity. The correct answer is **D**, because it relies on Statements I and IV. Choice **A** is wrong because it includes Statement II. Choice **B** is wrong because it includes Statement III, which is wrong. Choice **C** is wrong because it relies on Statement III, which is also wrong.

49. B An attorney is expected to take all reasonable and lawful steps available to him to "vindicate a client's cause or endeavor." MR 1.3 Comment [1]. On these facts, Sturdy may properly contact the local district attorney and request criminal action against Rough and Ready, which is described as committing many illegal collection practices. He may also advise Rough and Ready that he is about to file a civil complaint. His letter may serve to resolve the matter without litigation—an objective all lawyers are well advised to encourage. But Sturdy is probably not permitted to threaten the initiation of criminal charges in an effort to resolve Harry's civil complaint or to obtain an advantage over Rough and Ready. (The Model Code of Professional Responsibility specifically prohibited threats of criminal complaints to secure advantage in a civil matter. While there is no comparable provision in the Model Rules, the threat of criminal action to seek advantage in resolving a civil complaint continues to be frowned upon.) The threat of criminal complaint for civil advantage falls under the definition of the crime of extortion or coercion in some jurisdictions. In these jurisdictions, Sturdy may be committing a crime himself by threatening the criminal complaint. In that case, he will run afoul of Model Rules 8.4(b) and (d) (prohibiting conduct in violation of the Model Rules and the commission of criminal acts) and will be subject to discipline. The correct answer is Choice **B**, which relies on Statements I and II. Choice **A** is wrong because it identifies only Statement I. Choice **C** is wrong because it identifies only Statement II. Choice **D** is incorrect because it includes Statement III, which is wrong.

50. C A lawyer is often confronted with a dispute or disagreement between two persons with a common interest who are either his friends or clients, e.g., a husband and wife, or two partners in a commercial enterprise. He may be asked to use his good offices to resolve the dispute. In these circumstances, he is acting as intermediary. This role is proper so long as he can act as mediator and not as advocate for either party. MR 2.2 Comment [1]. The facts here tell us that Santori received the written authorization of both Jack and Jill to act as intermediary. Statement I is therefore not a basis for discipline. However, if during the course of the mediation, it becomes apparent that the differences between the parties cannot be resolved and that their interests have diverged, the attorney must withdraw and may not thereafter represent either party. MR 2.2(c) Comment [10]. Santori acted improperly in representing Jill once the efforts at mediation failed and the parties decided to litigate. He was also wrong to enter into a contingency agreement with Jill. Contingency agreements are not permitted in matrimonial matters. Society has no interest in promoting litigation between marriage partners. MR 1.5(d)(1). Under the circumstances described here, Santori did not act improperly when he discontinued his efforts at mediation. On the contrary, he was required to discontinue his efforts and to withdraw when it became clear the dispute between Jack and Jill could not be resolved and that each required separate counsel. The correct answer is **C**, which relies on Statements II and III. Choice **A** is wrong because it depends on Statement I, which is wrong. Choice **B** is wrong because it relies in part on Statement I. Choice **D** is wrong because it relies in part on Statement IV, which is wrong.

51. C The prime duty of a lawyer is to represent his client zealously and with reasonable diligence. MR 1.3. This duty carries with it the responsibility to present those arguments or positions which are most advantageous to the client's interests. If a lawyer has two clients whose interests do not conflict but who require inconsistent positions, he may take those positions under most circumstances. MR 1.7 Comment [9]. "Thus, it is ordinarily not improper to assert such [antagonistic] positions in cases pending in different trial courts, but it may be improper to do so in cases pending at the same time in an appellate court". The correct answer is **C**. Douglas is making his constitutional argument in each case on the trial court level. Whatever the decision of either judge, the constitutional issue will not be resolved finally at this level and Douglas has a duty to present the best arguments available to each client. The opposite rule would result either in the preference of one client over another or in the enforced withdrawal of Douglas from one or both of the matters. The correct answer is **C**. **A** is incorrect because a lawyer is permitted to argue contradictory positions on the same issue at the trial level so long as the interest of any client is not jeopardized. Choice **B** is incorrect for the same reason as **A**. A lawyer may be of record at the same time in two cases involving inconsistent theories. Choice **D** is incorrect. Douglas is not required to inform either judge that he has argued an inconsistent position in another, unrelated case.

52. B Provided the client is informed of the payment and consents to the arrangement, an attorney's fee may be paid by a third person. However, the attorney must ensure that her duty of loyalty to the client is not impaired. MR 1.7(b) Comment [10]. See also MR 1.8(f) Comment [4]. Tammy can take the case only if she gets David's informed consent to the payment of fees by his father and only if she genuinely believes that her representation of David will not be prejudiced by his father's interference. The correct answer is **B**. The fact that David's father is an attorney may make it more difficult for Tammy to maintain her independent judgment, but her duty to David includes her insistence on exercising her own judgment whenever it conflicts with the father's. Choice **C** is incorrect because it implies that Tammy must consult with David's father whenever she is confronted with a decision. This is not her duty, although she may, of course, listen to his recommendations and consider them in forming her own conclusion. Choice **A** is wrong because Tammy must at least undertake the representation and attempt to keep the father at a reasonable distance. Otherwise, David could not get independent representation from anyone. Choice **D** is wrong on the law. A third party may pay the lawyer's fees provided the lawyer's loyalties are not diverted from the client.

53. D The Model Rules do not prohibit advertising by lawyers on either radio or television, provided the message is neither false nor misleading, MR 7.1, 7.2(a) and provided that a copy of the message and a record of the medium used are kept for at least two years after the broadcast. Other media than radio and television are also permitted. There is no prohibition against the frequency of advertising. Statement I is therefore not a basis for disciplining Friendly. However, Friendly is subject to discipline in most jurisdictions for insisting that his clients agree in advance to waive any claims for malpractice. MR 1.8(h). (Note that this Rule does permit a waiver if permitted in the applicable jurisdiction and if the client is "independently represented in making the agreement".) Statement II therefore does state a basis for disciplining Friendly. Statement III does not state a disciplinable offense. A lawyer may charge fees lower than the local standard. A fee need only be reasonable. MR 1.5(a). Statement IV also does not state a disciplinable offense. Nothing in the Model Rules requires that a lawyer maintain malpractice insurance. However, a prudent lawyer will consult his local statutes and rules and his own sense of potential risk before deciding not to carry insurance. The correct answer is therefore **D**, which is the only answer that relies on Statement II. Choice **A** is wrong because it relies in part on Statement I. Choice **B** is wrong because it relies on two wrong Statements — I and III. Choice **C** is wrong because it relies on Statements I and IV.

54. B The Model Rules contain many provisions which are designed to insure that a client will be represented zealously and fairly by a lawyer who is not influenced by actual or potential conflicts of interest. Obviously when two lawyers who are closely related represent two separate clients with adverse interests, there is a potential for conflict. We may properly assume that a sister will be influenced as much by her affection for her sister as by her interest in protecting the client. Karen is subject to discipline for accepting the representation of Sharon when her sister was the prosecutor in the same matter. MR 1.8(i). The correct answer is **B**. Here, although Attorney Karen informed Sharon of the potential conflict, she did not ask for Sharon's consent to proceed "after consultation regarding the relationship." On the contrary, she attempted to deflect Sharon's concerns by assuring her that her defense would not be affected and that she no longer had any contact with her sister. This makes Choice **C** wrong. Choice **A** is wrong because Karen's belief is not important. The prohibition is objective and inflexible, not subjective. Choice **D** is wrong; the lack of contact between Karen and Marion is not controlling; their relationship as sisters is.

55. C The regulation of lawyers begins with the process by which they are tested in bar examinations and subjected to scrutiny by the bar examiners. This process is conducted on a state-by-state basis. The preservation of the admission process is vital to the administration of the law and of lawyers. For this reason, a lawyer is not permitted to practice in a state in which he has not been admitted. MR 5.5(a). In our complex and fluid society, it's not always easy to determine when a lawyer has crossed the line into another state. This dilemma may be especially relevant to general counsel for corporations or businesses with offices and interests in many states. But one prohibition is clear—a lawyer may not appear in a matter pending before a court in a state in which he is not admitted without petitioning for leave *pro hac vice* in accordance with the rules prevailing in that court. Ben should not have appeared for Bigtown in a court in State Delta, nor should he have argued before the court. However, only the state of Alpha in which Ben is admitted can subject him to disciplinary proceedings as an attorney. MR 8.5(a). He may have violated a criminal or disciplinary statute in

Delta, but he will be disciplined there not as an attorney but as any citizen who violates a local rule. However, the court in Delta may refer the matter to the disciplinary authority in Alpha. The correct answer is Choice **C**, which identifies only Statement II. Choice **A** is wrong because it identifies only Statement I and Ben is not subject to discipline in Delta. Choice **B** is wrong because it relies in part on Statement I. Choice **D** is wrong because it depends on Statement III, which is wrong. To adopt this statement would be to create a nation-wide system of licensing in the practice of law. This is not presently the American system.

56. B An attorney who serves as general counsel to an organization such as a large corporation sometimes has a difficult problem determining where his loyalties lie. This is not because the rules are not clear. On the contrary the Model Rules state quite clearly that the lawyer's sole duty is to "the organization...through its duly authorized constituents". MR 1.13(a).) But as the attorney acquires friendships and relationships with individual constituents of the organization, the line between loyalty to these constituents and duty to the organization can become obscured. The Rules make it clear that if the attorney becomes aware of an action by a constituent which is likely to result in injury to the organization, he shall proceed "as is reasonably necessary to the best interests of the organization." Here, Jerry was confronted by a set of facts disclosed by Dean, an executive of Franco, which would certainly work to the harm of Franco. His duty was to disclose these facts to Dean's superior. Choice **A** is therefore incorrect. Jerry did not have an obligation of confidentiality to Dean. Dean was not his client and the disclosures by Dean were not made in Dean's organizational capacity. MR 1.13 Comment [3]. (If they had been made in that capacity, they would have been protected as confidences under MR 1.6.) However, Jerry did have an obligation to advise Dean that he was making disclosures which were harmful to his own interests, that he should retain independent counsel and that his disclosures would not be privileged. He owed this duty to Dean not because Dean was his friend but because he was a constituent of Franco. MR 1.13 Comment [8]. The best answer is Choice **B**. Choice **C** is wrong because Jerry had another obligation than his obligation to Franco. He had an obligation to Dean as described above. Choice **D** is wrong because the fact that Dean was his good friend is immaterial to the basis on which Jerry's decision must be made.

57. **A** However abrupt and arbitrary the decision, an attorney must withdraw when discharged by her client. MR 1.16(a)(3) Comment [4]. The correct answer is **A**. The rule leaves no room for discretion. Even if Mary's discharge was wrongful, it was improper for her to continue performing any legal services on behalf of the Rancheros, however beneficial to the ballplayers, after she was told she was discharged. But nothing in the rules prevents her from protecting her own interests and she was perfectly within her rights to file suit for wrongful discharge. Choice **B** is therefore incorrect. Choice **C** is incorrect because it suggests that the discharged attorney can exercise her own judgment and discretion whether to accept the discharge. This is not the case; the client's decision can be arbitrary. The same reasoning makes Choice **D** incorrect. The place for Mary to test the reasonableness of her discharge was in the courts or administrative agencies, not in the offices of the Rancheros.

58. **B** In his responsibility to uphold the judicial system, a lawyer who engages in litigation must maintain his candor to the tribunal. MR 3.3. When his case turns on an issue of law, he must not fail to disclose legal authority which is adverse to his client's position. However, he is required to disclose only those cases "in the controlling jurisdiction" not disclosed by opposing counsel. MR 3.3(a)(3) Comment [3]. This does not mean, of course, that he cannot argue against or distinguish the adverse authority. On the contrary, he has a duty to do so if reasonable arguments are available. ABA Formal Opinion 146 (July 17, 1935.) On these facts, Sourseed had an obligation to disclose the adverse decision by Alpha's highest court (as well as the decision in the lower court of Alpha, unless the supreme court case considered and disposed of the lower court case). Choice **B** is therefore the correct answer. Choice **C** is wrong because Sourseed is not required to cite a decision from another state. Choice **D** is wrong because it includes Choice **B**. Choice **A** is wrong under most circumstances because the facts state the federal decision was by a federal court in another (therefore non-controlling) jurisdiction. However, if the decision in that court were on a federal or constitutional issue central and adverse to Roccocco's appeal, Sourseed would be required to disclose the federal decision.

59. **D** Lawyers must be careful not to inject their personal opinions about the culpability of a civil litigant or the guilt or innocence of an accused. The line between personal opinion and fair comment is often an elusive one, especially in closing arguments after a long and bitter criminal trial, but the duty is clear. MR 3.4(e). Further, a lawyer must not

engage in conduct which is intended to disrupt the tribunal. MR 3.5(c) Comment [2]. Here, Washington's characterization of Brutum as a "rabid rapist" and a "brute" and his use of the term "savage criminal" clearly crossed the line into forbidden and disciplinable territory. The correct answer is **D**. Washington's sensational language was not a fair comment on the evidence but a statement of his personal opinion intended to inflame the jury and disrupt the trial. Choice **A** is wrong because Washington is subject to discipline regardless of the outcome. Choice **B** is wrong. The failure of opposing counsel to object or of the court to intercede does not excuse Washington's conduct, which must be measured on its own terms. Choice **C** is wrong because Washington's beliefs only serve to confirm the inappropriateness of his remarks. Obviously, his beliefs lead to his personal opinions, and these are exactly the matters he is not permitted to express.

60. D Model Rule 3.6, which deals with trial publicity, was amended in 1994 in response to a decision by the Supreme Court which compelled greater regard for freedom of expression than was expressed in the previous Rule (*See, Gentile v. State Bar of Nevada*, 501 U.S. 1030 (1991)). In its present form, MR 3.6 contains a general prohibition against extrajudicial statements which have a substantial likelihood of materially prejudicing a trial. MR 3.6(a). It goes on to list 7 categories of statements which are permissible. MR 3.6(b)(1)-(7). The categories applicable to criminal cases include: the identity and occupation of the accused, the fact, time and place of the arrest, the length of the investigation, and the identities of investigating and arresting officers. The Comments to the Rule discuss the difficulty inherent in striking a balance between free expression and a fair trial. They go on to list several subjects which are essentially forbidden territory. These include (Comment [5]): the character or criminal record of a suspect in a criminal investigation; in a criminal case, the possibility of a plea of guilty or the contents of a confession; the prosecutor's opinion as to the guilt or innocence of the defendant; the fact that defendant has been charged with a crime, unless the disclosure is accompanied by a statement explaining that the charge is merely an accusation and that the defendant is assumed innocent until proven guilty. Here, Philips has clearly violated all these injunctions and has also expressed his own inflammatory opinion. Statements I, II and III all apply. The correct answer is therefore Choice **D**. Choices **A**, **B** and **C** are all incorrect because they include one or another of the three Statements.

61. A A prosecutor is often under pressure, especially in high-profile cases, to make public statements to the press. While he is free to do so in recognition of his right to freedom of expression (Statement III), his remarks to the press are governed by the provisions of Model Rule 3.6, entitled "Trial Publicity."" This lists in detail matters which the prosecutor may discuss and matters which he is not permitted to discuss. The general purpose of both is to prevent the spread of inflammatory press accounts which will make it difficult to select an impartial jury and to give the defendant a fair trial. The prosecutor may, for example, request the assistance of the public in obtaining evidence (Statement II). MR 3.6(b)(5). But he may not discuss the evidence against the accused. To permit him to do so would obviously work to subvert the jury's ability to hear the evidence for the first time under the protection of the rules of evidence and the guidance of the court. MR 3.6 Comment [5]. Statement I is therefore a basis upon which to discipline Philips. The correct answer is Choice **A**. Philips is subject to discipline under Statement I, but not under Statements II and III. A prosecutor is free to make a public statement announcing an arrest and he is also free to ask for the public's help in reporting new evidence about the crimes. Choice **B** is wrong because it relies on Statement II. Choice **C** is wrong because it relies on Statements II and III. Choice **D** is wrong because it fails to recognize that Statement I is a basis for discipline.

62. C In the present American climate in which media rights concerning the rich and famous are accorded enormous commercial value, there is an inevitable urge on the part of anyone who becomes associated with a public figure to "cash in" on the association. The temptation for a lawyer arises when he is asked to represent the defendant in a criminal matter which will receive wide press coverage and is almost certain to result in a book or movie. Anticipating this temptation, the Model Rules specifically reject any agreement between a lawyer and his client which gives the lawyer "literary or media rights to a portrayal or account based in substantial part on information relating to the representation." MR 1.8(d). Comment [3] tells us that the basis for this rule is the conflict between the interests of the client and the interests of the lawyer, e.g., the lawyer may wish to prolong and inflame the trial in order to increase the value of his media rights. The specific prohibition against the acquisition of media rights is in keeping with the general provisions of Model Rule 1.8, which state that a lawyer shall not enter into a business transaction with a client or knowingly acquire "...(a) pecuniary interest adverse to a client...". MR 1.8(a). The correct answer is Choice **C**. Choice **A** is wrong because the result on the appeal is immaterial to the issue raised by an agreement involving media rights.

As a matter of fact, the success of the appeal may well have increased the value of the media rights and makes the Adams-Huxtable agreement all the more objectionable. Choice **B** is wrong because it is wrong on the law. There are many restrictions on a lawyer's fees. First of all, all fees must be reasonable under the circumstances. MR 1.5. Secondly, agreements which measure fees by the value of the results are generally covered by contingency agreements, and these are regulated by the Model Rules, as well as by legislation in many jurisdictions. MR 1.5(c). Choice **D** is wrong. The fact that Huxtable was free to choose another attorney is immaterial. He was entitled to choose Adams if he wished, but Adams was not free to extract any price he wished.

63. B A lawyer is subject to discipline for professional misconduct even when that misconduct does not involve the practice of law or is committed under circumstances not related to the law. Any conduct, within or without the practice, which "reflects adversely on the lawyer's honesty, trustworthiness or fitness as a lawyer in other respects" or which involves "dishonesty, fraud, deceit or misrepresentation" will subject her to discipline. ABA Formal Opinion 336 (June 3, 1974); MR 8.4(c) Comment [1]. The correct answer is **B**. An attorney must maintain high standards of professional conduct, and cannot engage in conduct that calls into question her fitness to practice law. This standard applies at all times, not only when she is rendering legal services. Francine persuaded Investor to invest in a business venture without disclosing to him that she herself was not financially committed to the venture as an investor and that she was only nominally the producer. She was guilty of deceit and misrepresentation in withholding facts which were instrumental in Investor's decision whether or not to invest, especially since he told her specifically, "If you've got your money in, then I'm in too." Her conduct is clearly subject to discipline. Choice **A** is wrong because it's immaterial whether Investor thought of Francine as a lawyer or a non-lawyer. He did think of her as someone he could trust as a fellow investor, and she betrayed his trust. Choice **C** is wrong for the same basic reason. Her conduct reflects on her fitness to practice law. Choice **D** is wrong because an attorney can never escape from the standards expected of her profession, whether or not she is engaged in active practice.

64. D The relationship between lawyers and judges is a tenuous one fraught with many opportunities for misuse and undue pressure. The public must not be induced to think that judges are subject to pressure from the bar. Lawyers try cases and judges decide who wins and who loses. The potentials for abuse are built into the system. On the other hand, lawyers are presumed to know more about the abilities and qualifications of judges than any other group. In the interest of electing the most qualified judges and of encouraging free speech, lawyers must be free to comment on candidates for judicial office. On the other hand, their comments must be fair and truthful. MR 8.2(a) Comment [1]. Statement II describes activities which Smith may properly contribute in behalf of Smith. A lawyer may work to further the candidacy of a particular candidate for judgeship, and may compare his qualifications with those of another candidate, so long as his comments are truthful. Statement III also describes an activity which is permitted. Nimble may speak publicly in support of Smith. Nimble may also donate $5,000 to Smith's campaign committee (Statement IV). Nimble is bound as an attorney not to assist a judicial officer (or candidate) in conduct that is a violation of the Code of Judicial Conduct. MR 8.4(f). In making contributions to the campaign of a judicial candidate, he must conform to Canon 5 of the Code of Judicial Conduct. This Section permits contributions to committees organized to promote a judicial candidacy, but not to the candidate personally. CJC Canon 5C(2). The correct answer is **D**, which recognizes Statements II, III and IV, but excludes Statement I. Choice **A** is wrong because it includes Statement I, which is an improper activity. Choice **B** is wrong for the same reason. Choice **C** is wrong because it excludes Statement II.

65. A The correct answer is **A**. Alison has engaged in conduct which is clearly dishonest. She has issued false and deceitful invoices to ABC by misrepresenting the nature of the services and the time spent by her personally. In most jurisdictions, her actions probably constitute a crime. MR 8.4(b),(c). She could not properly describe her paralegal's time as her own. This was a patent falsehood and resulted in fraudulent overbilling. She is not helped by the fact that she was encouraged by Zabar to exaggerate her billing. MR 5.2(a) Comment [1]. Every lawyer is expected to know the rules of professional conduct and to follow them regardless of the instructions of his superior. Most firms have in place procedures which enable a young associate to seek guidance when he believes he is misdirected by a superior. Choice **B** is therefore incorrect. Choice **C** is wrong because the assumption contradicts the facts. It doesn't matter how long the work would have taken Alison. The point is that she didn't do the work and she may not adopt the paralegal's time as her own. Choice **D** is wrong because it creates a distinction without substance. Reprimand is one form of discipline which may be used against an attorney, but on these facts, the form of discipline would almost certainly be more severe than a reprimand.

Also, Alison's conduct was a major infraction. Dishonesty in billing strikes at the very heart of the lawyer-client relationship and of the integrity of the bar.

66. B The Model Rules contain an entire section dealing with the responsibilities both of a partner and of a supervising lawyer who is not a partner, for the acts of a non-lawyer. A paralegal is a non-lawyer and is not permitted to engage in the practice of law. Under these facts, Zabar permitted the paralegal to do all the work of a lawyer, including the review of contracts and the preparation of pleadings, with minimal or no supervision by her associate, Alison. MR 5.3(a),(b),(c). Statement I is a correct statement of the consequences to Zabar. Statement II is also a correct statement of the consequences to Zabar. Zabar encouraged Alison to "puff up" her bills to ABC by telling her that ABC never checked the firm's bills, that ABC had a "healthy budget", that their general counsel had worked for the firm, and that she was sure that Alison could "bill 70 hours every week." The effect was to encourage Alison to distort and misrepresent her work hours. This was a clear violation of the Rules. MR 5.1(a)-(c). The correct answer is therefore Choice **B**. Choice **A** is wrong because it cites only Statement I. Choice **C** is wrong because it relies on Statement III. Statement III is clearly wrong. A firm may not adopt professional standards which are different from those generally applicable to the bar as a whole. And a partner in a firm has an affirmative duty to ensure that the general standards are maintained. Statement IV is wrong. ABC's general counsel could not effectively condone Allison's inflated bills. On the contrary, he would be subject to discipline himself for complicity in the fraudulent billing to ABC if he approved and condoned the law firm's billing practices. Choice **D** is wrong because it relies in part on Statements III and IV.

67. C A lawyer who learns that another lawyer has committed a violation of the rules of professional conduct which raises a substantial question as to that lawyer's honesty, trustworthiness or fitness as a lawyer, has an obligation to inform the appropriate professional authorities. MR 8.3(a). If he has acquired the knowledge under circumstances protected by the rules of confidentiality (MR 1.6), he is not required to reveal the violation. MR 8.3(c). The correct answer is **C**. Charlie acted properly in reporting Alison's misconduct to the appropriate authorities (statement III). The appropriate authority in this instance was the chairman of the firm's disciplinary committee. That person would then have the responsibility to determine what further action to take to discipline Alison. The legal profession is self-regulating. To maintain the integrity of the profession, members must take seriously their duty to report incidents of misconduct . MR 8.3 Comment [1]. Each lawyer must use his own judgment whether the conduct is serious enough to report (MR 8.3 Comment [3]), but on these facts, Charlie had no other reasonable recourse. Choice **A** is wrong because it depends on Statement I. The duty of confidentiality applies to the attorney-client relationship. Alison and Charlie were not lawyer-client, but fellow lawyers and associates. Choice **B** is wrong because it depends on Statement II. Charlie did not owe a duty of loyalty to Alison. Nothing in their relationship operated to create this duty; in any event, where lawyers are concerned, the duty to disclose misconduct transcends the duty of loyalty. Choice **D** is wrong because it depends on Statements I and II.

68. C Lawyers are often asked or appointed to serve a counsel for indigent defendants. Generally, they have an affirmative duty to accept these appointments and to represent their clients with zeal and diligence. MR 1.3, MR 6.1. However, a lawyer who cannot, because of his own prejudices and beliefs, represent a client zealously, should ask to be relieved of the appointment. This is especially true when the client is personally repugnant to the lawyer or the circumstances of the alleged crime are so repugnant as to "impair the client-lawyer relationship or the lawyer's ability to represent the client." MR 6.2(c) Comments [1]. Here, it is reasonably clear that Neophyte cannot represent George zealously. She is not only repelled by criminals who use guns but has actively campaigned against them. It's doubtful that anyone with this background could act as George's wholehearted advocate. Under the circumstances, Neophyte could certainly consult with the grievance committee in her jurisdiction to be guided in her actions, and she could properly also ask the judge to relieve her of her appointment as George's counsel. The correct answer is Choice **C**, which adopts Statements II and III. Choice **A** is wrong. Under these facts, there would seem to be no way in which Neophyte could properly defend George. Choice **B** is wrong because it does not include Statement III. Choice **D** is wrong because it excludes Statement II.

69. D Over the last fifty years, the standards applicable to lawyer advertising have been loosened to condone advertising in all public media. MR 7.2. This approach is the result of Supreme Court decisions recognizing that lawyer advertising is protected as free expression. Within the general acceptance of the "anything goes" formula, two forms of control still survive. The most important is a stricture against false and misleading advertising. MR 7.1. An advertisement is false or misleading if it contains a material misrepresentation of fact or law or omits a fact necessary to make the ad truthful; if it is likely to create an unjustified expectation about results the lawyer can achieve; or if it compares the lawyer's services with the services of other lawyers. MR 7.1(a)-(c). The facts in this case require careful analysis to determine whether Attorney Shnazz has skirted the rules. The artificial props he uses (suit with tie, law books he rarely consults), may be troublesome but probably acceptable. Clients do generally expect lawyers to wear suits and to have bookcases full of books. His ad tells us that his fees are lower than most, but this statement is substantiated by the facts. The statements describing general client satisfaction come close to being excessive as suggesting unjustified expectations about results, but they do not rely on representations about specific prior results or promises of specific future results, and they are also substantially supported by the results of the questionnaires distributed by Shnazz. Shnazz's ad is skillfully worded and structured to bring it within the rules, but skillful ad copy is not itself disciplinable. The best answer is **D**, which depends on Statement IV. Because the ad is, at most, mere "puffery" and does not contain matter which is false or misleading, it is acceptable. Choice **A** is wrong because it depends on Statement I. Under the facts, it probably is not reasonable to conclude that Shnazz is creating unjustified expectations. Choice **B** is wrong because the rules do not strike at huckstering techniques, but against falsehoods and misstatements. Choice **C** is wrong because it depends on Statement III. Media advertising by lawyers is not unrestricted, as we have seen.

70. C The best answer is **C**. Clara may properly consider only the factors recited in Statements I and III in fixing her fee. A lawyer's fee must be reasonable under all the circumstances involved in the representation. MR 1.5(a). The Rule lists factors which the lawyer may properly review in determining whether a fee is reasonable. The first factors are the time and labor required, the novelty of the question involved, and the skill required to perform the services properly. Other factors are the fee customarily charged in the locality for similar services; the experience of the lawyer performing the services; the amount involved and the results obtained; and the nature and length of the relationship with the client. MR 1.5(a)(1)-(8). Under the circumstances described in these facts, Clara was probably right to feel some frustration at the size of her fee when measured by her long-term skill and knowledge and measured against her increasing value to Apco. She was not limited by the fees normally charged for general legal services in her area but could properly consider the larger fees charged by her colleagues in the representation of clients issuing securities (Statement I). She could also properly consider her own special knowledge, skill and experience (Statement III). However, she could not consider the compensation of non-lawyers, such as the broker described in Statement II. A lawyer's fee may not be measured by the standards of other professions and of commerce generally. Choice **A** is wrong because it adopts only Statement I. Choice **B** is wrong because it relies in part on Statement II. Choice **D** is wrong because it excludes Statements I and III. One final note: it probably would be prudent of Clara to discuss her increased fee with the management of Apco before submitting her invoice. Because she has never billed more than her $400 hourly rate, Apco may express dismay at the size of the increase and may wish to consider the implications for their ongoing relationship.

71. A We are told that Meccatown follows the Model Rules. The applicable rules are MR 7.1 and 7.4. MR 7.1 is the catch-all rule which enjoins false and misleading statements about a lawyer or his services. A lawyer's ad may not contain material misrepresentations of fact or law (MR 7.1(a)), create an unjustified expectation about results the lawyer can achieve (MR 7.1(b)), or compare the lawyer's services with the services of other lawyers (MR 7.1(c)). MR 7.4 deals with communications about fields of practice and the certification of specialists. It enjoins ads which state or imply that the lawyer has been recognized or certified as a specialist in a particular field of law, but it permits a lawyer who is admitted to practice before the U.S. Patent and Trademark Office to use the term "Patent Attorney." MR 7.4(a). A lawyer is permitted, however, "to communicate the fact that the lawyer does or does not practice in particular fields of law". MR 7.4. If we examine Farmer's ad under these provisions, we conclude that she was justified in describing herself as experienced in commercial and corporate law. (This makes Choice **B** wrong.) But she was not justified in stating that she specialized in patent litigation without also qualifying herself as a Patent Attorney. The facts do not suggest that she was admitted to engage in patent practice before the Patent Office, but only that she assisted Patent Attorneys in trial preparation. Her statement about specializing in patent litigation was therefore misleading (she was not entitled to make this statement if she could not describe herself as a Patent Attorney) and violates both MR 7.1 and 7.4. The correct answer is Choice **A**. As we have seen, Choice **B** is wrong. Choice **C** is wrong because Clara could advertise her experience in commercial and corporate law. Choice **D** is wrong because Choice **A** is right.

MULTIPLE-CHOICE ANSWERS

72. B The proper conduct of a lawyer in the course of a litigation or trial is described in MR 3.5. The Rule tells us that a lawyer shall not "engage in conduct intended to disrupt a tribunal". MR 3.5(c) Comment [2] amplifies on this general language. It specifies that the lawyer shall "refrain from abusive or obstreperous conduct"; avoid "reciprocation" against abuse by the judge; and exercise "patient firmness" rather than "belligerence or theatrics." "A lawyer may stand firm against abuse by a judge but should avoid reciprocation; the judge's default is no justification for similar dereliction." However aroused and upset Rembo may have been, his language was certainly excessive and intemperate enough to violate the Rule. A lawyer may not state that the judge is not fit to try the case or that he is "a disgrace to the judiciary." His recourse is to note the judge's prejudice and impropriety in the record to enable the appellate court to deal with his conduct. Also, if the judge has made improper rulings on his motions, he can preserve the record by making the necessary objections. Further, if he believes that the judge is actually guilty of bias and is unfit to serve, he has not only the right but the duty to present his beliefs to the proper authorities. MR 8.3(b). Statements I and II are the only correct statements. Rembo is subject to discipline for insulting the judge and if he does not report the judge to the proper authorities. His statements in open court obviously indicate that he believes the judge is biased and unfit, and he is required to follow through on his beliefs. Statement III is incorrect because his beliefs, reasonable or not, do not justify his conduct. He has other remedies to overcome the Judge's bias. Statement IV is wrong; Rembo will not be disciplined for disclosing his complaints against Judge Noitall; on the contrary, he is required to disclose them. The correct choice is **B**. The other choices are wrong because they depend on one or several of the wrong statements.

73. C A lawyer must not during a criminal trial state a personal opinion about the guilt or innocence of an accused. MR 3.4(e). Juliana's remarks to the jury clearly project to the jury her personal opinion of the defendant and of his culpability. She is permitted to analyze the evidence to prove Brad's guilt, but she may not say, "I've never seen a more heinous crime." Nor may she use such characterizations as "scourge" and "fiend", which are also reflective of her personal judgment and opinion. What are the judge's remedies? Certainly, he may report Juliana's conduct to the disciplinary authorities (Statement I). MR 8.3. Under the CJC, he has a duty to require courteous conduct from lawyers (CJC Canon 3B(4), and a duty to report violations of professional conduct by lawyers (CJC Canon 3D(2). He may also discipline Julia himself by censuring her on the record or by imposing monetary sanctions upon her. These steps will be governed by the rules of the court in which he sits. (Statement III). But he probably cannot direct Juliana not to act as prosecutor in the trial of Tad, unless the local rules or statutes provide to the contrary. The facts tell us that Juliana is the chief prosecutor in Poston City and that she has decided to try these cases herself. She has undoubtedly made herself familiar with all the facts of the case and it would be unfair to the state at this juncture to remove her and substitute another prosecutor. However, the Judge can control her closing arguments in the trial of Tad by admonishing Juliana and instructing her not to inject her personal opinions as to Tad's guilt and to stick to the evidence. Statement II is therefore wrong. The correct answer is Choice **C**, which depends on Statements I and III. Choice **A** is wrong because it recites only Statement I. Choice **B** is wrong because it depends on Statement II, which is wrong. Choice **D** is wrong because it depends only on Statement III.

74. **D** A lawyer is under a continuing duty to segregate and keep clients' funds in a special trust fund account. He must not commingle a client's funds with his own. MR 1.15(a),(b). Most jurisdictions have detailed legislation dealing with the lawyer's fiduciary obligations with respect to clients' funds. On these facts, Gregson acted correctly when he deposited all of the $1,200 in his Clients' Fund Account, because the money was not then his. Gregson has spent three hours on Defendant's matter at the rate of $200 per hour and has earned a fee of $600. However, Defendant is now disputing Gregson's fee on the grounds that his application was inadequate and he was unprepared at the license hearing. This has put the $600 fee in dispute. However, there is no dispute as to the $500 license fee or the $100 which Greyson has not earned, and that money should be returned to Mishna. MR 1.15(c). The correct answer is **D**. Gregson must leave $600 in his Clients' Fund Account until the dispute is resolved and return the rest of the money. Choice **A** is the worst of the choices. Gregson would be guilty of conversion if he transferred all the money to his Fee Account and would subject himself to discipline. Choices **B** and **C** are wrong because they do not preserve the integrity of the $600 until the dispute between Gregson and his client is resolved.

75. **C** A lawyer may not undertake to represent a client if there is a reasonable possibility that the lawyer's own interests will adversely affect the client or his interests. This is the general Conflicts of Interest Rule. MR 1.7. The critical issues presented by these facts are the importance to Jeffries of his stock ownership in Macronext and the extent to which he believes that Client's law suit will damage Macronext. Since both of

these issues are subjective to Jeffries, the only way in which he can reasonably resolve them is to disclose his interest to Client and obtain her consent to the representation after consultation. MR 1.7(b)(1),(2). It's not enough that Jeffries reasonably believe his representation will not be adverse to Client's interests; he must also get her consent after consultation. Choice **C** is the right answer. Choice **A** is wrong because a conflict may arise even if the lawyer does not actually represent the other side; the lawyer's own economic interests may create the conflict. Choice **B** is wrong because the critical measure is not the importance to Macronext of Jeffries' stock interest, but the importance to Jeffries himself; it's his self-interest that's at issue. Choice **D** is wrong because the consequence to the stock's value is immaterial. What we're concerned with is the potential for conflict in Jeffries' mind and the resulting influence on the diligence and zeal he will devote to Client's case.

76. C A prosecutor has a responsibility to ensure that the accused is given a fair trial. MR 3.8. Among her other duties, she must make timely disclosure to the defense "of all evidence...that tends to negate the guilt of the accused or mitigates the offense...." MR 3.8(d). This direction is a more explicit expression of the duty of all lawyers during trial. No lawyer may offer evidence which she knows to be false. If she has offered material evidence and learns of its falsity, she must take reasonable remedial measures. MR 3.3(a)(4) Comment [3]. See also MR 3.4(b). On these facts, as soon as the prosecutor learned that Sharon's neighbor had lied, she had an affirmative duty to disclose that fact to Henderson and to the court. The correct answer is **C**, which adopts Statement III. Choice **A**, which depends on Statement I, is wrong. Prosecutor was not free to exercise her own judgment about the consequences of the perjury. The disclosure of the perjury would give defense counsel the opportunity to move to remedy the impact of the perjury, and would also enable the court to select the appropriate remedy. The failure to disclose would deprive both of these rights. Choice **B** (which relies on Statement II) is also wrong. Prosecutor was not required to drop the charges. She might choose to do so if she decided her case against Butch was destroyed by the evidence contradicting the neighbor's, but she was not required to do so if her other evidence was sufficient to convict. Choice **D** is wrong because it relies in part on Statements I and II.

77. D Defense lawyers are sometimes put in Henderson's position of learning or suspecting after a criminal trial has resulted in a client's acquittal, that the client may well be guilty after all. Fortunately for lawyers caught up in this dilemma, the bar and public policy have determined that the greatest social interest is served by requiring the lawyer to observe the confidences of his client under almost all circumstances, even when he learns after the trial is over that the client may have committed perjury and is probably guilty. MR 1.6(a) Comments [1]-[6]. There are a small number of exceptions to the rigid duty of confidentialty (MR 1.6(b)), but they do not apply here. The duty to maintain Butch's confidences continued after the representation by Henderson had ended. MR 1.6 Comment [22]. On these facts, the best answer is **D**. Henderson should do nothing. He is not permitted to reveal Butch's perjury to the court (Choice **A**) and he may not notify Prosecutor that Butch was lying; Butch cannot be subjected to a new trial and no purpose would be served by making disclosure to the Prosecutor. Choice **B** is wrong because the memo might fall into the hands of someone who would not respect the confidence and had no duty to do so.

78. D Neither the attorney-client privilege nor the duty of confidentiality is absolute. Recently, the courts have made many inroads on both. One court has held that the privilege may not be asserted to avoid disclosure of continuing crimes. Another has held that the duty of confidentiality does not survive the death of the client who was the source of the confidences. The Model Rules recognize at least two exceptions to the duty of confidentiality: a lawyer may reveal confidential information if he reasonably believes disclosure is necessary: (1) to prevent the client from committing a criminal act that the lawyer believes is likely to result in imminent death or substantial bodily harm (MR 1.6(b)(1)); and (2) to establish a claim or defense by the lawyer in a controversy with the client or to establish a defense by the lawyer to a criminal charge based upon conduct in which the client was involved (MR 1.6(b)(2)). The facts recited here reveal a continuing and improper effort by Greater Neck Hospital to misuse the attorney-client privilege and the duty of confidentiality by systematically delivering to Lancelot all its files concerning negligence, to prevent their disclosure in litigation. The attorney-client privilege and the duty of confidentiality apply only to "representation of a client", i.e., to those papers and files which a lawyer has assembled and utilized in connection with his work for the client. They do not extend to client files and records merely because they are "parked" or "warehoused" in the lawyer's file room. The correct answer is **D**. Lance should carefully segregate those files related to his services as a lawyer and turn the rest back to the Hospital for disposition by it. Choice **A** is wrong. Lance should not allow himself to become an accomplice to the Hospital's deception by refusing to turn over those files which are not entitled to protection. Choice **B** is wrong because Lance does have an obligation to the Hospital to retain those files which would be protected by the attorney-client privilege. Choice **C** is not as good an answer as **D**. Under the circumstances, Lance's first obligation is still to his client, not the Department. He should turn the files over to the Hospital and let it decide which files to turn over to the Department.

79. C The American judicial system requires that a judge consider only those matters which are presented to him in an adversary setting. The outcome of a trial is determined, in effect, by the lawyers who present and challenge the evidence. Our system does not contemplate or permit independent, ex parte investigations by a judge. The essential purpose is to create and maintain a written and verifiable record of proceedings which will also serve as the record on appeal. It is improper for a judge to consider matters outside the presence of the parties. CJC Canon 3B(7). Judge Thomas was wrong to conduct his own independent research into the facts in the local library. He had to reach his decision on the basis of the evidence presented by the parties. Since each party presented several expert witnesses, the judge had an opportunity to examine these witnesses as extensively as he wished to develop all the facts. Choice **C** is the correct answer. Choice **A** is wrong. Judge Thomas is obligated only to help develop the truth to the best of his ability on the basis of admissible testimony. Our system may differ from other judicial systems, but it is our system. Choice **B** is wrong. If a judge suspects that a witness is guilty of perjury, he may interrogate the witness to develop the truth and he may then base his decision on the truth as he sees it, but he may not conduct his own research into the facts outside the courtroom. (He may, of course, conduct his own research into the law.) Choice **D** is wrong. Confronted by such an unusual disclosure by the judge, the lawyers in the matter would undoubtedly remind the judge that he was exceeding his prerogatives.

80. B The general rule is that material in a lawyer's files which is not his own work product belongs to the client. The client is entitled to his files whenever he asks for them. The lawyer is responsible to preserve and maintain the client's files as long as they remain in his custody and control. A law firm has a special responsibility which is described in this set of facts: because many lawyers may work on one matter, it's hard to identify the lawyer who is responsible to the client for the preservation of his files. The best solution, therefore, is to fix the responsibility for maintaining files on the entire firm as one continuing entity, rather than on any one partner. The well organized law firm will have in place a system and a set of rules for file maintenance. The firm has a continuing responsibility to keep all records intact. Most jurisdictions have rules of their own, prescribing how long and under what circumstances files must be kept. New York, for example, requires that certain records relating to the lawyers' dealings with their clients, be maintained for seven years. On this set of facts, my best advice to the firm would be Choice **B**. I would reject Choice **A** because it is too haphazard and fraught with many problems, especially conflicts over what clients belong to what partners. I would also reject Choice **C** because it might result in the dispersal of all records without adequate controls over the firm's obligations. I would also reject Choice **D** because of the difficulty of establishing, in some instances, the identity of the rightful custodian of the client's records. The Model Rules offer very little guidance on issues of record keeping.

81. B Dolly faces a conflict in attempting to represent Tennessee, an old friend and client. The conflict arises because Dibney, successor to Mountain Music, must be considered a former client of Dolly (Dibney has succeeded to the assets, files and interests of Mountain Music.) A lawyer may not represent a client with an interest adverse to a former client's interest in a matter substantially related to the representation. MR 1.9(a),(c). In her representation of Tennessee, Dolly would be forced to defend him against charges brought by Dibney. Clearly, her representation of Tennessee would be materially adverse to Dibney and would rely on facts and circumstances growing out of the merger itself. In a similar case, the New York Court of Appeals ordered that the law firm involved be disqualified from representing the sole shareholder of the acquired corporation. *Tekni-Plex, Inc. v. Meyner & Landis*, 674 N.E.2d 663 (N.Y. 1996). The best answer is **B**. Molly may represent Tennessee if she obtains the consent after consultation of her former client Dibney (successor to her client, Mountain Music), although on these facts Dibney is not likely to consent. MR 1.9(a). Choice **A** is wrong. She may not represent Tennessee without Dibney's consent. Choice **C** is wrong. The statement is true, but does not allow for the possibility that Dibney may nevertheless elect to consent. Choice **D** is wrong. She need not sever her relationships with Tennessee if she is successful in obtaining the consent of Dibney after consultation.

82. B High-low agreements were first discussed in an article by a New York State judge in 1975. Since then, they have come into increased use, especially in personal injury actions in which the injuries are substantial and the liability is questionable, i.e., where the plaintiff is concerned that he may not recover at all and the defendant, usually an insurance company, is afraid that the jury verdict will exceed coverage.

They are used in cases tried before juries. The agreement, usually in writing, prescribes the upper and lower limits of recovery, regardless of the jury verdict. Many commentators have suggested that the agreements are fraught with risks, especially that the attorneys will overlook such issues as interest and costs. One issue is whether the court should be informed of the agreement; some judges have set them aside when they were not informed. Certainly, the client should be told in great detail about the content and the implications of the agreement, and should be asked to give his consent in writing before the verdict is announced. The Model Rules do not deal with these agreements, and it does not appear that they are covered by the rules of any jurisdiction. Under the present circumstances, the best answer is Choice **B**. The high-low agreement would seem to be proper, but only if all clients have been fully consulted and have agreed in writing. Choice **A** is wrong; the agreement is not proper in the absence of clients' consent. Choice **C** is wrong in most jurisdictions. There is no requirement that they be approved by the court. Choice **D** is wrong. High-low agreements are not considered improper and some commentators encourage them as a legitimate way to resolve unpredictable verdicts, assure some recovery to the plaintiff and avoid the impact of run-away jury verdicts. It's easy to see why a high-low agreement may irritate a judge if he is not made aware of it until he's asked to amend the jury verdict to conform it to the agreement. He may feel that the entire trial process has been wasted or subverted. It's probably prudent, therefore, to advise the judge that a high-low agreement exists before the case goes to the jury. Nothing in the Model Rules appears to require this notice, however.

83. **C** "The practice of law is a profession, not merely a business. Clients are not commodities that can be purchased and sold at will." MR 1.17, Comment [1]. A lawyer's ability to sell all or any part of a law practice is severely limited. Most significantly, a lawyer may sell his practice only if he ceases to engage in the practice completely in the "area or jurisdiction" in which the practice has been conducted. Local law determines whether the boundary is the entire jurisdiction or a more limited area. A lawyer may move from one state to another, or he may be appointed or elected to a judgeship, or he may die. In all of these cases, sale would be proper. (In the event of death, the sale may be conducted by the personal representative of the deceased. Because the representative may not be a lawyer, the purchaser-lawyer is expected to comply with MR 1.17.) In any case, the sale must be to a single purchaser who purchases the entire practice. Also, actual written notice in advance of the sale must be given to each of the seller's clients regard-

ing the following: that a sale is proposed; the client's right to retain other counsel or to recover his files; any proposed change in fees; and the fact that the client's consent to the sale will be presumed if he fails to object within ninety days after receipt of the notice. MR 1.17. The correct answer is C. A law practice must be sold in its entirety. A is wrong because lawyers are not free to sell part or all of their practices freely. B is wrong because the letters by Ted and Roger were mailed after the fact and did not contain the requisite information. Choice D is wrong because the Rule is not concerned with the price paid for the practice but with insuring that the clients' interests are adequately protected. Note that Roger and Ted are both subject to discipline. The conditions of MR 1.17 apply to both lawyer-seller and lawyer-buyer.

84. B Many issues which confront disciplinary authorities do not have quick and easy answers. Which is paramount? The right of a judge to express his opinions freely in the same manner as any other citizen? Or the need to erase any doubts as to the judge's capacity to act impartially? Or the need to insure that a judge will avoid the appearance of endorsing a commercial enterprise? Many of the provisions of the Code of Judicial Conduct relate to these issues, but none is persuasive. Thus, "A judge shall act at all times in a manner that promotes public confidence in the integrity and impartiality of the judiciary." CJC Canon 2A. "A judge shall not allow...relationships to influence the judge's judicial conduct or judgment. A judge shall not lend the prestige of judicial office to advance the private interests of the judge or others; nor...convey or permit others to convey the impression that they are in a special position to influence the judge." CJC Canon 2B. "A judge shall conduct all of the judge's extra-judicial activities so that they do not cast reasonable doubt on the judge's capacity to act impartially, demean his office, or interfere with the performance of his duties." CJC Canon 4A. "A judge shall not engage in financial and business dealings that may reasonably be perceived to exploit his judicial position." CJC Canon 4D(1)(a). "A judge shall not accept...a gift, bequest, favor or loan from anyone except for:" (*Editor's note:* the exception is not applicable to these facts). On the other hand, "a judge may speak, write, lecture, teach and participate in other extrajudicial activities concerning the law, the legal system, the administration of justice and non-legal subjects, subject to the requirements of this Code." CJC Canon 4B. The dilemma presented by these facts was resolved by the New Jersey Supreme Court in favor of requiring a municipal judge to refrain from appearing as a commentator on the law on a regularly scheduled TV program. The court reasoned that the judge was commenting on pending cases and lending the prestige of his office to a commercial enterprise. The decision has been criticized by champions of a free press. The facts here are even more egregious than those in the New Jersey case. In that case, the judge was not paid for his appearance. On these facts, Judge Speaker will be paid a regular fee by an advertiser on the program. The potential for influence over the judge is much greater here. The best answer is Choice **B**. Choice **A** is not the best answer because a judge may have other sources of income so long as they do not reflect on his impartiality or freedom of judgment. Choice **C** does not appear to be correct, at least in New Jersey. If the issue arises again, as it probably will, other courts—including the U.S. Supreme Court—may decide the question differently. Choice **D** is wrong. A judge's right to speak freely is circumscribed in several respects by the Code.

85. C The correct answer to this question is clear and unequivocal. A judge is simply forbidden to engage in the practice of law. CJC Canon 4G. The prohibition is so broad as to permit only two exceptions: a judge may act *pro se* and he may give legal advice and review documents for his family—but ***without compensation.*** Judge Speaker has violated the most basic tenet of judicial integrity. The Judge has obviously performed the services of a lawyer in his help to John: he has reviewed and analyzed a legal document and has given legal advice. Furthermore, he has accepted compensation for his services. The Judge's conduct is highly improper and will subject him to discipline. Choice **A** is obviously wrong. Both of the activities described are essential ingredients of the practice of law, which is forbidden to the judge. Choice **B** is wrong. There is no exception for friends or former clients. Choice **D** is wrong. Reasonable or not, a judge may not accept compensation for legal services. The correct answer is **C**.

86. D What degree or level of loyalty does a lawyer owe to a former Client? The answer requires analysis of two ingredients: is the matter which the lawyer proposes to handle for a new client "the same or a substantially related matter" to the former representation? Will the interests of the new client in that matter be materially adverse to the interests of the former client? If the answer to both these ingredients is "no", the lawyer may proceed to take on the new matter. If the answer to either is "yes", the lawyer may not take on the new matter unless the former client consents after consultation. MR 1.9(a).Whether a client's interest is adverse to another's is covered by Model Rule 1.7. See MR 1.9 Comment [1]. Whether a matter is the same or substantially related to another matter depends on the facts of the particular situation or transaction. MR 1.9 Comment [2]. Under these facts, we do not appear to have a common or substantially related matter. Anthony's representation of Cleopatra involved a breach of contract action in which Niles was not involved. The new matter involves a suit in negligence. However adverse the interests of Cleopatra and Niles, they do not grow out of the same or a substantially related matter. However, the best answer is still **D**. The facts do not show any reason why Niles cannot take the prudent step of obtaining Cleopatra's consent after consultation. He may not be strictly required to do so, but it will avoid a lot of potential ill will and unnecessary bitterness if he does. In this regard, it should be noted that if Anthony does represent Niles, he is not permitted to use any information relating to the former matter to the disadvantage of Cleopatra. MR 1.9(c)(1). Choice **C** may be letter-of-the-law correct, but it is not the best answer because **D** is preferable for a prudent lawyer. Choice **A** is wrong because it oversimplifies the formula which determines the items which a lawyer must consider in contemplating a matter involving a former client. Choice **B** is wrong for the same reason.

87. D The Model Rules do not specify what disciplinary action should be taken against a lawyer for an infraction of the Rules. This decision is normally left to the local disciplinary authority or to the courts. In all jurisdictions, the most grievous infraction by a lawyer is the misuse of client funds. MR 1.15. Many jurisdictions have imposed controls which make it more difficult fora lawyer to misuse funds. However strict they may be, these controls are still violated from time to time. An attorney who faces discipline for misuse of funds must expect the most severe penalty, including suspension for a period of months or disbarment, usually with the right to reapply for admission at the end of a stated period (in New York, that period is seven years). Choices **A** and **B** correctly describe actions which the Committee may take in Sainsbury's case. Whether a lawyer may or should be disbarred for life and thereby deprived of the opportunity for rehabilitation and of professional employment presents a more difficult question, but one that is sometimes decided by the authorities adversely to the offender. The State of California has recently adopted lifetime disbarment as a remedy in cases of grievous misconduct. Choice **C** is also available to the Committee, but only in those jurisdictions which impose lifetime disbarment. However, the remedy described in Choice **D** is not available to the Committee, which may act only to control Sainsbury's actions as an attorney. It has no jurisdiction to extend its influence into her employment by the law school because the teaching of law is not the practice of law. However, Sainsbury may find that a condition of employment at Podunk for an adjunct law professor is good standing at the bar. The correct answer is **D**.

88. A Lawyers who function as in-house counsel to businesses often cross the subtle line between their work as lawyers and their other functions within the firm. Some examples: a lawyer who participates in new-product research; a lawyer who engages in legislative lobbying; a lawyer who participates in high-level policy managerial meetings on new investments or acquisitions. Another example is furnished by these facts. Adam certainly performs the duties of a lawyer in most of his work, but when he sits in on board and committee meetings and acts only as scrivener or recorder, he is not acting as a lawyer. To the extent that his files contain information or disclosures of HCN which he has received and maintained in his function as an attorney, he must respect the client's right to the attorney-client privilege and his duty of confidentiality and refuse to turn over the files. MR 1.6(a). The correct answer is Choice **A**. Choice **B** is not the correct answer because it implies that the attorney-client privilege and the right to confidentiality belong to the attorney. They belong only to the client and may be waived by it. Choice **C** is wrong. Adam may not turn over his attorney-client files unless HCN consents after consultation. Choice **D** is also wrong. Adam is not privileged to make his own decision as to which portions of the minutes are relevant to the State's investigation.

89. C We must distinguish between Adam's function as counsel to HCN and his function as recording secretary and scrivener of Board and committee meetings. In the first function, he receives information to which he must accord two duties: the duty to observe the attorney-client privilege and the duty of confidentiality. They are not the same, as the Model Rules make clear. MR 1.6 Comment [5]. The attorney-client privilege applies when the lawyer is called upon to act as witness or a source of evidence about the client in a judicial or other proceeding. The duty of confidentiality applies in all circumstances in which a lawyer's information is sought other than "through compulsion of law." The latter duty extends to all matters related to the representation, not only matters communicated by the client. On these facts, the information contained in the minutes recorded by Adam was not acquired by him in his role as attorney. It doesn't take a lawyer to write minutes. And a lawyer does not wear a cloak of secrecy wherever he goes or whatever he does. The correct answer is Choice **C**. Adam must turn the minutes over to the Attorney General. Choice **A** is wrong because the minutes are not covered by the attorney-client privilege because they were not related to Adam's role as counsel. Choice **B** is wrong because they are not covered by the duty of confidentiality. Under the Model Rules definition, the duty of confidentiality is not the correct basis on which to resist the subpoena in any event. Because the subpoena represents "compulsion of law", the correct basis for a lawyer's refusal to obey a subpoena to produce client's papers is the attorney-client privilege. Choice **D** is wrong because in his role as non-lawyer scrivener, Adam must obey the subpoena whether or not the Board authorizes it.

90. D Individual practitioners and lawyers in small firms sometimes overreach and accept too many cases, or cases which they are not qualified to handle. Their problems than take on a classic pattern: missed appointments, unanswered phone calls, neglected correspondence, forgotten court dates, inadequate preparation, bad research, client complaints to the grievance committee. Over time, the lawyer not only loses cases and clients, but violates several of the prevailing rules of professional responsibility. He fails to act with reasonable diligence and promptness. MR 1.3. He fails to keep his client reasonably informed about the status of a matter and to comply with reasonable requests for information, or to explain matters to the extent necessary to enable the client to make informed decisions. MR 1.4(a),(b). He rejects the notion that he may not have the skill or knowledge necessary for the representation—or he may recognize his inadequacy and proceed to ignore it. MR 1.1. He fails to recognize danger signals which would require him to withdraw from the matter and to recommend that new counsel be engaged. MR 1.16(a). And he may even resort to excuses and fabrications which constitute "conduct involving dishonesty, fraud, deceit or misrepresentation" or conduct that is "prejudicial to the administration of justice." MR 8.4(c),(d). The litany of problems resulting from Biddle's effort to take on a matter too complicated for his office to handle shows what can happen if the lawyer loses control of a matter. The Committee is likely to charge Biddle with all the violations described in Choices **A**, **B** and **C**. The correct answer is therefore Choice **D**. Each of the other choices states a correct conclusion but is not the best choice when standing by itself. Choice **D** is correct because it recognizes that all the conduct described is disciplinable.

91. B The facts presents an issue which often confronts a large law firm. Assume the firm has represented a client over several matters. Or a new client is referred to the firm by another lawyer. In either event, a series of circumstances has conspired to make the client repugnant and offensive to many of the lawyers in the firm. How does the firm resolve the dilemma and determine whether or not to represent the client? An individual practitioner may withdraw from representing a client if the client insists on pursuing an objective that the lawyer considers repugnant or imprudent. MR 1.16(b)(3). But how does a multi-lawyer firm reach a consensus on a question which is essentially subjective. One sensible and defensible answer is a democratic vote among the partners. The firm in these facts has complied with this process and cannot be criticized for its decision. What is the resulting obligation of the lawyer-associates who are asked to work on the matter but who find the client or the client's cause personally repugnant and reprehensible? The best answer is that they should be expected to put aside their personal judgments and proceed to fulfill their obligation to represent the client diligently and competently. MR 1.1, 1.3. Any other rule would make it impossible for the firm to proceed. The best answer is Choice **B**. This is a better answer than **A** only because it reflects the way in which firms generally operate. Associates take their instructions from the partner in charge of the matter. Choice **A** would be a defensible Choice, but it is not as good as **B**. Choice **C** is wrong in this case. Although it may be a general statement of a sound basic principle for a solo practitioner, it has no application to a multi-lawyer firm which has reached a democratic consensus. Choice **D** is not correct because although it, too, states a valid general principle, it is also the fact that an individual lawyer is not required to represent a client whose objectives are repugnant to him. (*Editor's Note:* a major law firm was recently confronted with a dispute among partners whether or not to represent a client with a questionable history. The issue was resolved in favor of the representation by a vote of the partners.)

92. **A** A lawyer is sometimes confronted with a problem in ethics which is still being debated among lawyers and scholars and is essentially unresolved. The facts in this case illustrate one such problem. The conflict here is between zealous representation of a client (MR 1.1, 1.3) and the essential impropriety of utilizing information harmful to the other side which comes into the possession of the lawyer not through legal means but through the negligence or inadvertence of the adversary. One commentator has even suggested that a lawyer who does not take advantage of these slips by the adversary may subject herself to an action for malpractice by her client. Although the Model Rules do not deal specifically with these issues, it may be argued that the use of misdirected communications violates the spirit, if not the letter, of the provisions dealing with Candor Toward the Tribunal (MR 3.3) and Fairness to Opposing Party and Counsel (MR 3.4). Several states per-

mit the use of misdirected material, but some courts have banned its use. It should be noted that even if the lawyer who receives the misdirected item decides not to use it as such, she will inevitably be influenced by the knowledge she derives from it in the conduct of the trial. Because the ABA would take apparently the position that misdirected documents should not be used, the best current answer is Choice **A**. Lindsey will be subject to discipline for introducing the fax into evidence. Once it's determined that Choice **A** is correct, Choice **B** is wrong because it misstates the basis for disciplining Lindsey. Choice **C** is wrong on our analysis, although some commentators and some courts will disagree. Choice **D** is wrong because the issue is the very use of the material, not the manner in which it falls into the lawyer's hands.

93. D The conduct of judges is controlled by the ABA Code of Judicial Conduct, which was last revised in 1990. The Code speaks more in terms of general admonitions and standards than in precise definitions of wrong and right, although some of its provisions are quite precise. CJC Canon 1A instructs all judges to "participate in establishing, maintaining and enforcing high standards of conduct," and to "personally observe these standards so that the integrity and independence of the judiciary will be preserved." CJC Canon 2A directs all judges to respect and comply with the law and to act at all times to promote public confidence in the integrity and impartiality of the judiciary. CJC Canon 4A, which deals with a judge's extra-judicial activities, tells him to conduct these activities so as to insure that they do not (1) cast reasonable doubt on his capacity to act impartially as a judge; (2) demean the judicial office; and (3) interfere with the proper performance of judicial duties. Judge Thorndike's conduct in refusing a summons, refusing a breathalizer test, threatening a police officer, and taking advantage of his office by resort to a display of his badge, violates one or another of all these provisions and will subject him to discipline. The correct answer is Choice **D**. Choice **A** is wrong. A judge must be scrupulous in the conduct of his extra-judicial activities as well as in his conduct on the bench. Choice **B** is incorrect because the CJC does not attempt to define precisely all possible infractions of judicial standards but to act as a moral and ethical guide. Choice **C** is wrong because the conduct described was not a minor infraction. On the contrary, it reflects Judge Thorndike's disrespect for the entire process by which all citizens, regardless of rank or position, become subject to society's rules and procedures. (*Editor's Note:* the facts in this question adopt the facts involved in a recent proceeding to discipline an appellate judge serving in a midwestern state.)

MULTIPLE-CHOICE ANSWERS

94. C Each jurisdiction has in place a body which initiates or receives complaints against judges and then investigates and disposes of these complaints, generally after an evidentiary hearing. The body may be called a Judicial Ethics Committee, a Commission on Judicial Conduct, or another similar name indicative of its purpose and function. After consideration of all relevant factors, the body is usually empowered to take the action appropriate to the judge's conduct. Because the conduct under investigation is a judge's conduct, not that of a lawyer-practitioner, the sanctions are directed at the judge's status as a judicial officer, not at his status as a member of the bar. Accordingly, the judge who is being disciplined may be admonished, reprimanded (Statement I), censured, suspended (Statement II), removed from office (Statement IV), or retired for mental or physical disability which prevents the proper performance of his judicial duties. In most jurisdictions, the body reviewing a judge's conduct will not have the power to disbar the judge (Statement III). Disbarment is a function usually reserved to another body—a court or a judicial or administrative agency—which maintains supervision over all lawyers. The standards for measuring a judge's conduct are different from those measuring a lawyer's conduct. Statement III is therefore incorrect. The correct answer is Choice **C**, which depends on Statements I, II and IV. Choice **D** is wrong because it includes Statement III. Choice **A** is wrong because it omits Statements II and IV. Choice **B** is wrong because it omits Statement IV.

95. C The Model Rules are somwhat ambiguous on the question of a trial lawyer's right to contact jurors after they have been discharged by the court. The Rules do specify that a lawyer may not "seek to influence a...juror, prospective juror...by means prohibited by law." MR 3.5(a). Because the descriptive word is "influence", it would appear that the draftsmen intended to strike only at conduct before and during the trial, not following it. The Rules do also forbid a lawyer to communicate ex parte with a juror "except as permitted by law", but this language also is ambiguous enough to leave a question whether contact after the trial is included in the prohibition. MR 3.5(b). The draftsmen apparently intended to leave the issue of post-trial contact for determination by each state. Several states, including New York, have retained the language of the Model Code of Professional Responsibility, which forbade questions or statements "calculated to harass or embarrass the juror." Other states permit post-trial contact when it is made with the court's permission and involves an inquiry into whether the verdict was tainted by extrinsic matters. In virtually every state, Randy's conduct is improper because it definitely served to harass and embarrass the four jurors whom Randy confronted. The best answer is **C**. Choice **A** is wrong because Randy's conduct is wrong whether or not opposing counsel is present; further, there is no procedure for joint interview of jurors by trial counsel following the verdict. Choice **B** is wrong under MR 3.5(b) because most jurisdictions impose restrictions on juror contact even after the jury is discharged. Choice **D** is wrong. Whether or not this jurisdiction permits post-trial contact with jurors after approval by the court, Randy's remarks were abusive, harassing and embarrassing and therefore improper.

96. B Lawyers are held accountable for their actions in representing clients in two ways: if they violate the standards of professional responsibility imposed in the jurisdiction in which they are licensed to practice, they become subject to discipline by the appropriate authorities; and if they act unreasonably as that term is defined by general principles of tort law, they become liable in damages measured by the injury to the client. In representing a client, a lawyer has the capacity to exert enormous influence on the client's judgment. MR 1.8 Comment [1]. Especially where the lawyer's self-interest is involved, a lawyer must be careful not to prefer his interest to the interest of the client. On these facts, Attorney Wheaton has caused Client Lenape at least $150,000 in measurable damages by ignoring the statute of limitations. He is not permitted to negotiate a settlement or release of these damages without first advising Lenape *in writing* that it is appropriate under the circumstances for her to seek independent representation. MR 1.8(h). The correct answer is Choice **B**. Choice **A** is wrong because the responsibility not to negotiate a settlement of claims without the proper written notice applies to former clients as well as current clients; besides, Lenape's letter was not only a notice terminating the attorney-client relationship, but also a demand for redress. Choice **C** is wrong; although it is a high-sounding statement of a broad general principle, it does not satisfy the lawyer's obligation to give the client the opportunity after written notice to retain independent counsel to protect her interests. Choice **D** is wrong for the obvious reason that Lenape's consent would be uninformed without the opportunity to discuss the matter with independent counsel.

97. A Lawyers who represent the accused in criminal prosecutions face special problems in following the narrow line between the duty of confidentiality and the crime of obstruction of justice. The line becomes obscured when the lawyer learns from his client that there is physical evidence connecting the client to the crime and that the client expects the lawyer to protect the evidence itself as part of his duty of confidentiality. What should the lawyer do under these circumstances. The answer is reasonably clear. The lawyer may inspect the evidence, but he must leave it in place. He must not under any circumstances remove or secrete it. If the client attempts to deliver it to him for safekeeping, he must reject it. It doesn't matter whether the physical evidence is the "fruit or instrumentality" of the crime. As long as it has probative value or has any tendency to link the accused to the crime, the lawyer must decline to take it, hold it or keep it. MR 3.4(a). The correct answer on these facts is Choice **A**. Choice **B** is wrong because, as we have stated, the duty of confidentiality is destroyed as soon as the lawyer controls or takes custody of the physical evidence. Choice **C** is wrong; the attorney-client privilege is not applicable on these facts. The privilege applies only when the lawyer is required to give testimony or evidence concerning the client; the privilege cannot be used by the lawyer to protect himself against discipline for hiding evidence. (*Editor's note:* the Model Rules distinguish between the attorney-client privilege and the duty of confidentiality. MR 1.6 Comment [5]). Choice **D** is wrong. Although in the strictest sense the tapes were not the fruit or instrumentality of the crime of sexual assault, they constitute evidence linking Defendant to the crime and may not be secreted by Stevens. (See *People v. Belge,* 372 N.Y.S.2d 798, *aff'd,* 376 N.Y.S.2d 771 (1975); *In re Ryder,* 263 F. Supp. 360 (E.D. Va.), *aff'd,* 381 F.2d 713 (4th Cir. 1967); *People v. Meredith,* 29 Cal. 3d 682, 631 P.2d 46 (1981). (*Editor's note:* the facts in this question follow the facts of a case which recently occurred in Ontario, Canada.)

98. C The law may be a noble profession with lofty ideals and standards, but it is also the means by which each lawyer earns his daily bread. The profession as a whole has an interest in promoting the financial health of each practitioner. A sound practitioner is more apt to avoid and resist the temptations that inevitably flow from contact with and control over the property and money of clients. The Model Rules prohibit agreements which tend to restrict a lawyer's right to practice upon termination of an employment or partnership relationship. The only exception is an agreement which deals with retirement benefits. MR 5.6(a). Agreements which restrict the freedom of practice limit the autonomy of lawyers and also limit the freedom of each client to choose a lawyer. MR 5.6 Comment [1]. The rule does not apply in the case of the sale of a law practice, but only if the sale complies with the terms specifically recited. MR 1.17 Comments [1]-[4]. The correct answer is Choice **C**. Choice **A** is wrong. The agreement is not valid under the Model Rules because it prevents Blumberg from practicing in the very area in which his clients and potential clients probably reside. The agreement violates the substance of the rule against practice restrictions in that it forces Blumberg's client to choose another lawyer. Choice **B** is wrong. The firm is not entitled to enforce the agreement by this showing. The clients must be free to do as they wish when Blumberg leaves the firm. Choice **D** is wrong because it is an overstatement of the Rule. Nothing prevents a firm from placing work restrictions on a partner or associate. Each firm is entitled to establish its own internal employment policies and rules, but these may not include restraints on the right to practice.

99. C Essentially, the rationale behind the requirements imposed upon lawyers to keep and maintain records is three-fold: (1) to provide access to information important to the client; (2) to police the handling by the lawyer of the money and property of his clients; and (3) to give to disciplinary authorities the machinery for conducting inquiries and investigations into the lawyer's conduct. A wise lawyer will maintain scrupulous records and files and comply with all the record- and bookkeeping requirements of his jurisdiction. The Model Rules do not specify a period during which files and records must be kept, but many jurisdictions have adopted their own rules which do impose varying time periods. [New York, for example, requires the lawyer to keep a variety of records (bank records, copies of retainer and fee agreements, copies of invoices and statements to clients, copies of payment records, copies of all retainer and closing statements, etc.) for seven years after the event. New York Code of Professional Responsibility, DR 9-102(D),(H)]. Because the Model Rules impose no fixed period, the lawyer is under an obligation to monitor and maintain his files long enough to ensure that his clients always have access to information they need. MR 1.4; MR 1.15. This would seem to require that a lawyer retain his files and records indefinitely, or, with respect to any one client, at least until there is demonstrably no further interest by that client in his files. On these facts, the best answer is **C**, which depends on Statement I. However jaded and fatigued he may be, Fosdick has an obligation to protect the interests of his clients. The best way to do this would be to make an effort to contact each client before destroying his files. Choice **B** is wrong because Statement IV is wrong. Fosdick has no obligation to deliver the files to another lawyer; nor may he shed his own responsibilities by designating another lawyer as keeper of his files. (Of course, if he sold his practice to another lawyer in compliance with Model Rule 1.17, then that other lawyer could succeed to the files of those clients who consented to the transfer of files after notice.) Choice **A** is wrong because it depends in part on Statement II, which is wrong only because the Model Rules do not impose a fixed period for file retention. Choice **D** is wrong because all of the Statements are wrong except Statement I.

100. A One of the key principles of the lawyer-client relationship is that a lawyer may not personally solicit the representation of a client who is not a member of his family or with whom he does not have a prior professional relationship. MR 7.3(a). (Note, however, that the Supreme Court has permitted solicitation by mail in the case of persons "who need legal services of the kind provided by the lawyer in a particular matter." *Shapero v. Kentucky Bar Association,* 486 U.S. 466 (1988); but the Court also upheld a Florida statute which prohibited targeted mailing to accident victims for a period of 30 days after the accident. *Florida Bar v. Went for It, Inc.,* 515 U.S. 618 (1995).) The issue in this case is whether a lawyer may solicit through a non-lawyer agent who is in his employ or under his control. The Model Rules are not specific on this issue, but many provisions suggest the correct answer. For example, a lawyer may not share his fees with a non-lawyer. MR 5.4(a). A lawyer may not give anything of value to any person for recommending his services (with certain exceptions which are not applicable here). MR 7.2(c). A lawyer may not by in-person or telephone contact solicit professional employment from a prospective client (again, with inapplicable exceptions.) MR 7.3. Many jurisdictions have rules and statutes which make solicitation, either in person or through agents, a crime. (See New York Judiciary Law §481, 482.) On these facts, both Brenda and Brian are clearly subject to discipline. The remaining question is: in which jurisdiction will they be disciplined? A lawyer is subject to discipline as a lawyer only in the state(s) in which he is licensed to practice. MR 8.5(a). The correct answer is **A**. Brenda and Brian are subject to discipline in Iroquois but not in Sioux because they are not admitted in Sioux (they may, however, have committed a crime in Sioux if Sioux has a statute similar to New York's). Choice **B** is wrong for the reason stated. Choice **C** is wrong for the same reason. Choice **D** is wrong because the vice is the act of solicitation. It doesn't matter whether the prospective client "signed up" or not.

Table of References to the Model Rules

Preamble, Scope 7 145
1.1 .... 49, 68, 144, 146, 192, 193
1.1 Comment 2 49
1.1 Comment 1 146
1.1 Comment 2 .... 145, 146
1.10 81
1.11(a) 73
1.11(a)(1) 74
1.11(b) 74
1.11(c)(2) 73
1.13 76
1.13(a) 76, 171
1.13(b) 76
1.13 Comment 3 171
1.13 Comment 8 171
1.15 .... 161, 190, 198
1.15(a) 68, 154, 182
1.15(b) 154, 182
1.15(b) Comment 2 154
1.15(c) 68, 154, 182
1.15(c) Comment 2 154
1.16 .... 70, 148
1.16(a) 192
1.16(a)(1) 71, 150
1.16(a)(1) Comment 1 163
1.16(a)(3) Comment 4 .... 163, 172
1.16(b) 150
1.16(b)(3) 193
1.16(d) 150
1.17 .... 188, 198
1.17 Comment 1 .... 187, 197
1.17 Comment 2 197
1.17 Comment 3 197
1.17 Comment 4 197
1.2 .... 68, 75
1.2(a) 45, 72, 78, 147, 148, 162
1.2(d) 47, 146
1.2(d) Comment 6 146
1.2(d) Comment 7 146
1.2(d) Comment 8 146
1.2(d) Comment 9 146
1.3 ...... 45, 51, 68, 75, 82, 168, 178, 192, 193
1.3 Comment 2 51
1.3 Comment 1 167
1.3 Comment 2 155
1.4 .... 51, 78, 198
1.4(a) 78, 192

1.4(b) 51, 163, 192
1.5 .... 50, 59, 67, 81, 94
1.5(a) 150, 164, 169, 174, 179
1.5(a)(1) 179
1.5(a)(2) 179
1.5(a)(3) 164, 179
1.5(a)(4) 179
1.5(a)(5) 179
1.5(a)(6) 179
1.5(a)(7) 164, 179
1.5(a)(8) 179
1.5(a) Comment 2 150
1.5(b) 67
1.5(c) 59, 67, 68, 94, 153
.... , 161, 162, 164, 175
1.5(d) 59, 67
1.5(d)(1) 168
1.5 Comment 5 154
1.6 .... 47, 50, 53, 56, 60, 171, 177
1.6 Comment 21 160
1.6 Comment 9 60
1.6(a) 144, 147, 160, 191
1.6(a) Comment 1 .... 152, 184
1.6(a) Comment 2 .... 152, 184
1.6(a) Comment 3 .... 152, 184
1.6(a) Comment 4 .... 152, 184
1.6(a) Comment 5 .... 152, 184
1.6(a) Comment 6 184
1.6(b) 184
1.6(b)(1) 60, 151, 184
1.6(b)(2) 145, 153, 154, 184
1.6 Comment 1 151
1.6 Comment 11 147
1.6 Comment 12 153
1.6 Comment 2 151
1.6 Comment 21 .... 145, 184
1.6 Comment 3 .... 151, 156
1.6 Comment 4 .... 151, 156
1.6 Comment 5 ...... 144, 151, 156, 191, 197
1.7 .... 69, 182, 189
1.7 Comment 12 69
1.7(b) 71, 157
1.7(b)(1) 183
1.7(b)(2) 183
1.7(b) Comment 10 169
1.7 Comment 71
1.7 Comment 9 168

TABLES

1.8	174
1.8 Comment 1	58
1.8(a)	77
1.8(b) Comment 1	162
1.8(c)	58
1.8(d)	77, 174
1.8(d) Comment 3	174
1.8(e)	59, 67
1.8(e)(1)	163
1.8(f)	70, 71
1.8(f) Comment 4	169
1.8(h)	169, 196
1.8(i)	170
1.8 Comment 1	196
1.9	81
1.9(a)	58, 80, 163, 186, 189
1.9(c)	186
1.9(c)(1)	163, 190
1.9 Comment 1	189
1.9 Comment 2	189
2.2(a)(3)(c) Comment 10	168
2.2 Comment 1	168
3.1	75
3.1 Comment 2	75, 149
3.3	45, 47, 193
3.3 Comments 7-10	47
3.3(a)(4) Comment 11	161
3.3(a)(3) Comment 3	172
3.3(a)(4)	45, 46, 47
3.3(a)(4) Comment 3	183
3.3 Comment 7	152
3.4	45, 193
3.4 Comment 2	46
3.4(a)	45, 46, 61, 82, 145, 197
3.4(a) Comment 2	151
3.4(b)	91, 163, 183
3.4(c)	181
3.4(d)	75
3.4(e)	83, 91, 172
3.5	83
3.5(a)	195
3.5(b)	158, 195
3.5(c) Comment 2	173, 181
3.6	63, 173, 174
3.6(a)	91, 166, 173
3.6(b)(1)	173
3.6(b)(2)	173
3.6(b)(3)	173
3.6(b)(4)	173
3.6(b)(5)	173, 174
3.6(b)(6)	173
3.6(b)(7)	173
3.6 Comment 5	173, 174
3.7	77, 78, 80
3.8	143, 183
4.1(a)	143
4.2	77, 82
4.4	143
5.1(a)	177
5.2(a) Comment 1	176
5.3(a)	177
5.3(b)	56, 61, 177
5.3(c)	56, 177
5.4(a)	199
5.4(b)	55, 165
5.4(c)	165
5.5	93
5.5(a)	170
5.5(b)	55, 177
5.5 Comment	166
5.6(a)	197
5.6 Comment 1	197
6.1	178
6.2(c) Comment 1	178
6.2(c) Comment 2	178
7.1	63, 65, 92, 166, 169, 178, 180
7.1(a)	92, 179, 180
7.1(b)	63, 90, 92, 179, 180
7.1(c)	66, 179, 180
7.2	65, 166, 178
7.2(a)	169
7.2(b)	64
7.2(c)	64, 165, 199
7.3	65, 92, 199
7.3 Comment 1	90
7.3(a)	63, 90, 165, 199
7.3(a) Comment 4	149
7.3(b)(1)	157
7.3(b)(2)	90, 157
7.3(c)	66, 157
7.4	66, 180
7.4(a)	180
7.5	63
7.5(d)	55
8.1	53, 149
8.1(a)	52, 160
8.1(b)	52, 160
8.1 Comment 1	160
8.2(a) Comment 1	176
8.2(b)	164
8.3 Comment 4	53
8.3(a)	52, 159, 177, 181
8.3(b)	181
8.3(c)	53, 160, 177

8.3 Comment 1 178
8.3 Comment 3 178
8.4 .... 59, 143
8.4(b) 78, 83, 167, 176
8.4(c) 56, 159, 176, 192
8.4(c) Comment 1 175
8.4(d) 56, 84, 167, 183, 192
8.4(e) 56
8.4(f) 84, 87, 176
8.5 143
8.5(2)(ii) 143
8.5(a) 94, 170, 199

Table of References to the Code of Judicial Conduct

§ 1A	194	§ 4D(5)(d)	87
§ 2A	188, 194	§ 4G	89, 189
§ 2B	85, 188	§ 4H	159
§ 2C	85	§ 4H(1)	158
§ 3B(4)	181	§ 4H(1)(b)	158
§ 3B(7)	185	§ 4H(2)	159
§ 3D(2)	181	§ 5A(1)(b)	86
§ 3E(1)(a)	84, 89	§ 5A(1)(d)	164
§ 4A	188, 194	§ 5A(3)(d)(i)	88
§ 4B	156, 188	§ 5A(3)(d)(ii)	85
§ 4C(1)	156	§ 5C(1)	88
§ 4C(3)	156	§ 5C(1)(a)(ii)	164
§ 4C(3)(b)(i)	156	§ 5C(1)(b)(i)	164
§ 4D(1)(a)	188	§ 5C(1)(b)(iv)	86
§ 4D(5)	84, 87	§ 5C(2)	87, 88, 164, 176
§ 4D(5)(c)	84		

Index

References are to the number of the question raising the issue.
"E" indicates an Essay Question; "M" indicates a Multiple-Choice Question

Abusive conduct before tribunal, M72

Advertising
See also Solicitation
False or misleading communications, E8, E20, M47, M53, M69, M71
Specialization, fields of, M71

Advocate-witness rule, E14, E15

Alteration of evidence
See Concealment, Alteration or Destruction of Evidence

Application for bar admission, E3

Appointment to represent indigent defendant, M68

Attorney-client privilege
See also Confidentiality
Generally, E4, M2, M5, M19, M28
Continuing crimes, M78
Corporate counsel, E13, M55, M88, M89
Death of client, effect of, M78
Information not related to performance of legal services, M78
Report of another lawyer's violation of rules of professional conduct, E3
Will, testimony of lawyer regarding drafting of, E15

Attorney-client relationship, change in law after termination of, M12

Bar admissions
Applications, E3
Character references, M35
Confidentiality, M35
False statement of material fact on application, E3
Recommendation letters, M13, M34

Belge, People v., M97

Bequest, acceptance by judge, E17, E18

Business transactions with clients, E14

Campaigns for judicial office, E18, M43, M64

Candor to tribunal, E1, M20, M58, M92

Cases
Belge, People v., M97
Ficker v. Curran, M30
Florida Bar v. Went For It, M30, M100
Meredith, People v., M97
Miranda v. Arizona, M1
Ryder, In re, M97
Shapero v. Kentucky Bar Ass'n, E8, M30, M100
Tekni-Plex, Inc. v. Meyner & Landis, M81

Character references, bar admissions, M35

Closing arguments, statement of personal opinion, E16, M59, M73

Commercial enterprise, lending prestige of judicial office to, E17, M84

Communication, E2

Compensation
See Fees

Competent representation, E2, E9, E13, M4, M6, M90
See also Malpractice

Concealment, alteration or destruction of evidence
Generally, E1, E6, M6
Production of documents, illegible photocopies, E16

Confidentiality
See also Attorney-Client Privilege
Generally, E1, E4, E6, M3, M8
Bar admissions, M35
Consent to association with another counsel, E2
Fee controversy, M23
Future crime, intent of client to commit, E6, M17, M78

Information not related to performance of legal services, M78
Intercom system, leaving turned on, E6
Report of another lawyer's violation of rules of professional conduct, E3
Third party, statement to lawyer made by, M28

Conflicts of interest
See also Confidentiality
Corporate counsel, E13, M55
Criminal cases, representation of multiple clients, E11
Death of client, representation of third party in related matter after, E15
Family relationship of opposing attorneys, M54
Fees, E10, E14
Financial assistance to client in connection with litigation, E5
Former client, case against, E5, M41, M81, M86
Former government lawyers, E12
Gift from client to lawyer, preparation of instrument which gives, E5
Government lawyer, acceptance of employment with private party, E12
Informed consent, E10, E11, E12, E15, M41, M81, M86
Literary or media rights, payment of fee by assignment of, E14
Loyalty, E10, E15
Multiple clients, representation of, E10, E11, M50
Negotiations, E10
Partnerships, E15
Profiting from information revealed by client, M39
Stock, ownership of stock in opposing corporate party, M75
Withdrawal of attorney upon appearance of conflict, E10

Consent
Association with another counsel, E2
Conflicts of interest, E10, E11, E12, E15, M41, M81, M86

Consultation, fee for, E15

Contingent fees
Generally, E5
Criminal cases, E9, M22
Discharge, entitlement of attorney to fee after, M40
Domestic relations matters, E9, M22, M50
Reasonableness, E9, E20, M22
Written agreements, E9, E20

Continuing crimes, disclosure of, M78

Contracts, unauthorized practice of law, M48

Convention, speaking before, M47

Corporate counsel
Attorney-client privilege, E13, M55, M88, M89
Conflicts of interest, E13, M55

Crimes
Avoidance of detection, advice regarding, M8
Commission of criminal act by lawyer, E14

Criminal cases
See also Perjury
Contingent fees, E9, M22
Decisions of client, abiding by, E14, M9, M10
Defendant, testimony of, E1
Exculpatory evidence, disclosure by prosecutor, M1, M76
Initiation of case, request for, M49
Malpractice, instructions regarding trial tactics by third party, E11
Multiple clients, representation of, E11
Physical evidence in possession of defense counsel, turning over to prosecution, E1, E6, M18, M97
Probable cause to institute proceedings, M1
Publicity regarding criminal record of defendant, M60
Right to counsel, M1
Trial tactics, E11, M9, M10

Death of client
Attorney-client privilege, effect on, M78
Representation of third party in related matter after, E15

Decisions of client, abiding by
Civil cases, E13, M11, M38
Criminal cases, E14, M9, M10

INDEX

Destruction of evidence
See Concealment, Alteration or Destruction of Evidence

Diligence, E1, E2, E9, E13, E14, M26, M51, M90

Discharge of lawyer
Generally, M57
Contingency fee, entitlement to, M40

Discourteous conduct before tribunal, E16, M72

Discovery, engaging in, E13

Discredit upon lawyer and profession, avoidance of, M2

Discrimination, membership of judge in club or organization that practices, E17

Disqualification of judge for lack of impartiality, E18

Disqualification of lawyer, advocate-witness rule, E14

Disruption of tribunal, M72

Dissolution of firm, preservation of files upon, M80

Domestic relations, contingent fees, E9, M22, M50

Exculpatory evidence, disclosure by prosecutor, M1, M76

Expenses of judge in connection with public speech, reimbursement of, M32

Expert witnesses, compensation and expenses of, M42

Fairness to opposing party and counsel, E1, M92

False advertising, E8, E20, M47, M53, M69, M71

False evidence, presentation of, E1

Family relationship of opposing attorneys, M54

Favor, acceptance by judge, E17, E18

Fees
See also Contingent Fees
Communication of fee to client, E2
Confidentiality, fee controversy, M23
Conflicts of interest, E10, E14
Consultation fees, E15
Customary charges, M70
Invoice, submission of false, M65, M66
Judges, public speeches by, M32
Literary or media rights, E14, E62
Options for fee structure, E9
Reasonableness, E2, E15, E20, M16, M44, M70
Special knowledge, skill and experience, M70
Suit against client for fee, M23
Third party, payment by, E11, M52
Trust accounts, retention of disputed fee in, E9, M23, M24, M74
Written agreements, E2, M44

Ficker v. Curran, M30

Fitness as lawyer
See Honesty, Trustworthiness or Fitness as Lawyer

Florida Bar v. Went For It, M30, M100

Former government lawyers, conflicts of interest, E12

Fraud and misrepresentation
Advertising, E8, E20, M47, M53, M69, M71
Bar admissions, false statement of material fact on application, E3
Business venture, conduct pertaining to, M63
Revelation of client's fraud by attorney, M21
Solicitation, E19

Friends, acceptance by judge of gift, bequest, favor or loan from, E17, E18

Frivolous claims
Generally, E13
Harassment and intimidation, E13, M14
Withdrawal of attorney, material adverse effect on client caused by, M15

Fund raising activities for nonprofit organizations, participation of judge in, M27

Future crime, intent of client to commit, E6, M17, M78

Gifts
Judge, acceptance by, E17, E18
Preparation of instrument which gives gift from client to lawyer, E5

Government lawyer, acceptance of employment with private party, E12

Grand jury, right to counsel, M1

Harassment, frivolous claims, E13, M14

High-low agreements, M82, M83

Honesty, trustworthiness or fitness as lawyer
Criminal act, commission of, E14
Report of another lawyer's violation of rules of professional conduct, E3, M33, M67

"How To" books, unauthorized practice of law, E20

Impartiality of judge, M93

Inconsistent positions, argument in separate cases, M51

Indigent defendants, representation of, M68

Informing client of status of matter, M90

Insurance, malpractice, M53

Intimidation, frivolous claims, M14

Invitation by attorney to judge, E17

Invoice, submission of false, M65, M66

Judges
Acceptance of gift, bequest, favor or loan, E17, E18
Campaigns for office, E18, M43, M64
Club or organization that practices discrimination, membership in, E17
Commercial enterprise, lending prestige of office to, E17, M84
Compensation and reimbursement of expenses for public speeches, M32
Disqualification for lack of impartiality, E18
Ex parte investigation of case, M79
Fund raising activities for nonprofit organizations, participation in, M27
High standards of conduct, M93
Impartiality, M93
Nonprofit organizations, participation in, M27
Political activity, E17
Practice of law by judge, E18, M85
Public hearings, appearance at, M27
Report regarding compensation and reimbursement of expenses for public speeches, M32
Report to proper authorities regarding conduct of judge, M72
Respect and compliance with law, M93
Sanctions for misconduct, M94
Speaking, writing, lecturing and teaching, M27

Jurors
End of trial, communications after, M95
Ex parte communication with juror, M31, M95
Harassment or embarrassment, M95

Jury trial, waiver of, M10

Law Practice, Sale of, M83

Legal authority, disclosure of adverse, M58

Legal journal, writing article for, M47

Literary rights, payment of fee by assignment of, E14, M62

Loan, acceptance by judge, E17, E18

Local rules, applicability of, M25

Loyalty, conflicts of interest, E10, E15

Mail, solicitation by, M30

Malice, frivolous proceedings, E13

Malpractice
See also Competent Representation
Criminal case, instructions regarding trial tactics by third party, E11
Insurance, M53
Nonlawyer subordinates, supervision of, E4
Settlement of claim, advice to client to obtain independent representation in connection with, M96
Waiver of liability from client, M53

Matrimonial matters, contingent fees, E9, M22, M50

INDEX

Media rights, payment of fee by assignment of, E14, M62

Media, payment for publicity in news item, E7

Meredith, People v., M97

Miranda v. Arizona, M1

Misdirected material, use of, M92

Misrepresentation
See Fraud and Misrepresentation

Multiple clients, representation of, E10, E11, M50

Negotiations, conflicts of interest, E10

Noncompetition agreements, partnerships, M98

Nonlawyer subordinates, supervision of, E4, E6

Nonlawyer, partnership with, E4, M46

Nonprofit organizations, participation of judge in, M27

Obstreperous conduct before tribunal, M72

Obstruction of access to evidence
Generally, E1, E6, M6
Production of documents, illegible photocopies, E16

Obstruction of justice, M97

Opening statement, statements not supported by admissible evidence, E19

Paralegals, unauthorized practice of law, M66

Partnerships
Conflicts of interest, E15
Dissolution of firm, preservation of files upon, M80
Noncompetition agreements, M98
Nonlawyer, partnership with, E4, M46
Orders of partner, refusal of associate to obey, M91
Wrongful implication of partnership, E4

Perjury
Confidential remonstration with client, M37
Defendant, testimony of, E1, M77
Discovery of perjury after trial, M77
Prosecution witness, disclosure of perjury by prosecutor, M76
Withdrawal of attorney, E1, M20, M37

Personal opinion
Statement before tribunal, E16, M59, M73
Statement to media, M60

Place of disciplinary action, E20, M1, M55, M100

Plea bargain, discussion with client, E14

Political activity of judges, E17

Political view, public expression of view differing from that of client, M29

Pro se **claims, unauthorized practice of law,** E20, M48

Probable cause to institute criminal proceeding, M1

Production of documents, illegible photocopies, E16

Promptness, E9, M26

Publicity in news item, payment for, E7

Publicity regarding case, E19, M47, M60, M61

Racial discrimination, membership of judge in club or organization that practices, E17

Reasonableness of fees, E2, E15, E20, M16, M44, M70

Recommendation letters, bar admissions, M13, M34

Recommendation of lawyer's services, payment for, E7

Records, preservation of, M80, M99

Recusal of judge, E17

Referrals from nonlawyers, M46

Relatives, acceptance by judge of gift, bequest, favor or loan from, E17, E18

Religious discrimination, membership of judge in club or organization that practices, E17

Report of another lawyer's violation of rules of professional conduct, E3, M33, M67

Represented party, communication with, E14, E16

Right to counsel, M1

Ryder, In re, M97

Sale of Law Practice, M83

Self-incrimination, grant of immunity, M1

Settlement of claim
Generally, E9
Decisions of client, abiding by, M11
Malpractice, advice to client to obtain independent representation, M96
Offer, communication with client regarding, M38
Trust account, deposit in, E9, M36

Sex discrimination, membership of judge in club or organization that practices, E17

Shapero v. Kentucky Bar Ass'n, E8, M30, M100

Small claims court, pro se appearance before, M48

Social hospitality, acceptance by judge of gift, bequest, favor or loan, E17, E18

Solicitation
See also Advertising
Generally, E8
False or misleading statements, E19
Former clients, M45
In-person solicitation, E19, M100
Live telephone solicitation, E7, E19
Mail, solicitation by, M30
Nonlawyer agent, in-person solicitation by, M100
Relatives, M45
Television talk show, appearance on, E7

Specialization, advertising, M71

Stock, ownership of stock in opposing corporate party, M75

Tekni-Plex, Inc. v. Meyner & Landis, M81

Television show, appearance on, E7, M47

Threat of criminal prosecution to advance interests of client, E4, E16, M48

Trust accounts
Disputed fee, retention in trust account, E9, M23, M24, M74
Misuse, sanctions for, M87
Settlement, deposit of, E9, M36

Trustworthiness
See Honesty, Trustworthiness or Fitness as Lawyer

Unauthorized practice of law
Generally, E4
Contract, drafting of, M48
"How To" books, E20
Paralegals, M66
Pro se claims, E20, M48
Small claims court, pro se appearance before, M48
State in which lawyer is not licensed, appearance in, E20, M55
Will, drafting of, M48

Undignified conduct before tribunal, E16, M72

Waiver of malpractice liability from client, M53

Wills
Drafting, testimony of lawyer regarding, E15
Unauthorized practice of law, M48

Withdrawal of attorney
Competent representation, failure to give, E1, M6
Conflict of interest, appearance of, E10
Material adverse effect on client, M15
Perjury by client or witness, E1, M20, M37

Zealous representation, E1, E13, E14, M20, M51, M68, M92

Quality companion products for students in law school!

Also available from Aspen Law & Business

Emanuel Law Outline Series
Each outline in the series is the work of Steven Emanuel. Each is packed with features that take you from next-day preparation to night-before-the-exam review. Outlines are available for all major law school subjects and many are revised annually.

Available titles:
Civil Procedure
Constitutional Law
Contracts
Corporations
Criminal Law
Criminal Procedure
Environmental Law
Evidence
Property
Property (Dukeminier Ed.)
Secured Credit
Torts (General Ed.)
Torts (Prosser Ed.)
Wills, Trusts, and Estates (Dukeminier Ed.)

Law In A Flash Series
Flashcards add a dimension to law school study which cannot be matched by any other study aid, and these are the acknowledged leader in flashcards. They make legal issues and answers stick to your mind like glue. Each Law In A Flash card set contains 350-625 cards arranged to give you black-letter principles first. Then they teach you all the subtleties by taking you through a series of hypotheticals filled with mnemonics and checklists. Excellent for exam preparation.

Available titles:
Civil Procedure 1
Civil Procedure 2
Constitutional Law
Contracts
Corporations
Criminal Law
Criminal Procedure
Evidence
Federal Income Taxation
Future Interests
Professional Responsibility
Real Property
Sales (UCC Article 2)
Torts
Wills & Trusts

Available at your local bookstore or from us directly at **www.aspenpublishers.com**